Changing Families

An Ethnographic Approach to Divorce and Separation

Bob Simpson

Oxford • New York

First published in 1998 by
Berg
Editorial offices:
150 Cowley Road, Oxford, OX4 1JJ, UK
70 Washington Square South, New York, NY 10012, USA

Berg is the imprint of Oxford International Publishers Ltd.

Library of Congress Cataloging-in-Publication Data

A catalogue record for this book is available from the Library of Congress

British Library Cataloguing-in-Publication Date

A catalogue record for this book is available from the British Library

ISBN 1 85973 914 8 (Cloth)
1 85973 919 9 (Paper)

Typeset by JS Typesetting, Wellingborough, Northants.
Printed in the United Kingdom by WBC Book Manufacturers, Bridgend,
Mid Glamorgan.

Contents

Contents

Preface: Divorcing in the Late 1980s

In English law, in order to become divorced it is first necessary to have been married. The evidence of marriage that is required by the courts is a marriage certificate and, unless some such document is produced, a divorce cannot proceed. The marriage certificate is thus a kind of touchstone without which the activation of 400 years of English civil divorce law cannot proceed. To see and handle these once treasured and celebrated pieces of paper, as I did many times as a researcher into divorce and separation, was a poignant experience, especially when they were sandwiched between petitions and affidavits heavy with allegation, recrimination and distress. The marriage certificates indicated weddings in small rural Methodist chapels, large urban Anglican and catholic churches, registry offices and marriages 'according to the usages of the Jews'.[1] For each case one could readily visualise ceremonies and celebrations attended by families and friends to witness and to mark in some way this major transition in adult life. One might further assume that in each case the act of getting married involved the couple in some understanding, if not of each other, then of the roles, expectations and obligations the act of marrying creates. Each of these now defunct marriages began with an anticipated future in which the longer-term project of living together, creating a separate domestic unit, pooling labour and resources and producing offspring was unsullied by the prospect of divorce. In short, those who marry express a commitment to creating a relatively permanent fragment of the wider social order. Whilst the marriage certificates revealed that the ways people had ritually marked their entry into long-term conjugal commitment were massively varied, their presence, pinned and rudely stapled to the standard letters and pro formas of the Lord Chancellor's Department would suggest that they were all filing out through the same door.[2] Diversity of entry in terms of class, region and religious background contrasts starkly with apparent uniformity of exit.

The rise in the numbers of couples whose marriages end in divorce represents possibly the most profound change in the pattern of family life in the western world in recent times. Divorce rates which were marginal at the turn of the century have become central demographic features of most European countries (Phillips 1988; Goode 1993). Within this European-wide trend, British divorce rates have risen in spectacular fashion. In 1911, the number of divorces in England and Wales was a mere 700 couples. The number of divorces increased sixfold in the period between 1960 and 1980 (*Marriage & Divorce Statistics* 1990) and went on to peak at over 171,000 divorces in 1991 (*Social Trends* 1994). This was equivalent to one divorce for every two marriages. Since then, the number of divorces has remained more or less at this level, giving Britain the highest divorce rate in Europe. Furthermore, marriages would appear to be getting shorter in duration (Haskey 1989) with the process of marital breakdown beginning for many people within three years of their wedding day (Dormor 1992: 22). Rising divorce rates are further reflected in the numbers of marriages which are in fact re-marriages. It is estimated that one-third of all marriages are re-marriages (*Marriage and Divorce Statistics* 1994).

Just over half (55 per cent) of couples who divorced in 1990 had at least one child under the age of sixteen. Official statistics indicate that some 153,000 children under the age of sixteen experienced their parents divorce in 1990 (*Marriage & Divorce Statistics* 1990). On present trends it has been estimated that by the turn of the century in England and Wales 3.7 million children will have experienced at least one parental divorce (Haskey 1988; also see De'Ath 1992). The inclusion of the breakdown of non-jural relationships in which there are offspring would undoubtedly swell these figures even further. Statistics such as these are no doubt striking but they give little hint of the immense conflict, distress and despair which is unleashed into individual lives when the nuclear family undergoes fission. Disillusionment with the people and circumstances which the institution of marriage has created and a deep desire to seek alternative partners, life-styles and living arrangements brings with it a chaotic backwash of altered personal and family circumstances.

The Divorce Reform Act of 1969 which forms the basis of current divorce law in England and Wales was intended to ameliorate the consequences of marital breakdown by taking the sting out of divorce proceedings. Most notable in this regard was the shift from 'matrimonial offence' to 'irretrievable breakdown' through the introduction of less stringent grounds for divorce (Davis and Murch 1988; Gibson 1994). Courts had to be satisfied that 'irretrievable breakdown' had taken place and this was evidenced by one of five 'specified facts': adultery, unreasonable behaviour, desertion, separation after two years by consent and separation after five without consent. In the context of the arguments put forward in this book, two trends are of particular note in the period since the 1969 Divorce Law Reform Act came into being. Firstly, there has been a spectacular increase in the use of 'unreasonable behaviour' as the specified fact in divorce petitions. This rose from 18 per cent of all divorces in 1971 to 45 per cent in 1990 (Gibson 1994: 170). Secondly, it would appear that throughout the 1970s and 1980s it has been women who have petitioned for divorce in increasing numbers. By 1990, 72 per cent of all petitions were initiated by women. Within the category of women petitioners, those seeking divorce on the grounds of 'unreasonable behaviour' had risen from 28 per cent of all decrees granted to women in 1971 to 51 per cent of such decrees in 1986 (*Marriage and Divorce Statistics* 1977 & 1988). 'Unreasonable behaviour' petitions more than any other reveal, often in painful detail, precisely what happens when the over-charged circuit of family life finally blows. Allegations of violence, alcoholism, sexual abuse, lack of consideration, failure to be a 'good' husband and father, failure to be a 'good' wife and mother and a host of other alleged actions and in-actions provide public declarations that a marriage is fatally flawed and that the one chosen as a lifelong helpmate is no longer fit to live with (Corlyon *et al.* 1991). In earlier generations the incidents which appear in divorce petitions might have been taken as part of the inevitable rough and tumble of married life and to which endurance was the only response. Nowadays, however, many of the legal and economic barriers to divorce have been removed and exit is a readily available option.

Consideration of these developments and the forms they took in the late 1980s is the focus of this book. In Britain at this time many projects of the New Right initiated in the early days of the Thatcher administration were coming to florescence. Words such as 'privatisation', 'efficiency', 'Victorian values', 'the right-to-buy', 'law and order' and 'enterprise' entered everyday political discourse as part of a wholesale assault on things public and collective. Central to the Thatcherite project was a ubiquitous familism which provided a rich fund of appealing and easily accessible metaphors – as Thatcher once remarked 'it (the family) is a nursery, a school, a hospital, a leisure centre, a place of refuge, a place of rest. It encompasses the whole of society' (Conservative Women's Conference 1988 cited in Franklin *et al.* 1991: 38). This reification of the family effectively drew attention away from the more ominous project of dismantling civic and public culture and letting the market reign. In her famous statement that 'there is no such thing as society. There are individual men and women and there are families' (cited in Strathern 1992a: 144) Thatcher simultaneously staked the outer limits of social concern and the locus of enterprise, choice and consumption. The ideological support for and celebration of the family in its nuclear, heterosexual, co-resident, stable, monogamous form created a strong sense of the naturalness, universality and self-evidence of these arrangements. To fall outside this arrangement was to indulge in lifestyles perceived as problematic and potentially deviant. Of particular concern to those on the right was the growing number of women who became single parents either because they chose to divorce or because they opted never to marry in the first place. Concerns were moral and economic. Could women bring up children properly on their own? Should the State be expected to subsidise the housing and welfare needs of what were invariably portrayed as partial and pretended families? Linked to these concerns was a more profound unease at the fact that men were apparently being ousted from a domain in which they had hitherto reigned supreme. Their departure, 'a case of unfair dismissal' as one pundit characterised this development (Morgan 1986), was readily linked to the economic plight of single parent families and seen as creating a dangerous moral vacuum in which children were increasingly likely to be raised. In the ideology of the 'new right', the crises facing Britain in the late 1980s were thus linked explicitly with the fate of the traditional nuclear family with blame being apportioned to gays, single parents, selfish mothers, feckless fathers and cohabitees. Divorce in particular was readily identified as a source of current social problems and future catastrophes.

Despite these dire assessments however, divorce and its consequences had become a common feature of the landscape of contemporary domestic life. Indeed, in social and cultural terms, the statistics described earlier indicate a spectacular shift in the way that relationships are organised and private lives are conducted. Yet, this is a development which has hardly been considered in sociological, let alone anthropological terms. The present work sets about filling this hiatus by describing fundamental shifts in the way that domestic and private lives are conducted. It explores the increasingly common circumstance in which key social arrangements are no longer built on the institution of long-term conjugality but on complex and convoluted patterns of inter-personal commitment, dependency and exchange. It is my intention in this work to cast an ethnographic eye on these arrangements and to begin to map the chaos and turmoil which tend to follow the passage of men, women and their children out of the emotional, social, legal and economic edifice of marriage. Building on nearly a decade of research into divorce, divorcing and the divorced, I explore what happens when people undertake a radical re-routing of personal trajectories and move out of marriage and into new and alternative patternings of domestic and personal life.

One of the central themes of the book is the notion that, for couples with children who undergo divorce, there are a range of fundamental issues which necessarily have to be resolved or at the very least accommodated into post-divorce life. This accommodation takes the form of a number of uneasy truces. The process of arriving at a *modus vivendi* after divorce entails complex and protracted negotiations about relationships, property and persons which are a central feature of the assembly of arrangements I have dubbed the unclear family.[3] This term is not intended to refer to actual configurations of people as such but aims to capture the form and character of the complex and processual relationship continuities which persist after the nuclear family fragments. Rather than being held together by some apparently natural binding agent, or what Meyer Fortes once referred to as 'the axiom of amity' (Fortes 1969), former family members are linked in ways that are contested and contradictory; their social relations are fashioned out of dispute, distrust, conflict and stark economic considerations which often sit alongside the sentiments more typically identified with family such as trust, love, respect, duty, mutual accommodation and selflessness. The domestic and social arrangements which evolve from the mingling of positive and negative sentiments expressed between husbands and wives, mothers and fathers and parents and children might well be complex and unclear but, I go on to argue, they are still expressions of human kinship and are therefore of primary anthropological concern. This concern is not merely theoretical in that it identifies questions surrounding the meaning of kinship in human relations but serves a more substantive purpose in that it carries the anthropological study of kinship to the centre of some of the most important policy debates of the day. These debates concern issues such as the future of the monogamous, nuclear family, the regulation of private life by law and economic policy, the nature of morality and responsibility and the changing status of gendered family roles in contemporary society. However, as I set about weaving insights drawn from socio-legal studies and the sociology of the family into the anthropological study of kinship, I cannot claim to do any more than touch on these major issues and political concerns. In this sense, the present work is nothing more than a prolegomenon for the study of family and kinship relations in the late twentieth century.

In accumulating the data and arriving at the insights contained in this book I have drawn on the help, support and inspiration of many people. My wife, Joanna, has been a ready source of support and good advice over the years. Judy Corlyon, Pete McCarthy and Jan Walker with whom I worked at Newcastle University proved to be not just good colleagues but good friends and each of them has made a major contribution to the development of my writing and thinking on divorce and separation over the years. The interview programmes were carried out with Judy Corlyon who was an excellent companion during some arduous stints in the field. Thanks also go to colleagues who worked on the original Conciliation Project Unit and whose influence has fed into the present work in diverse ways; these include Anthony Ogus, Michael Jones Lee, Sarah Wray and Bill Cole. Earlier drafts of certain chapters have appeared elsewhere and have benefited enormously from peer review and general feedback enabling these sections to be improved and significantly expanded. Chapter 2 first appeared as 'Bringing the unclear family into focus' in The Journal of the Royal Anthropological Institute (1994). Sections of chapter 6 appeared in *After Writing Culture* edited by James Hockey, and Dawson (1997) in an essay entitled 'Representations and Representation of Family: An Analysis of Divorce Narratives'. Chapter 5 first appeared as 'On Gifts Payments and Disputes after Divorce' in The Journal of the Royal Anthropological Institute (1997). The manuscript, in part and whole, has benefited enormously from the comments of Sandra Bell, the late David Brooks, James Carrier, Michael Carrithers, Jack Goody, Erica Haimes, Allison James, Peter McCarthy, Peter Phillimore, Marilyn Strathern and Jan Walker. Finally I would like to express my sincere thanks to all those people into whose unclear families I was briefly welcomed and who provided an intimate glimpse of their lives, often at a time of great distress and turmoil.

Notes

1. Among court files were also to be found marriages sacralised by the Vedic fire ceremony of the Hindus and according to Urhobo native laws along with many others from ethnic minority groups. The implications of ethnic divorces in English courts are an important issue which has been given very little attention in research terms, however, it is one which lies beyond the scope of the present work.
2. This point was not lost on the newspapers who seized on the granting of a *decree absolute* to the Prince and Princess of Wales in August 1996 as a newsworthy item. Many papers at the time featured a photograph of the court list on which the royal couple appeared largely undistinguishable from the day-to-day run of 'Smith v Smith's'.

3. I cannot claim credit for the term 'unclear family'. The main contenders are co-researcher Judy Corlyon, whose son reportedly came up with it in conversation, an exhibition organised by the photographer Richard Grassick which appeared in Crook, County Durham in 1992 entitled 'Unclear Families' and finally an article by Andrew Marr entitled 'Troubled by the Unclear Family' which appeared in the *Independent* newspaper in November 1993.

Divorce: Towards an Anthropology of Endings

... what you do from that moment (of separation) are very strange things and you kind of make a decision one week based on something that's happened. In hindsight it's a very higgledy-piggledy state of affairs and you realise that perhaps you don't act quite rationally at the time because there are so many pressures and so many things going on, you know. But the thing is that you are ... I think you are both trying to come out of it as sort of like, as ... not respectably as possible but you're trying to survive out of something that's like a holocaust you know, it's an indignity and a sort of ... it does change you but if you're trying to say to people 'well look, I'm alright, I'm ok' so you know but I mean you're fighting like hell underneath because ... because you are always alongside, you see ... couples who've made it and life is hunky dory.

Ostensibly, the ethnographic and theoretical focus of the book is upon divorce in contemporary Britain. However, the implications of what I have to say go much further. They relate to fundamental changes in the way that people conduct their intimate social lives in the late twentieth century; the study of divorce is merely an aperture through which to glimpse these changes. At its simplest, divorce refers to the legal mechanisms for dissolving a legally constituted marriage. In broader terms divorce legislation provides the legal framework to direct, manage and regulate the movement of people and property in relation to one another once a marriage has ended. Yet, divorce is also a highly complex social process which is apt to be mistaken for a simple legal event. Talk of divorce thus tends to draw attention to endings, termination and dissolution in ways which conflate legal processes with complex social, emotional and economic circumstances. For example, it is still common in Britain for lawyers to strive to engineer a 'clean break' for their clients and for government policy documents to refer to 'absent fathers' denying at a stroke the continuities which straddle the households which emerge when a previously co-resident family unit undergoes fission. The simple fact is that throughout the western world, for the many thousands of couples who formally end their marriages, divorce does not spell the end of their relationship but a new phase of 'post-marital marriage' (Beck and Beck-Gernsheim 1995: 147) or familiality (Buisson & Mermet 1986).[1] The quest for pure, honest, authentic, satisfying, stimulating inter-personal relationships which motivates increasing numbers of men and women to exit from their marriages is one that leaves a complex tangle of ongoing and disputed ties, obligations and dependencies in its wake. For an anthropologist interested in kinship, this tangle is a source of considerable fascination. What appears again and again is the fact that divorce is not simply about endings and the fragmentation of once seemingly wholesome chunks of social organisation but that it also generates vital continuities in the way that one generation passes on its status, property, identity and accumulated wisdom and folly to the next. Evidence of continuity is to be seen in commitments to ongoing parenting arrangements, the transfer of resources, the re-negotiation of roles and the re-ordering of patterns of kinship which take place after divorce. Such continuities are cast against the backdrop of common and deeply interwoven biographies and have economic and emotional repercussions long after a couple receive the final statement of legal dissolution. Thus, despite apocalyptic accounts of the breakdown of the family, and the moral and social unravelling of society which is believed to follow inexorably in its wake, fundamental continuities do persist and their form and content ought to be understood. At a time when British society is politically, bureaucratically and to a large extent intellectually attuned to the nuclear family, it is my aim to bring the unclear family into analytical and methodological focus (Simpson 1994b). My exposition of family life after divorce provides an alternative perspective to the tendency to see the fate of kinship relationships as perpetually contracting and shrinking, as for example in Dizard and Gadlin's account of the 'minimal family' (Dizard and Gadlin 1990), rather than undergoing a continual transformation and re-working to fit prevailing social and economic conditions. In this respect, the present work falls within a broader vision of social relationships intimated by Giddens:

> The post-traditional society is an ending; but it is also a beginning, a genuinely new social universe of action and experience. What type of social order is it, or might it become? It is, as I have said, a global society, not in the sense of a world society but as one of 'indefinite space'. It is one where social bonds have effectively to be made, rather than inherited from the past – on the personal and more collective levels this is a fraught and difficult enterprise, but one which also holds out the promise of great rewards. It is de-centred in terms of

authorities, but re-centred in terms of opportunities and dilemmas, because focused on new forms of inter-dependence. To regard narcissism, or even individualism, as the core of post-traditional order is a mistake – certainly in terms of the potentials for the future that it contains (1994: 106).

The extent to which the enterprise is 'fraught and difficult' is revealed in the accounts which form the basis of this book and which show how divorcing men and women set about bringing order and stability in the midst of the considerable personal conflict, confusion, pain and chaos which follows divorce. For some couples, such issues might be resolved quickly and relatively painlessly; but, for the majority, enormous efforts have to be made to construct and sustain the overlapping and conflicting social networks, boundaries and identities. These endeavours take on a particular significance where there are children of the marriage. In such cases, the process of maintaining continuities is far from straightforward as individuals struggle to contain, manage or win conflicts that arise from the deeper structural tensions surrounding gender, identity and power in the late twentieth century. Indeed, many people are unaccustomed to the corrosion and contagion which inter-personal conflict and dispute unleash following divorce. The quest for stability or 'a peaceful life', as it is often characterised by those caught in the maelstom, brings with it uncomfortable processes of adjustment to and accommodation of a variety of unwanted but nonetheless significant others as all try to make sense of this increasingly common transition in the modern life-cycle.

Divorcing couples, however, are not a separate species. The problems with which they must wrestle in order to live as coherent, competent moral and social beings are different in magnitude but not in kind from those that confront most people in contemporary western society. As such, this work offers a parable of contemporary social life. The form and character of conflict and unpredictability evident in the transition from conventional family arrangements to a host of alternative arrangements reveal a style of interaction which is rapidly becoming the dominant characteristic of social relationships throughout contemporary society. Changing patterns of family life are symptomatic of more fundamental changes in the social and cultural organisation of western society and point to a growing individualisation and fluidity in the conduct of social life.

Framed within the debates on the globalisation of capital, information and lifestyles, changes in the organisation of family life might well be construed as further evidence of the post-modern condition. In the stories which people tell of their experiences after divorce we can find evidence of the 'saturation' of the self (Gergen 1991) as multiple sets of relationships are integrated and overlaid. There is also concern at the loss or questioning of independent universal standards of morality and aesthetics surrounding family and parenting. Previous certainties seem to disintegrate and family-life is apt to appear as little more than a culturally constructed life-style possibility (see Davies 1993). Finally, one can also detect a growing difficulty when people try to locate themselves in an ongoing social history as they become distanced from the former imperatives of the family life-cycle. Rapport has suggested that in an age of mass mobility and migration 'home' might be more appropriately located in movement rather than in stasis (Rapport 1997); similarly, it may well be that what passes for family is increasingly located in a kaleidoscopic flux of relationships over time rather than in stable structures predicated upon long-term relationships of consanguinity and affinity (Scanzioni *et al.* 1989). Whether such changes should be labelled post-modern (Harvey 1989), or subsumed within the paradigms of high or late-modernity (Giddens 1991) is a moot point. What is less in dispute is that radical transformations are indeed taking place in the meaning, content and expression of intimate social relations in contemporary society and about which we have little by way of detailed ethnographic description.

Works exploring the new and alternative family structures arising because of divorce in Britain have tended to focus on second families and the problems they experience in achieving an identity as a second, step-, reconstituted or recombinant family (Burgoyne & Clarke 1984; De'Ath 1992). The present work offers a radically different perspective on the same phenomena in that it seeks to identify an altogether different plane of social activity. It addresses specifically the networks of social relationships which persist after divorce between husbands and wives and which usually centre on the children of their former marriage. The move from the apparently simple order of the nuclear family household in which people, resources and relationships were located in a powerful concentricity is followed by a bewildering and stressful opening out and unfolding of relational possibilities. The burgeoning of complexity in human relationships is accompanied by a corresponding move towards uncertainty, unpredictability, conflict and dispute over the basic currencies of human interaction. Radical personal change engendered by divorce must be synchronised with other developments such as the maturation of children, the arrival of new partners, the birth of new children, unemploy-ment, employment, re-location, increases in prosperity or decreases in prosperity all of which have considerable potential to add to the unpredictable and contested nature of relationships after divorce. What Harré has referred to as the 'standard dramatic scenarios' (1986: 13) which shape and direct emotion in any particular cultural setting, are still far from clear when it comes to the turbulent and disordered aftermath of divorce. For most people there is little sense of how one ought to be with former family members after divorce: the desire for peaceful and harmonious relations with a former partner and his or her kin often sits uncomfortably with powerful feelings of anger, guilt, antipathy and recrimination.[2] The former certainties surrounding rights, roles, responsibilities, norms and expectations give way to uncertainty surrounding how to proceed in relationships which might once have been self-evident and even natural in their character. The 'kinscripts' (Stack and Burton 1994) by which people might make sense of these relationships are still in the process of being written. Conflict and dispute are common, as is evidenced by the burgeoning machinery available to adjudicate, arbitrate or mediate in family disputes. But, despite the efforts of courts, solicitors, mediators and counsellors, the contours of post-divorce family life are rarely stable. Whilst some of these disputes are taken into the courts for an ultimate adjudication and yet others are resolved by the parties themselves, I would contend that the majority fall somewhere in between and become the subject of uneasy compromises and lived contradictions. In an era when order, predictability and simplicity are conditions to which many aspire, the complexity of post-divorce relationships is in itself often associated with feelings of failure to achieve a satisfactory aesthetic of family life. The grand narrative of personal meaning as it is located within the modern family would appear to be breaking down and giving way to a whole series of *petits récits*, or little stories, which do not reveal the social order so much as illuminate the multiplicity of ways that social ordering is achieved during the late twentieth century.

Beyond the Axiom of Amity

The breakdown of the grand narrative of modern family life is further revealed in the considerable fascination, popular and intellectual, with the formation and maintenance of intimate relationships in western society. It would seem that there is a growing desire to dissect in ever greater detail the material and emotional structures which precede, shape and under-pin family life. Those interested in the 'making and unmaking' (Stacey 1990) of the modern family focus their concerns on the tension between traditional family and parenting arrangements on the one hand and the pursuit of individualistic needs and desires on the other. At root, the problem which must be addressed is a classic paradox of western social thought. How do configurations of separate and existentially unique individuals interact to produce arrangements in which the whole, whether it be society, community, culture or an organisation, is considerably greater than the sum of its parts? Implicit in this question is a secondary concern: how can the benefits and values of these various social synergies be prevented from compromising and erasing the autonomy of their members?

Let me begin with those domestic and intimate relationships which in the West engender particularly powerful, distinctive and identifiable constructions such as 'the couple', 'married life', 'the home' and 'the family', which are the very things that are 'broken' and 'split' by divorce. In a study carried out by Mansfield and Collard (1988) among newly weds in Britain, for example, the tension between individuality and collectivity is captured in the confusion that couples experienced in talking about 'we', 'me' and 'us' in relation to their lives together. Couples interviewed in that study were keen to bring their personal relationships into line with the public institution of marriage and thereby submit to the shared construct of coupledom and family life. The expected pay-off for participation in this powerful collectivity is the extent to which those who embark on the long-term project of family life are able to find security, love, affection and future stability. The unanticipated costs are the extent to which public and private expectations of being a husband and father or wife and mother run counter to those of the individual.

The relationship between parts and wholes has been a persistent motif in accounts of western marriage and family life. Throughout many of these accounts the emphasis has been squarely on the way that the parts achieve and sustain a kind of wholeness which is readily identifiable and persists through time. Burgess, for example, one of the founders of what later became the field of 'family sociology', spoke of the family as 'a unity of interacting personalities' (Burgess 1926). In the accounts of the family which were to emerge and hold sway, this 'unity' lay at the heart of the social order. Unlike family structures to be found in earlier times and more distant places, the modern western family was seen as held together by positive psychological and emotional forces believed to promote warmth and internal cohesion for the family. As such a striking contrast was drawn with families prior to the impact of industrialisation and mass migration in which it was external pressures that held people together, simply corralling them into functional domestic arrangements. Similarly, Berger and Kellner (1964), in their classic article 'Marriage and the Construction of Reality', described marriage as an ongoing conversation or dialogue between family members and particularly a husband and wife. It is through the ongoing conduct of this dialogue that a 'consistent reality' (ibid: 5) is maintained. Through this reality, family members can realise a mutual affirmation which, Berger and Kellner suggest, cannot be achieved in other less intimate settings beyond the family. In a more ambitious analogy Reiss (1981) portrays the interior of the family as a 'small group culture'. Following Kuhn's model of scientific revolutions, Reiss proposes the idea of family paradigms with each family developing mechanisms of 'shared construal' when it comes to dealing with the social worlds beyond its boundaries. In each of these characterisations there is a fundamental assumption about the extent to which individuals are submerged and subsumed in a bounded collectivity which can be thought of as the family.

The central concern in each of the above accounts is with the reproducibility of familial arrangements. However, this concern is not so much with the external conditions which lead to the reproduction of certain family formations and structures, as it might be in a Marxist or feminist analysis, but with the stable and orderly reproduction of roles and relationships through the day-to-day functioning of the family. In such accounts, marriage and family are not seen simply as objects to which essentialist doctrines can be applied but are processes made up of social interactions and tangible arrangements of people which are assumed to evolve regular and predictable patterns over long periods of time. The continuity of these arrangements provides the basis for family members to think and talk about their relationships and underpins the powerful cognitive and emotional realities which result. Such approaches have been critically assessed and seen as contributing to a pervasive psychologism of the family (Osmond 1986) which has tended to cast the family as some kind of 'super personality' (Gubrium & Holstein 1990). A healthy family, like a healthy personality, is thus one in which divergent needs, interests and drives are more or less integrated into a coherent and socially acceptable form. Implicit in the notion of family are behaviours, attitudes and expectations which converge to produce worlds that are commonsense, self-evident, natural and ultimately stable. It is hardly surprising therefore that within the sociology of the family, concepts of marriage and the family came to be centrally implicated in questions of how persons achieved their sense of ontological security and mutual predictability. Going about the daily business of talking, feeding, giving, receiving, eating, sleeping, loving and all the other myriad exchanges that go on within the family provide the web of meaning upon which the most fundamental of human relationships appear to be hung. The character of these arrangements is captured in Fletcher's definition of the western family as:

a small relatively permanent group of people, related to each other in the most intimate way, bound together by the most personal aspects of life, who experience amongst themselves the whole range of human emotions . . . who experience continual responsibilities and obligations towards each other; who experience the sense of 'belonging' to each other in the most intimately felt sense of the word (Fletcher 1973: 26–7).

The notion that the family constitutes a particularly dense site of exchanges and interactions, however, is not confined to the study of western families but has featured as a crucial element in the study of family and kinship cross-culturally. The separation of more or less privileged or special domains of human interaction is part of a much more pervasive view of the role of kinship in human society and particularly as it relates to domestic arrangements. In his highly influential writings on kinship, Fortes developed a theoretical perspective in which kinship relations were distinguished from other more instrumental kinds of social relationship. Kin relations were to be distinguished by their essentially moral character:

the domain of familial and kinship relations, institutions and values is structurally discrete . . . founded on principles and processes that are irreducible . . . a critical feature of this domain, intrinsic to its constitution and distinctive of its manifestation in social life is a set of normative premises . . . focused on a general and fundamental axiom which I call amity (Fortes 1969: 250–1).

Derived ultimately from a Durkheimian view of social solidarity, Fortes' approach attributes the moral imperatives of kinship with a central role in binding society together. The site in which the axiom of amity reveals its most potent expression is in the domestic domain, an analytical yet rather amorphous construct which covers the field of personal relations centred on household, reproduction and parenting. Thus, in the African societies which Fortes studied, predominantly male kinship activities which took place in the domains of law, politics and the management of power were seen as underpinned by predominantly female kinship activities focused on discrete, co-resident, family groupings.[3] Implicit in this notion of the domestic domain is the view that what people do with their kin and how they act towards them cannot be explained by resort to individual materialistic or instrumental considerations alone but involves the evocation of higher order human capacities which are fundamentally social in character. In this sense, the axiom of amity is nothing less than a convenient shorthand for those complex social operations involving questions of morality, conscience, obligation, belonging and identity which enable human beings to conduct meaningful and enduring social relations.

Exemplary in this regard are parental relations which, in all societies, have resulted in the expression and maintenance of powerful linkages across the generations. Furthermore, the act of marrying was seen universally as the occasion on which the main pillars of these enduring and axiomatic relations were secured in position; nature was, in effect, simply being given a legalistic gloss by the rites of marriage.

In the approaches identified above, whether marriage, family or the broader frameworks of kinship are under consideration, a strongly integrationist imperative is in evidence. Such accounts draw attention to a discrete clustering of interactions which centre upon the domestic unit in which identities and values are assumed to converge into normative and stable arrangements. Critiques of this approach to family and kinship have developed from a variety of perspectives: feminist, Marxist and psycho-analytic (see Morgan 1985 for a review of these). My intention here is to present a further challenge to this dominant perspective through a detailed consideration of what happens when adults who were once committed to the long-term ideals of marriage, parenthood and cohabitation take the decision to part and initiate a process of disintegration and disengagement. What happens when 'shared construal' is no longer shared, the ongoing 'marital conversation' stops and 'small group culture' breaks down? In making long-term relationships in western society, the traditional pattern is one in which attraction precedes courtship, which precedes marriage, which precedes home-making, which precedes parenthood, or some rough approximation of this ordering. Little is known about the increasingly common situation in which the delights and compulsions which guide and direct the consolidation of relationships are thrown into reverse. What happens when the desire for integration is replaced by the painful and drawn-out stratagems of separation and former intimates set about disentangling themselves from the 'super-personality' which was formerly their marriage and family? A deeply tangled history of relationships, emotions and exchanges carries a considerable momentum and is not easily erased. Familial relationships, in some form or other, tend to continue long after the apparent finality of marital breakdown. The dominant paradigms of kinship and family in western society have bequeathed only a limited conceptual and analytical vocabulary with which to consider these continuities. Family and household are all too often treated synonymously and the complex kindreds which emerge over time following divorce are not easily characterised.

At one level, therefore, the present work can be seen as an attempt to throw light on aspects of family and kinship which have largely escaped the attention of researchers: a body of ethnographic and qualitative data relating to divorce and separation is examined for what it tells us about relationships which do not fit neatly within the theoretical paradigms which have dominated accounts of the western family. At a rather more grand theoretical level, however, consideration of the fate of familial relationships after divorce might also be seen as an attempt to go beyond the axiom of amity and to consider some of the more enduring features of human relationships. We can begin to explore the wider reaches of intimate human relationships by moving beyond a view which sees social life as firmly and solely located in ongoing, positive and active contacts to one which encompasses a broader range of relational possibilities and, incidentally, one which is more consistent with the pattern of human relationships which has prevailed for most people throughout most of human history. The vicissitudes of human existence have meant that the need to care and nurture subsequent generations, or the 'social organisation of human reproduction' as Robertson (1991) refers to it, has always been character- ised by flexible and fluid adult relationships. In extreme circumstances, communities have lived through crises such as war, migration, natural catastrophe or slavery and experienced conflict, separation and loss yet, despite the radically altered circumstances of personal existence, continuities of family life prevail (see for example Gutman 1984; Harris 1995). To consider these added and perhaps unconventional dimensions of social life is to recognise that who we are is not simply determined by the positive relations we have with those that surround us but that ongoing negative relationships as well as the absence, the memory and the former significance of others also play their part in who we are and who we might become. What the testimonies of those who were interviewed in this study repeatedly reveal is that beyond the apparent finality of relationship breakdown is an ongoing struggle to rise above havoc and distress and to fashion kin relations afresh.

I would suggest that in order to understand the full social and cultural significance of these developments in relation to the modern western family we have to move beyond the axiom of amity and to countenance more complex and multi-layered views of social life. For example, long after powerfully normative notions of marriage, amity and morality have been rendered redundant through separation, other imperatives of human sociality persist. Former husbands and wives still have to be part of one another's social worlds despite the fact that their changed circumstances mean that they are mostly absent from one another. They might thus encounter one another as an actual physical presence or in the imagination, as former intimates who are implicated in one another's biography rather more than is comfortable. In other words, the transformation of family life which divorce sets in train does not relieve people of the need to make sense of themselves in relation to one another and this process of 'making sense' is still fundamentally social in character. An ethnographic exploration of these continuities must therefore adopt a radically different perspective from that espoused by conventional sociologies of the family. Bringing the unclear family into focus necessitates a consideration of the ways in which people assert and express continuities between themselves after divorce.

In order to produce an ethnographic account of the continuities, concrete and abstract, which persist after divorce I have explored three closely related theoretical themes. These themes are networks, disputes and narratives and it will be useful to say a little about each of these in order to highlight the distinctive uses to which I have pressed these concepts. The idea of social networks has proved a productive and persuasive metaphor for understanding social relations in general and kinship relations in particular (Mitchell 1969; Bott 1971; Cochrane *et al.* 1990). Network approaches provide on the one hand a methodology for mapping and enumerating relationships and on the other a theoretical framework within which sets of relationships can be conceptualised. In this sense networks are the patterns of relationship which arise out of empirically identifiable social interactions. My own use of the concept of networks combines insights derived from classic network theory with those of more recent approaches to the study of processes of social ordering as found in the work of actor network theorists (e.g. Law 1994). In the approach of the latter, networks are not seen as stable, final configurations of individual actors but as processes in which actors (and in actor network theory they may not even be human actors) make and re-make networks by attributing characteristics, distributing properties, making connections and circulating objects and information. The potential of actor network theory in the context of divorce is that it offers a way of making sense of the distinctive relations and diverse spatial arrangements that emerge after divorce; it gives us some clues as to how we might talk about a father's relationship with a daughter or son with whom he does not live or a mother's relationship with an ex-husband's new wife or any one of a number of de-centralised and de-localised family relationships. Thus, networks are not to be treated as things which exist independent of the actions which make them up; they are more akin to narrational fields which come into effect as people assert claims upon, and interests in, the people and things which are important to them.

My attempts to develop what is in effect a social constructivist perspective on familial deconstruction is exemplified at numerous points throughout the present work. For example, in chapter 2, informants' accounts of relationships after divorce are considered. These accounts reveal the way that important continuities are maintained after divorce. The chapter provides two extended narrations of post-divorce kinship each of which demonstrates a radically different strategy for the organisation of relationships after divorce. In one, the 'nuclear family mould', family members are constrained to replicate former family structures in a way which minimises or plays down the connections which persist between them. In the second account, the 'extending family', there is an evident passion for accretion and expansion of relationships across the conjugal divide. In both cases, people begin with the basic currencies of Euro-American kinship but in each one the emergent networks are constrained rather differently by material circumstance. In chapters 3, 4 and 5 the notion of disputes is taken up. In the expression and maintenance of continuities after divorce disputes play a vital role. Considerable energy is put into anticipating, plotting, confronting and reacting to a variety of actual and assumed adversaries. The two main sites of dispute considered here are access to children by their fathers and payment of child support to mothers by their former husbands. Children and money constitute just two of the many points at which parties are likely to engage in dispute and thereby invest considerable energies in the maintenance of social relationships, albeit negative and somewhat acrimonious ones. By considering in detail what people fall out about, why they fall out about these things and the way they express their grievances and disputes, light is thrown onto the ideological factors which motivate and shape people's concerns for the integrity of their kinship relations once they separate. Crucial in this regard is a fundamental tension between patrifiliation and matrifocality with men expressing their concern and often their despera-tion at finding themselves on the outside looking in when it comes to parenting their children after divorce. In the penultimate chapter, attention turns explicitly to narrative and its role in enabling us to understand the emergence of new patterns of relationships and roles after divorce. The chapter provides a detailed analysis of interview material drawn from different members of two former nuclear family units. The analysis extends notions of network to incorporate the dialogical nature of informants' accounts and goes on to illustrate the ways in which real and imagined relationships are woven together in the stories they tell about their present and former circumstances. Through these acts of narration can be seen the rich social and mental life which holds members of a former nuclear family suspended in ongoing webs of emotional and economic dependence in the wake of divorce.

Analysis of networks, disputes and narratives after divorce takes us beyond the axiom of amity. However, before such a move, it is necessary to consider briefly the context in which the data upon which my analysis is based were collected.

Picking through the Wreckage

The data upon which this book is based have been brought together from many sources. The bulk of the empirical data I have drawn upon were generated during a prolonged sojourn in the world of socio-legal research. Between 1985 and 1992 I worked as an anthropologist in a multidisciplinary team which at various points in its development was comprised of sociologists, lawyers, economists and social policy analysts. A considerable body of data was generated by this research team, most of which related to the emotional, economic and social wreckage left when the conjugal family runs aground. Over a seven-year period and under the auspices of a variety of research centres I was engaged in projects related to divorce and spent many hundreds of hours in discussion with divorcing and divorced men, women and occasionally their children. I attended court hearings and appointments; observed conciliation appointments and interviewed conciliators and court welfare officers. Research projects undertaken covered post-divorce issues such as custody and access,[4] the use of welfare and legal services, housing, conflict and dispute resolution and most recently a study of post-divorce fatherhood[5] (see for example Ogus *et al.* 1989; McCarthy & Simpson 1991; Corlyon *et al.* 1991; McCarthy *et al.* 1991; Simpson *et al.* 1995).

The research projects undertaken during this period were to a large extent driven by the policy agenda of the time. High on this agenda, then as now, were the unprecedented levels of divorce in England and Wales and the substantial costs engendered by changes in the way that families are structured and resourced after divorce. Of particular interest to those responsible for dealing with divorce and its consequences was the question of conflict. In the UK, as in most other countries in the western world, the social and economic costs of dealing with divorce related conflicts have risen inexorably over the last twenty years. Disputes over children, finances and property have found their way in increasing numbers to the doors of the courts and of welfare agencies. Expenditure on legal aid for matrimonial and family proceedings in England and Wales was rising steadily throughout the 1980s and was £133 million in 1989–90. This trend continued and by 1993–4 this had more than doubled reaching £332 million (Legal Aid Board 1994). Similarly, issues of maintenance and child support were prominent in the policy concerns of that period. The Child Support Agency ostensibly brought into operation in 1993 in order to press recalcitrant non-custodial parents to maintain their offspring incurred an estimated start-up cost of £150 million and running costs of £115 million in its first year (Child Support Agency 1994). Substantial costs such as these did not rest easily alongside the policies of a Conservative government which was at once committed to the 'traditional family', to reducing state intervention in people's private lives and to cutting taxes. Hardly surprising therefore that the costs and benefits of changing family structures received close research attention.

The research which began my own involvement in the area of divorce commenced in 1985 when I was employed on a major project funded by the Lord Chancellor's Department. The task of the project was to evaluate the costs and effectiveness of divorce conciliation in England and Wales. In order to do this a sample of couples was identified as they passed through divorce courts and conciliation services. These couples were subsequently monitored as they jumped over hurdles and passed through hoops to unpick their once cherished ideals of marriage and family life. As questionnaires, interviews and correspondence revealed, those with whom we were in contact expressed strong feelings of shame, anger, guilt and sadness but rather more powerful was the desire, at least on the part of one of the parties, to wrench free of the constraints and impediments of married life and embark upon the painful and challenging process of constructing self and family anew. For many of the individuals who filled in our questionnaires, sat through our interviews and generally gave us access to their lives during this most delicate period, the applications and petitions to the courts were their point of entry into our research. The initial sample identified in order to carry out research into divorce conciliation was made up of 1143 cases which were passing through the divorce courts in 1985. These cases were selected on the basis that there was some indication of dispute or disagreement over the children of the marriage. The majority of these cases were linked to divorce petitions of which we were able to identify a total of 1047. It is worthwhile reflecting for a moment on what this institutional data revealed about the initial sample.

In 70 per cent of cases the divorce petition had been filed by the wife. Husbands were more likely to have taken the initiative in applying for divorce if they had custody of the children. There were 182 cases (19 per cent) in which fathers had custody of the children and in two-thirds of these cases he was the petitioner. The court sample involved a total of 2281 children. In 80 per cent of cases there were two or less children. In

67 per cent of the cases the children were living with their mother at the time of the petition or application. In 18 per cent they were living with their father and in the remaining cases some arrangement involving both parents was indicated, typically with both parents occupying the former matrimonial home. The 'specified facts' cited in the divorce petitions were predominantly 'fault' related with 31 per cent of petitioners citing adultery and 60 per cent alleging 'unreasonable behaviour'. Adultery was a more common complaint on petitions lodged by men whereas 'unreasonable behaviour' featured more regularly on women's petitions. The sample differed from the national average in that 'unreasonable behaviour' petitions were over-represented (the 1986 average for England and Wales was 45 per cent). Petitions citing separation after two years by consent and five years without consent were correspondingly under-represented. The choice of 'fact' often reflects the difficulty of divorce, for example unilateral allegations of 'unreasonable behaviour' suggest a different approach to divorce than an agreed separation after two years. The deviations from the national average regarding the 'specified facts' are thus a further indication that the sample we identified was rather more conflicted than the average divorce case.

This brief profile is in no way meant to be a comprehensive accounting of what proved to be a very complicated sampling and pick-up procedure (Ogus *et al.* 1989 chapter 10). It is no more than a general indication of the baseline from which other samples were subsequently identified. Suffice it to say that the 1143 cases were contacted and resulted in responses from 482 individuals agreeing to be actively involved in the research. A further 249 cases were identified from conciliation services operating independently of the courts and from these 306 individual positive responses were received. All respondents who had opted into the research were sent a series of questionnaires and a sub-sample was selected for interview. In the event the initial interview cohort consisted of 75 men and 76 women of which 33 were double cases, that is, ones in which both parties were interviewed. The Conciliation Project Unit sample then became the basis of several future projects for which we returned to our respondents. Variations on this sample were approached regarding their experience of housing (1989), their experience of petitioning for divorce on the grounds of unreasonable behaviour (1989), their experience of relationships four years after their initial contact with the courts (1990), and finally a project focusing on fathers after divorce was carried out (1991). What accumulated over the years was thus an important and unique corpus of longitudinal data relating to a sample of divorced people. The present work is an attempt to examine this data set as a totality and to draw out threads relating to individual lives and families. In particular, I have focused in some depth on the interview material generated throughout this period and this data forms the main basis for my account of kinship continuities after divorce.

To turn data collected specifically for one purpose to serve a rather different one is a risky undertaking unless the inherent limitations and particular characteristics of the data are made explicit from the outset. Principal in this respect is the simple fact that those talked about in this book are all people who were formerly married. As Goode (1993: 163) has pointed out, the characteristics of those who are married are systematically different from those who co-habit and these differences have significant implications at divorce. At divorce, married couples are likely to have lived together longer, to have one or more children and accumulated more property than cohabiting couples. Wives are more likely to have altered their employment patterns in order to fit in with the demands of mothering rather than have maintained full-time continuous employment like their co-habiting equivalents. Partners to a marriage are also more likely to have merged money, assets, friendship networks and kin than co-habitees (op. cit.). These important distinctions are worthwhile bearing in mind throughout this work as the original commitment to marriage by those in the sample and their subsequent attempt to live according to certain ideals and aspirations engenders a particularly complex task of disentangling issues, emotions and entitlements which may not be so apparent among cohabitees who terminate established relationships.

It is also important to bear in mind that the initial data set was generated as part of a study whose brief was to evaluate the costs and effectiveness of family conciliation (Ogus *et al.* 1989). The sampling procedure for this research involved tracking individuals through courts and conciliation services in no less than twelve different areas of England and Wales. The data collection commenced in 1985 and potential research cases were identified using a wide variety of triggers to indicate whether or not there were conflicts which might require the services of conciliation or a court adjudication. The main focus of the research was to evaluate the relative effectiveness of the various dispute resolution procedures using measures which included rates of settlement, lastingness of agreement and satisfaction with outcomes. Typically, these conflicts concerned child custody and access (or residence and contact as they have been referred to since the Children Act of 1989). Immediately, therefore, four important characteristics of the data need to be highlighted.

First, the cases which I will be discussing in the present work originate in a sample explicitly selected for the fact that the parties were formerly married couples who were in dispute or disagreement over their children at the time of divorce. This is potentially problematic given that the thesis I present identifies conflict as central to ongoing social relationships after divorce and separation. However, I would contend that the difference between this population and the divorcing population in general when it comes to conflict is a difference of order rather than of kind, especially when the conflict is over children. The samples from which many of my illustrations are drawn are simply more stark renditions of the problems faced by many people in the aftermath of divorce. Despite the growing numbers of people who divorce, the conflict free divorce is still the exception and, given the deep economic and emotional commitments that individuals make to one another, is likely to be the case into the foreseeable future. Contrary to the views of some commentators who suggest an increasingly frivolous escape from marriage, it appears that divorcing couples only rarely give up their marriage without long and painful deliberation.

Second, the conflicts identified in the original study were between couples over their children. Whilst conflict and children represent abiding and closely related themes in most divorce cases these should not be assumed to be present at the ending of every marriage and likewise the pattern of dispute among couples without children who divorce is very different from those described in this work. To focus on child disputes is thus to highlight continuities of a particular kind. They are ones in which questions of kinship, resources, identity and the future are placed centre stage. However, in terms of gender the continuities are not neutral. Whilst in a small minority of cases children were resident with their fathers after divorce, in the vast majority of cases they were resident with their mothers on a day-to-day basis and visited their fathers at weekends and at holiday time. Questionnaire responses reveal that throughout the five years of study over four-fifths of women reported having custody of all their children. At the outset of the study approximately one-quarter of men reported having custody of all their children and by the final survey in 1989 this had risen to approximately one-third (McCarthy *et al.* 1991: 4).

Thirdly, the fact that the couples who were interviewed in this sample were going through divorce courts or conciliation services in 1985 identifies them with a particular period of family law. It comes after the 1984 Matrimonial and Family Proceedings Act. This Act relieved men of the obligation to maintain their wives and opened the way for creative exchanges in which many women traded off their right to spousal maintenance in return for equity tied up in the matrimonial home. This legislation was part of the much vaunted move towards a 'clean break' at divorce and was aimed at reducing the financial entanglements of husbands and wives after divorce. However, the sample is pre-Children Act 1989, pre-Child Support Act 1991 and pre-the divorce law reform heralded in the White Paper *Looking to the Future: Mediation and the Ground for Divorce* published by the Lord Chancellor's Department in April 1995. Each of these legislative developments aims to steer the responsibility for dealing with the consequences of divorce away from the state and back onto the parties. Indeed, the views and experiences of the families that were identified as the original Conciliation Project Unit sample have in some small ways fed into these three important changes in divorce legislation. Nonetheless, the sample identified was very much of the period. This is perhaps best summed up in terms of an expectation amongst those who comprised the sample of a high level of state intervention, direction and paternalism at a time when the dominant political ethos was consistently working in the opposite direction.

The final feature of the sample to be borne in mind concerns the motivation for research participants to have stayed involved for the length of time that they did. As different phases of the research were carried out and requests were made for further information from informants in the form of questionnaires and interviews there was an inevitable attrition. Parties resolved their problems and felt that they were no longer of interest to the research, in some cases disputes took a turn for the worse and parties felt they could not share their anger and their grief even if it was in the cause of research, whilst others moved house and did not leave forwarding addresses. The result was a core of highly dependable and co-operative individuals about whom a considerable amount of information was generated regarding this major transition in their lives. But, as in any social research, the element of self-selection is liable to introduce distortions. It is worthwhile noting that over time the attrition was likely to have moved the samples in the direction of a more educated and articulate group than would have appeared by random chance (see Table 1 in McCarthy *et al.* 1991: 4). However, I would maintain that the breadth of the data considered still gives a uniquely detailed and intimate insight into this painful and deeply sensitive transition in people's personal lives.

A Note on Method

In each of the research projects on which I worked, information was collected to answer specific, policy-oriented questions. However, the model of the policy machine lubricated and adjusted with the benefit of research input is idealistic to say the least. An apparent hunger for information to service the policy process is contradicted by the fact that government is highly selective and discriminating in what is appropriate material when it comes to policy considerations (cf. Weiss 1986: 221–3). Inevitably, attempts to formulate research agenda with these possibilities and constraints in mind have an effect on the kinds of questions one might come up with. For example, to obtain funding, research must address clearly identifiable questions, it has to be turned around quickly, its methodologies have to be crisp and results easily condensed. In applied research terms, divorce as a complex, contingent, situated process will therefore tend to be re-cast as a simple mechanistic process for which we can assume a range of commonalities from case to case. Geertz captures the distinction implied here in his contrast between extensive and intensive data; the former refers to a kind of data collection which cuts across temporal and social continuities whereas the latter pays full attention to the deep and convoluted nature of social life through time (Leach 1967; Geertz 1983).

In the original analysis of the qualitative data collected during these projects many of these temporal and social continuities were overlooked. The approach to analysis in the early days of the research was, to use Geertz's phrase, 'experience distant', that is, seeking to extract common-alities from samples of men and women created as a result of having the shared characteristic of passing through the divorce courts in 1985. The present work is based on a re-examination of the mass of taped interviews accumulated by Judy Corlyon and me throughout these projects with an eye upon the way that individual actor's narratives show divorced people re-organising their interests and claims in relation to one another. The substantial corpus of data assembled was extensively transcribed and analysed at the time but inevitably only a fraction found its way into formal reports and publications at the end of each project.

Consideration of these interviews, as discursive talk and narrative rather than as sources of factual information, opened up the possibility of exploring 'experience near' concepts, that is, ones which are used 'naturally and effortlessly' by an informant to make sense of experience (Geertz 1983: 57). Significant in this regard is the fact that we had returned to particular individuals on a regular basis over and over again and considerable rapport had been established with many of our informants. In re-visiting the tapes and transcripts, it was therefore possible to examine informant accounts unfolding over time. Also, we had interviewed not just divorced individuals but divorced couples in many cases and therefore had generated a particularly special and unique form of data. In these 'double cases', as we came to refer to them, emerge parallel accounts which provide important glimpses of the way in which men and women set about the business of disentangling themselves from one another. Their narratives emerge not only over time but in relation to one another. As such, the interviews invite consideration of the complex and contradictory perspectives on events, motives, relationships and expectations which emerge once the project of family is derailed. In these Rashoman-like versions lies an antidote to the simplistic piling up of accounts in the direction of one interest or another which often characterises divorce research. The interviews are thus not simply instances of a one to one communication but reveal a complex, multiplanar account of how family relationships, as a special kind of social relationship, are ordered and maintained after divorce.

The encounter between interviewer and informant is in many ways a peculiar one. A relative stranger appears in your living room. They invite you to 'tell the story' about a personal and often deeply painful series of events. These events are more than likely to have changed your life and are still in the process of changing it in a profound and irreversible way. Not surprisingly, respondents were typically in an emotionally raw state when we interviewed them with some trying, perhaps years after the event, to make sense of an untidy and tangled mess of people, emotions and things and the energies that were formerly invested in them. Awareness of a 'normal' world in which neatness, economy and precision in inter-personal relationships were assumed to be the common currency made informants all the more sensitive about their plight. A thought that often crossed my mind during interviews was why, given these circumstances, people seemed 'happy' to meet with a researcher. On the occasions when I actually asked informants this question I received two types of response; one official, 'frontstage' and impersonal and the other unofficial, 'backstage' and deeply personal. The official response was something along the lines that divorce is an event that causes great sadness and can easily cause even greater sadness if handled badly by the parties, the courts and the authorities and therefore, as a typical example of a person experiencing divorce, I am glad to be of service to your university, and therefore to a legitimate (i.e. not sensational, voyeuristic, profit-making or amateur) piece of research which might ultimately help others. This rather altruistic response no doubt arises in part from the appeal for 'help' requested in the various letters sent to informants on university headed notepaper. For the purposes of the research, what we asked for and what adults undergoing divorce and separation tried to articulate to us were simple, honest accounts that were in a sense typical yet exemplary. The informal response, not voiced directly, but often lying behind the formal response was something along the lines: I rarely get the chance to talk about these issues and I value the fact that I can rehearse my accounts of events, I can sound off about things and I can show emotion in the knowledge that none of it will ever find its way back into the turbulent disequilibrium which now characterises some of the most significant relationships in my life. The interviews were thus a straightforward and perhaps rare occasion to talk without pressure about the personal consequences of divorce. After all, the minutiae of access arrangements or financial wrangles whilst crucial in their every detail to the parties involved can be deadly boring to those for whom family life is largely implicit, self-evident and self-ordering. The presence of an empathetic researcher who is concerned to grasp this detail could be a surprising and fortuitous encounter. In terms of the research methodology adopted, the successful interview was thus one in which a shift in dominance was to a greater or lesser extent brought about. The interviewer might begin by controlling the content and direction of communication consistent with the interviewee's formal expectations surrounding participation in an interview but ideally, by the end, the interviewer should have been able to transfer this sense of dominance to the interviewee who would be encouraged to take control of the topics and progressively increase their amount of talk (cf. Linell 1990).

Embedded in the interviews then, are not just facts but stories, evaluations, interpretations, speculations and illustrations which shed light on the way people go about reviewing and making sense of complex changes. So, for example, the informant might tell a story of what happened, sometimes in a few lines and at other times through a lengthy and detailed disquisition taking hours. As the creator or author of such an account the interviewee can place themselves within their story in whatever spatial or temporal position they wish. The story can begin with an injustice experienced many years ago within the marriage or it can relate to a phone call received in the last twenty-four hours; it can relate to a child who the person sees everyday or to someone who has not been spoken to for many years. The interview can thus be seen as an opportunity for the informant to engage in networking activities in which he or she ranges widely and revealingly across a universe of past, present and indeed future social interactions. To capture this experience and its social consequences in ethnographic terms is the primary reason for re-analysing this corpus of data.

Finally, the failure of the companionate ideal of marriage and all that this entails for self, children and wider kin is rarely something that can be passed off lightly. The interview provides an important illustration of the quest for coherence (cf. Riessman 1990 & 1993 also Linde 1993). In weaving their particular narrative the interviewee is constructing what is essentially a moral account justifying why they became divorced and why they have acted in the way that they have before, during and after divorce. The interview thus provides the respondent with an opportunity to develop 'a self-representation that persuades self and others that the teller is a good person' (Goffman 1969). It is interesting to note in this regard that in many of the interviews carried out the meeting was seen by the informant as an important chance to correct mis-representations, assumed or actual, perpetrated by ex-partners, solicitors or the community at large. The opportunity to produce a self-representation unimpeded or criticised was clearly a welcome one offering a means to expression, expiation and occasionally confession. Despite the fact that informants were aware that their self-centred tellings would not be conveyed beyond the research context they often commented on how valuable it had been simply to tell their story (cf. Day-Sclater 1997). Indeed, with some male informants I was acutely aware that there was nobody else who they had talked to or could talk to about issues which were clearly occupying a disproportionate space in their minds and consequently in their day-to-day activities.

Notes

1. I am grateful to Leena Alanen of the University of Jyväskylä, Finland for alerting me to the work of Buisson and Mermet (1986 also see Alanen 1993: 7) on new forms of familial socialisation. In their analysis, the notion of *familialité* (familiality) is developed to capture the quality and character of the arrangements that parents arrive at after divorce. Their analysis identifies a blurring of public (social) and private (familial) domains in the organisation of parental and former spousal relationships. Their account of *familialité* has clear resonances with the notion of the unclear family developed in the present work.

2. This problem has recently been writ large for the British monarchy as they struggled to find an appropriate response after the death of Diana, Princess of Wales. As the former wife of the heir to the throne and mother of the next heir she was in any case an anomaly; as a deceased, former wife how she should be treated became profoundly problematic as the alleged disagreements between Prince Charles and the Queen

and the subsequent media pressure on the Royal Family to modify funeral arrangements would seem to confirm.

3. The opposition between public and domestic domains as useful analytical categories has been challenged by a number of writers including Yanagisako and Collier (1979); Strathern (1984) and Moore (1988).

4. The terms custody and access are used throughout this work. Despite the fact that these terms were replaced by the less emotive labels of 'residence' and 'contact' in the 1989 Children Act. I have retained custody and access as these were the terms that research participants used and understood. North American readers will be more familiar with the term visitation rather than access.

5. The housing and divorce research was funded by The Joseph Rowntree Memorial Foundation (see McCarthy & Simpson 1991); the divorce petitions project was funded by The Nuffield Foundation (see Corlyon *et al.* 1989); the longitudinal study of relationships after divorce was funded by The Ford Foundation (see McCarthy *et al.* 1991) and the fatherhood research was funded by The Nuffield Foundation (see Simpson *et al.* 1995).

2

Plotting the Contours of the 'Unclear' Family

Rising rates of divorce and separation in Britain over the last twenty years have generated a considerable amount of debate and engaged the perspectives of lawyers, sociologists, theologians, feminists, politicians and policy-makers. The ground over which this highly contested discourse ranges takes in changes in familial residential patterns, gender roles, socialisation and patterns of inheritance, as well as the way in which changes in each of these relate to broader patterns of cultural and social interaction. In other words, precisely the area which anthropologists tend to subsume under the heading of kinship.

To date however, discussion of divorce has been solidly cast in the idiom of family and, as I have suggested in the introduction, this ideologically loaded concept proves wholly inadequate to capture the social complexities it is made to encompass. To talk of family in a non-contested and uncritical way is to obscure the creative possibilities inherent in kinship for the structuring and organisation of inter-personal relations (cf. Weston 1991). The study of divorce as a cultural expression of kinship rather than a social problem with the family demonstrates the distinctiveness of western patterns of relational organisation and transformation; it offers the prospect of locating distinctively Euro-American (Edwards *et al.* 1993: 7–8) ideas of parenthood, relatedness and the transmission of identity within the wider continuum of societies studied by anthropologists. In this chapter consideration is given to the kinship implications of divorce and re-marriage. Consideration of the way in which particular kinds of networks are asserted and maintained after divorce enables us to begin the process of plotting the contours of the unclear family. First, however, it is important to locate the study of divorce within the anthropological study of family and kinship.

Anthropological Perspectives on Divorce

Divorce has long been a pre-occupation of social anthropologists studying non-western societies. Classical structural-functionalist concerns with the reproduction and maintenance of social and political order meant that marriage and its dissolution were of central importance. Just as marriages, in a general sense might be said to be formally marked by the transfer of goods, rights and people, so the ending of marriages involves the realloc-ation of these. The strategies for this reallocation proved illuminating for understanding broader questions of filiation, legitimacy, inheritance and authority in traditional societies. Apparent differences in the stability of marriage across cultures, and particularly those of African tribal societies, were noted and attempts made to explain these in terms of the variability of bridewealth practices. Large bridewealth meant that a substantial bundle of rights were acquired by a husband and his kin in the productive and reproductive capacities of a woman and this, in turn, tended to produce 'low divorce' societies. This contention laid the grounds for the much vaunted and latterly much criticised 'bridewealth and stability of marriage' debate which raged throughout the 1950s (see Comaroff 1980 and Hutchinson 1990 for a review of the issues). Although this debate is instructive in that it focuses on the question of how rights and obligations are reallocated following marital dissolution, in other ways it is singularly unhelpful. Its predominantly jural focus and concomitant concern with male rights obscures the processual aspects of marital dissolution and the extent to which women act as agents within these processes (Hutchinson 1990: 394). The anthropological interest in divorce was thus in terms of what it revealed about marriage in broadly functionalist terms rather than as a process in itself which involved actual relationships and arrangements concerning people and property, negotiated in particular contexts of power and gender relationships. An important exception to this view is to be found in Esther Goody's seminal piece on separation and divorce among the Gonja (1962). In this work, the place of divorce within the develop-mental cycle of the domestic group is made clear, as are the strategies for incorporating its consequences into everyday life (cf. also Stenning 1958 & Cohen 1971). Marriages are ended either *de facto* or *de jure* at various points in the life-cycle and this results in dispersal of kin; a woman may return to her natal village, perhaps with young children, but leaving older ones with their father and his kin.

What is of note here is that in Goody's account, divorce relocates people and relationships in space and time. It does not result in the ending of all relationships between the separating couple. The ties created by the birth of children, for example, continue to bind parents long after they cease to live together. The particular dynamics of Gonja kinship also mean that the splitting of the sibling group is common and this gives rise to a wide range of parenting and caring arrangements. The Gonja case provides a useful illustration of what Goode describes as a 'stable high divorce rate system' (Goode 1993: 16). As he points out, even though the instability of individual marriages is very high in such systems the overall patterning of relationships is remarkably stable for the simple reason that customary arrangements are in place to deal with the economic and kinship consequences of marital dissolution.

The interest in divorce in traditional societies is in stark contrast to the lack of attention paid to divorce in contemporary western society; anthropologists have been slow to respond to the kinship implications of large-scale divorce in contemporary western society.[1] This is a serious omission. Kinship provides a context in which people make sense of the relational dimensions of their lives. Divorce entails a fundamental re-ordering of this context which invites public and private concern. However, given the way that anthropologists have tended to approach the study of English kinship it is hardly surprising that radical changes in this system have escaped attention. As Bouquet has highlighted (1993: 13), the centrality of the study of kinship within the British anthropological tradition makes for a revealing contrast when placed alongside the relative paucity of anthropological studies of English kinship. In a similar, and somewhat wry observation, Barnes (1980: 297) contrasts the study of kinship by anthropologists with the study of family by sociologists. For the former, the study of kinship in non-western societies is a rather serious and esoteric pursuit which forms one of the central planks of the discipline. For the latter, the study of the family has often been treated as rather more lightweight and marginal to central sociological concerns with class, mobility and industrialisation in modern society. Suffice it to say that for a long time anthropologists were not particularly aware that there was anything to study under the heading of kinship in English society. Notable exceptions are the classic monographs of Firth and his colleagues (Firth, Hubert and Forge 1969) who mapped middle-class kinship in London and Young and Willmott who tracked working-class communities in transition with a particular eye on kinship (Young and Willmott 1957). However, the dominant view appears to have been that the family was best left to the attentions of sociologists and psychologists. Beyond the nuclear family in western societies, relations seemed to fall into the rag-bag of bilateral or cognatic systems with an emphasis on fluidity in the ascription of roles and identities. The rich vocabulary of classical anthropological kinship studies, with its ideological focus on descent and group formation, could offer little by way of illumination when considering western kinship in general and English kinship in particular. As a result, English kinship and its consequences for ideas of personhood, community and economy was for a long time lost to anthropological enquiry to the extent that Bouquet has deemed it necessary to 'reclaim' it (1993). Indeed, the lack of analytical rigour in the area of family studies has obscured more than it has revealed about the operations of kinship and household in contemporary society. In a recent review of A.F. Roberston's book *Beyond the Family*, Paul Bohannan was moved to point out the diffuse and unsatisfactory nature of literature on the western family: 'almost never have the lurking assumptions been examined' (1993: 175). In similar vein, Wilson and Pahl (1988) have drawn attention to the overly narrow focus on conjugal and parental roles within the family. Some family sociologists, such as Bernardes (1988) and Scanzioni (Scanzioni *et al.* 1989), have gone so far as to advocate the total abandonment of family as a meaningful concept in sociological discourse.

The anthropological study of divorce and separation put forward here is in some senses part and parcel of the reclamation process advocated by Bouquet (ibid). As such, consideration of divorce as a revealing manifestation of kinship has strong affinities with the study of other domestic and inter-personal contexts in contemporary British society. As Strathern has suggested there is a 'vanishing effect' in operation. The point at which kinship 'disappears' into class or consumption (Strathern 1992a) or into the classrooms of Portuguese undergraduates (Bouquet 1993) is the point at which the implicit is made explicit. Divorce provides a similar occasion for analytical reflection and revelation. Divorce is the point at which marriage is officially dissolved but is also the point at which the principles, assumptions, values, attitudes and expectations surrounding marriage, family and parenting are made explicit. The reason they are made explicit is that these fundamental and implicit cultural tenets are all, in one way or another, confounded and conflicted and have to become the subject of a rather public and painful process of negotiation and calculation. The apparent certainties of the life-cycle are rapidly and irreversibly replaced by the vicissitudes of an individualised life-course. We, along with our informants, can no longer assume that kinship and biology provide immutable, common-sense baselines for the understanding of contemporary English kinship but must endeavour to construct our knowledge of human relations 'after nature' (Strathern 1992a), that is, as a kaleidoscope of connected cultural contexts rather than as a layering of discourses upon a solid foundation of immutable connections. For example, the rhetoric of the enterprise culture, so fundamental to British conservatism throughout the 1980s, provides just such a context. Freedom, fulfilment and authenticity of the individual are shaped through choice. The enterprising self (Rose 1992) is but one step away from enterprising kinship (Strathern 1992b) and the expansion of choice in the conduct of personal relations carries profound implications for the way that we think of relationships of intimacy and friendship, nurture and parenthood as well as obligations to kin in general. Recent efforts to illuminate these processes include Strathern's comprehensive account of new reproductive technologies and their impact on conceptualisations of kinship relations (Strathern 1991, 1992a, 1992b; Edwards *et al.* 1993). La Fontaine has provided a detailed analysis of child abuse in the light of anthropological theories of incest avoidance as well as a broader commentary on changing family (La Fontaine 1985, 1988, 1990). Such studies provide an important point of departure for the study of divorce in that they begin to probe the culturally distinct patterns of procreation, nurture and parenthood found in Britain which have hitherto been treated as opaque and self-evident in most social science discourse.

Important as studies of new reproductive technologies, sexual abuse and incest undoubtedly are, they do tend to reproduce an anthropological preoccupation with the marginal if not the exotic. Divorce and its longer-term consequences on the other hand are pervasive and are bringing about fundamental transformations in patterns of kinship, parenting and what is thought of as family life in contemporary Britain. Yet, these transformations are ones about which we know relatively little. In many ways the debates which currently surround the family suggest a point similar to the one identified in the 1970s by Pahl (1984) regarding unemployment. In the preface to *Divisions of Labour* he points to the absence at that time of any clear understanding regarding the relationship between work and household provisioning on the one hand and unemployment on the other. Then, as now, the absence of good ethnographic research on a politically loaded topic makes it difficult to separate what is actually happening from the fog of ideological pronouncements about what might be happening or, as is more often the case, what pundits feel should be happening on the ground.

What is readily apparent from even a cursory examination of recent divorce statistics is that divorce has become an increasingly common part of the life-course for men and women in contemporary society. In the not too distant past divorce was a relatively isolated and anomalous incident in a world of 'normal' families. It was perceived as evidence of deviance and pathology and invited attention of a therapeutic kind (Dominian 1965).

Nowadays, this sense of anomaly and stigma has been greatly diluted. Today, divorce and family reconstitution are an increasingly distinctive weft running through the fabric of society, linking households through the movement of children and property from former marital relationships and generating new and complex variations in the ordering of kinship relations. The result for many divorced men and women is that they find themselves at the centre of extensive kindreds based as much on the negative affinities of divorce, as on the positive relationships one normally attributes to relations between kin. Connections, albeit negative and unwelcome, must be directly or indirectly incorporated into networks based on more conventional notions of family and kinship. Unlike the compact and predictable sociality of the nuclear family, the post-divorce kindred is fashioned out of a dispersed and rather less predictable sociality in which kinship, residence and the economics of household are substantially refigured. From the perspective of any one individual several layers of kin may have to be ordered as new constellations of relatives appear and disappear as a result of divorce and re-marriage. But, just as families are zipped together through acts of recombination they may be just as easily unzipped at some later date compounding even further the confusions over the significance of others. Similarly, the discrete family residence may for the child become radically de-centred as children pass through multiple family spaces in which they might well also have their own private spaces. Indeed, the identification of the post-divorce family with two or even more households is presented in many divorce 'self-help' books as the 'ideal' solution to the problem of ensuring parental continuity in the face of conjugal discontinuity (Ricci 1980; Burrett 1993). Resourcing the family may be similarly fragmented with household income a patchwork of wage, state benefits and the formal and informal inter-household transfer of money, labour and commodities. Such arrangements I have dubbed the unclear family.

The Unclear Family: a Case in Point

Steve is a man in his mid thirties. He is a local government caretaker living in tied accommodation and, by his own estimation, 'happily' married to Karen. They have three children. This is the family as it would appear to be on a tax return or census form or on a typical evening in front of the television. However, when Steve met Karen she was a single-parent caring for her daughter (see Figure 2.1). She was not in contact with the child's father. When they married in 1990, Steve took on the role of 'father' to Karen's daughter, that is, by virtue of co-residence, his marriage to Karen and his economic support for the two of them, he became what is commonly referred to as the child's step-father or, rather more formally, her *pater*. Steve and Karen went on to have two children together. Steve also came to the marriage with previous commitments. He was earlier married to Kath, from whom he divorced in 1985. Together they had produced two daughters with whom Steve was still in regular contact and who came to stay with Steve and Karen on a regular basis. Steve also spoke of a relationship he had had in his teens which resulted in the birth of a son who lived close by and whom he saw from time to time. However, he neither lived with the boy's mother nor had had any permanent relationship with her.

Kath   Steve   Karen

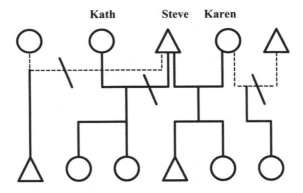

Figure 2.1. Kinship diagram showing the marriages and children of Steve. (divorces are shown by oblique lines. Dotted lines represent non-marital relationships)

Steve's narration of his 'family life' places him at the centre of a network of relationships which carry varying loads in terms of affect and commitment. For example, he sees himself as a 'father' to six children. However, the way in which fatherhood is expressed and experienced by Steve in relation to each of his children is variable. The simple label 'father' condenses and conceals varying levels of financial and emotional commitment, different residential arrangements and variable quantities of contact with these six children.

In being a 'father' to his children, Steve also comes into contact with the three women who are the mothers of the five children to whom he is *genitor*. He co-habits with his present wife Karen but also regularly meets with his ex-wife, Kath and has helped her with domestic and relationship problems. He also sees the mother of his eldest son from time to time, with whom he claims to 'get on well'. To complete the picture, he also claims to have good relationships with the current partners of both his ex-partners, that is, the step-fathers of the children who do not live with him.

Steve also likes to present his children as being part of 'one big happy family'. He encourages them to treat the various full-, half- and step-sibling relationships as if they were all 'brothers and sisters'. He sees this as having considerable potential when it comes to future patterns of friendship, support and obligation between them. However, not everyone understands and interprets the pattern and meaning of sibling relations as Steve does. From the perspective of grandparents, for example, there is considerable impetus to deny such patterns as they seek to establish their own sense of boundary and structure to their 'family' after divorce. Steve's parents speak of having six grandchildren while Karen's parents speak of having three. This discrepancy in reckoning has become a source of conflict between Steve and his in-laws, because it translates into actions on their part which Steve sees as divisive of the sibling group. The principle of treating all the children equally, which is espoused by Steve and Karen, is contradicted when Karen's mother ignores Steve's children from his earlier marriage and only gives treats and gifts to the children actually born to Karen. The children for their part can find themselves with four, six or possibly eight relatives at the grandparental level.

Steve provides us with a summary account of what constitutes family life for a growing number of men, women and children in Britain today. Measured against the cereal-packet norm of the nuclear family it is complex, with children and resources linking households across space and time, in ways which render the identification of family with a single, discrete household wholly misleading. Indeed, the whole vocabulary of western kinship is woefully inadequate when it comes to making intelligible the complex arrangements which lie beneath the simple notions of mother, father, family, home, son and daughter in contemporary contexts.

What was once part of the habitus of domestic organisation – 'a system of durable transposable dispositions' (Bourdieu 1977) – must, because of divorce, necessarily be transposed in such a way that structures and values are made conscious and explicit. The practical mastery of the domestic habitus is undermined; actions, strategies and intentions have to be thought about in ways that would not normally occur in the family prior to divorce. Pragmatic decisions have to be taken about where children should live, how often they should see the other parent, who should support whom and at what level. Emotional and economic contributions previously invisible in the implicit and private ordering of home and hearth become subject to exacting and explicit public classification and calculation; they are described and transformed by a whole new vocabulary. For example, a father's contribution to the domestic budget thus becomes 'maintenance' or 'support' while his role as a parent is likely to be expressed as 'access' or 'contact'. There is nothing new in the distinction between *pater* and *genitor* which emerges from these transformations and neither is there anything new in the idea that the tenuousness of physiological paternity is apt to render its social constructions somewhat diverse across cultures (Barnes 1973). What is new in this account is the way essentialist notions of fatherhood, as a coherent repertoire of assumptions, attitudes, emotions and relationships, are rendered partial and fragmented. The emerging patterns of serial monogamy mean that fatherhood is enacted and embodied differently according to situation and circumstance. Fatherhood is thus simultaneously a grand iconic image as well as a multiplicity of situated and specifiable possibilities. Steve's account of fatherhood can thus be seen as an attempt to orchestrate multiple narratives relating to other marriages, other relationships and other parenting, within a single narrative. As I demonstrate in considerably more detail in later chapters, the cultural scripts which shape how such narratives ought to be are highly contested. Steve provides one version of how ideas of hegemonic masculinity (Carrigan *et al.* 1985; Cornwall and Lindisfarne 1994) and the emergent habitus of family life after divorce are brought together in practice.

Where familial arrangements fall outside the temporally stable, co-resident, nuclear model, external and normative factors such as the form and extent of state economic and welfare support following marital breakdown or the legal machinery to process divorce and civil dispute come into play to shape relational continuities. Adjusting to relationship breakdown and divorce, despite the illusion of private ordering, thus amounts to a series of personal choices and negotiations conducted within state-controlled parameters about the way that kinship ought to be. Just what these parameters are, and the models to which people turn in order to make sense of their circumstances in the wake of divorce, are only beginning to emerge.

Continuity and Discontinuity after Divorce

Marital breakdown necessitates dismantling the joint edifice of family life and divorce is the legal mechanism sanctioning this process. Putting asunder, however, does not have the dire consequences that it had in the nineteenth century when divorce brought shame and ostracism, particularly to women. Far from being the social death that it once was, divorce is nowadays more likely to be framed in terms of liberation and social rebirth; 'an acute version of the process of "finding oneself" which the social conditions of modernity force upon us all' (Giddens 1991: 12). However, divorce is not entirely the unfettered quest for personal freedom and individual autonomy which such comments imply. On the contrary, personal destiny and family history are deeply entwined and in practice divorce is just as likely to reproduce continuities in social relationships as it is to establish discontinuities. From an anthropological perspective the interesting problem is what continues and what does not, what kin relations are preserved and developed and which ones attenuate and atrophy? The terminologies applied in popular discourse tend to mask such continuities whilst emphasising the discrete households and family forms that emerge. Categories such as 'lone' or 'single' parent, 'second family' and 'absent father' all emphasise the separateness of persons rather than the ways in which they retain connections economically, socially and emotionally after divorce.

In terms of the wider network of relatives the patterns are difficult to predict and often run counter to expectations of a conjugal chasm held by onlookers or, indeed, by participants themselves. In a study of middle-class families in London, a case is presented in which the person a woman was closest to after divorce was her ex-husband's sister and her daughter (Firth *et al.* 1969: 288). This rather arbitrary process has been referred to by Finch as 'working out' (Finch 1989: 194–211); it is a process of evaluating relationships on the basis of shared histories and future expectations rather than rigid role prescriptions. The networks which are established once a couple cut loose from the moorings of affinity thus appear to owe more to voluntarism than to expectation: more to process than to structure. However, 'working out' relationships and identifying an ego-centred post-divorce kindred is not without its problems for there are no clear expectations as to how one should treat an ex-husband's new wife or what one's attitudes should be to affines who were, prior to divorce, close and supportive relatives (Finch and Mason 1990). Indeed, for a divorcing couple 'working out' is far too neat a description of this process and the idea of disentangling or disaggregating social relations might be a better conceptualisation. Speaking of notions of personhood among the Are'are of Melanesia, Strathern sees this process as being achieved 'via funerary, bridewealth and similar prestations, transactions that lay out the person in terms of the claims diverse others have' (Strathern 1996: 527). Divorce necessitates similar processes of disaggregating persons in terms of their interests, rights and claims in one another. Such processes are invariably characterised by high levels of confusion and ambivalence over how and whether these processes should take place. The difficulties raised by this process are further compounded by the form which Euro-American kinship takes. The capacity for extension of the kinship network is an important feature of bilateral kinship systems; they appear to have 'no in built boundaries' (Strathern 1996: 529). Chains of potential relationships span out from the individual person in all directions and can be activated according to a wide range of apparently arbitrary contingencies. The capacity for relatives to become 'distant', 'lost' or 'forgotten' is an important indicator of this process in operation. The prevalence of divorce has now added the kin prefix 'ex-' to this list. Just as marriage generates a universe of kin who are like one's consanguineous kin but are related 'in-law', divorce converts these relatives into 'ex' relations. People will thus talk of their 'ex-mother-in-law' or 'ex-sister-in-law'. Conversely, relatives also retain their potential for resurrection at some point in the future despite the absence of active contact or communication. As the following examples illustrate, disaggregating persons is not simply a linear process but one in which parties may have radically different ideas about how networks and boundaries should be constituted.

In the first example, the couple in question had evolved a reasonably communicative relationship despite a painful and highly conflicted divorce some six years earlier. In the passage below the man is reflecting on his ex-wife's relationship with his relatives:

> The only thing that is odd is that Kate [ex-wife] tends to pop up at my family gatherings . I find that most odd. To me it's a source of extreme resentment. It makes T [new partner] feel terribly awkward. I find it embarrassing. I used to say 'I can't go to any formal occasion without that bloody woman being there!' During the time that we were married she tried to draw me away from my family and into her family and she put all sorts of obstacles in the way of us going to any kind of functions with my family. Yet as soon as we separate she's trying to home in on my family – it's most odd. And I find it insensitive of the people sending the invitations to invite her. And secondly I find it insensitive of her to accept the invitations.

His ex-wife, for her part, claimed not to see her husband's family very often – *'we haven't fallen out or anything, we just don't keep in touch'*. However, she did point out that one of her ex-husband's sisters does still consider her *'as family'* and invites her to family functions such as weddings and christenings. Her occasional inclusion in collective family rituals amounts to an uncomfortable blurring of boundaries for her ex-husband who is anxious to incorporate his new partner and children publicly into his wider network of relatives without the anomalous presence of his ex-wife. He is quick to attribute to his former wife a proactive rather than a reactive role in this and sees her as wishing '*to home in*' on his family.

In a second example, a similar unease is in evidence as the woman interviewed questions her ex-husband's motives for visiting her parents:

... he's cultivated my mother and father since the break up and he often goes to see them on a Sunday afternoon with the boys, so that's very cosy. Now he hadn't that much time for them when we were married, so again it's a sort of ingratiating way of niggling me I suppose because I think 'well why is he doing that?' The boys see my parents as often as they want. They ought really to go of their own account and actually see their grandparents.

The implication is clear. The woman's ex-husband's visits to her parents with her sons create the blurring of a boundary which she would rather keep as discrete: the affection, interaction and exchange which animate his networks run on in ways which spill into the networks of his former wife. Furthermore, this unwelcome overlap of networks causes tensions with her own parents who still, much to the woman's chagrin, continue to keep up relationships that grew out of the first marriage:

Well it does annoy me because even after John (her new husband) and I were married, for a good 18 months my mother wouldn't let me bring him to the house – even when were married. And although she idolises Keith (the child of her second marriage) . . . [ ] . . . I found that very hurtful, and she said 'well, you know I've got nothing against him (first husband) and he didn't do anything wrong to us, you were the one that wanted the marriage ended, you know 'why should I turn my back on him?' and I said 'well, don't you really . . . can't you see my side of it, that you're actually keeping away Keith's father and my husband' you know, 'excluding him in favour of someone who, you know, didn't particularly have a great deal of er, social graces, when you used to come and visit us'.

Examples such as these illustrate the divergence of perspectives over the meaning and significance of adult kin relations and contacts between relatives after divorce. Whereas at one time marriage brought a set of seemingly indissoluble relationships, with divorce there is the possibility for individuals to make particular selections from this set. This is no doubt part of a broader pattern of uncouplings in which sex has been largely uncoupled from marriage and marriage uncoupled from reproduction. With the advent of New Reproductive Technologies, the uncoupling of sex from reproduction is now also an option. With divorce the options available appear to be getting wider, such that, as in the example above, one might have in-laws even though one no longer has a spouse. Indeed, it would appear that an important expression of personal progress and development after divorce is the right to construct one's network of significant others. Good, wholesome, gratifying relationships can be preserved whereas the people to whom one was previously yoked by the mere accident of affinal relationship can be distanced and forgotten.

As we have seen, the making and un-making of networks is achieved through statements of inclusion and exclusion which are likely to prove highly contentious. Nevertheless, where a former partner's kin are concerned a sense of personal history rather than a sense of duty or ascribed role would appear to prevail. However, where kin relationships involving children are at issue, questions of continuity and discontinuity become significantly more contentious and emotive. The desire to construct networks which maximise inclusion of one's children yet limit the inclusion of a former partner is particularly acute. As we shall see in the next chapter, these circumstances makes all the more difficult the business of disaggregating persons from the rights, interests and responsibilities in which they were previously enmeshed. First, however, it is necessary to consider some of the cultural under-pinnings of parent-child relationships after divorce.

Disentangling 'Love' from 'Blood'

For couples without children who divorce, the separation might well be total and the process of adjustment an entirely personal affair achieved without reference to a former partner. It is often characterised by those concerned as 'sad', rather than as a problem which invites wider public concern. Where there are children from a marriage, however, the problem is acute. Notions of continuity, connectedness and extension are fundamental to kinship and hence to the relational context through which people identify themselves. These must be disentangled from the notions of curtailment, discontinuity and severance which it is the object of divorce to achieve. Feelings and sentiments which previously flowed more or less freely are subject to multiple and conflicting interpretations. Furthermore, attempts to clarify, or at least make workable, relationships between mothers and fathers and their children after divorce are the objective of a wide range of informal and statutory agencies to say nothing of parents and children themselves.

Schneider's account (1968: 1984) of American kinship is a useful starting point in an attempt to understand this problem, not least because it invites reflection upon the cultural construction of western kinship systems. The account is premised on two major constructs. One corresponds to the order of nature, metaphorically expressed as ties of blood, and otherwise referred to as consanguinity or descent. The other corresponds to the order of law, in which culture is contrasted with nature. In the order of law the formation of relationships is based upon affinity and the extension of kin networks is through marriage. This particular construct is paradigmatic in the organisation and development of western family law. Schneider goes on to describe two kinds of 'love', conjugal and cognatic, both of which he considers are central to American kinship. The latter is associated with parental ties and the former with adult conjugal relationships. These strands are woven together and subsumed under the elastic and common-sense label of 'family'; within which they come all of a piece. The integration of marriage, procreation and parenthood lies at the heart of the western tradition of 'family' and has been evident in philosophical discourse at least since the time of Aquinas (Blustein 1982: 234). Human offspring need attention and nurturance for greater lengths of time than non-human counterparts and the indissolubility of marriage, as a divinely ordained construct, strengthens conjugal love in a way that promotes the collaborative and long-term endeavour of procreation and parenting. However, what happens at divorce, amongst other things, is that these two closely integrated polarities of kinship, the legal and the natural, the conjugal and the cognatic, the affinal and the consanguineal, have to be unpicked with the result that the roles of mother, father, and parent are constructed anew. There is continuity, yet also transformation. Conjugal relationships are sanctioned by law and are therefore capable of reversal, that is, the married can return to being unmarried. However, these must be disentangled from those relationships which are seen as essentially irreversible, that is, the set of *natural* relationships which are brought into being by the birth of a child.

Viewed in these terms, the history of divorce is one of a growing reversibility of affinal relationships. In the past, relationships, whether consanguineal or affinal, were never reversible – Christian marriage was indeed 'till death us do part' with the couple, in terms of identity and estate, becoming 'one flesh'. The possibilities of the legal reversal of what were hitherto irreversible ties of procreative marriage has gradually widened from obscure grounds based on the failure to consummate, argued in the ecclesiastical courts of the Middle Ages, through eighteenth-century acts of parliament which enabled adulterous aristocrats to divorce and on into the humiliating and inquisitorial divorce courts of the 1940s and 1950s intent on divining 'fault' amongst errant middle-class couples. However, replacement of 'fault' with the notion of 'irretrievable breakdown' in the 1969 Divorce Reform Act meant the way was virtually open for the pursuit of individual fulfilment beyond marriage, unfettered by legal and moral constraints. As Wolfram (1987: 148) has argued, what was previously available only to the rich has, since the Matrimonial Causes Act of 1857, gradually been made more available, through legal reform and liberalisation, to all sections of society.

However, along with these changes have also come changes in ideas about parental rights and responsibilities. In the nineteenth century, the legal position of fathers vis-à-vis their legitimate children was unassailable with that of mothers correspondingly weak. Lowe (1982) cites the case of R. v De Manneville 1804 in which a man who had separated from his wife 'forcibly removed an eight month old child while it was actually at the breast and carried it away almost naked in an open carriage in inclement weather. Despite this the court said it could draw no inferences to the disadvantage of the father and upheld his right to custody' (Lowe 1982: 27). Over the last fifty years the pendulum has swung in the opposite direction with mothers experiencing a seemingly natural ascendancy when it comes to decisions over custody. It is estimated that as many as 90 per cent of fathers who divorce do not retain custody of their children (Richards and Dyson 1982).

With this increasing reversibility of affinal ties the perceived irreversibility of consanguineal relations has become problematic, especially for a society with high investment in the ideology of patriarchy and patrifiliation (La Fontaine 1980: 340). What should be the relationship between a non-resident father and his children from a former marriage? As we shall see the answers of mothers, fathers and children to this question are often seriously at odds. However, the 'official' solution to the question of parental continuities and discontinuities after divorce is neatly summed up by a judge with whom I was able to sit during his day long processing of Children's Appointments (also known at that time as Section 41 Appointments). Such meetings normally took place in his chambers; there were no wigs and no oaths, just a few minutes' avuncular chat in which the judge elicited more information from a sad and often fearful parade of mothers and fathers about their proposed arrangements for their children after the divorce. In the absence of a more rigorous divination, the arrangements so described are quickly rubber-stamped and one case ushered out as the next is ushered in. However, this judge ended each of his meetings with his own particular incantation: 'you may not be husband and wife anymore but you are mum and dad for the rest of your lives'.

The judge's statement carries with it an important cultural expectation about patterns of kinship post-divorce. Being 'mum and dad for the rest of your lives' invites reflection on the perceived irreversibility of certain relationships and consideration of their long-term implications. The distinction is one that parents who divorce readily articulate: 'I mean he's a good father to him (the son) but he were a bad husband.' Indeed, it is likely to be the basis for parents to rationalise their separation in the first place as one young woman recalled:

> Dad carted off Anna (sister) and I for a walk along the sea front with the dog and he explained that, although he loved us very dearly, he couldn't stand living with mother anymore and he was moving out . . .

However, being 'mum and dad for the rest of your lives' handed down as free advice from on high is easy to say but notoriously difficult to achieve in practice. Maintaining relationships with children across the conjugal divide is often stressful and unsatisfactory for all participants (Simpson *et al.* 1995). Under these circumstances, parenting all too easily becomes an exhausting round of conflict and attrition rather than the rewarding and constructive experience described in the 'how to do it' books. Navigating the life-course after divorce can be a perilous undertaking with many important reference points rendered dysfunctional or entirely absent. In the next section some of the predominant ways in which post-divorce relations are patterned are considered. This exploration of the distinctive ways that new relationships are grafted onto the old is developed with reference to two extended case studies of the post-divorce kindred.

Two Variants of the Unclear family

The post-divorce kindred may take many forms. It is shaped and re-shaped over time by an interplay of emotions and public and private interests. To plot this complex social form in space and over time will be a major theoretical and methodological challenge for the study of kinship in contemporary European society in the years to come. As a preliminary move in this direction, the remainder of this chapter is taken up with a discussion of two forms of post-divorce family relations which appear to be at opposite ends of a spectrum. At one end of the spectrum there is a propensity for discontinuities in post-divorce relations, at the other, choice and the possibilities for continuity in social relations would appear to be maximised. The first account is given by Sally Thomas, a working-class housewife living in council accommodation. The second account is provided by Stuart Smith, a middle-class, self-employed builder living in the home of his new partner. Each case demonstrates how cultural expectations and economic constraints shape relational possibilities in practice. Each typifies a pattern of kinship which is clearly derivative of family life before the separation but which is, in crucial ways, also distinct and emergent.

The Nuclear Mould: The Case of Sally Thomas

When Sally married Stephen Thomas he had been married before and already had a young daughter, Sharon. Sally took on the role of primary carer for Sharon (see Figure 2.2.) and the couple went on to have two children together, Andrew and Dawn. Towards the latter stages, their marriage became increasingly problematic because in Sally's view Stephen was mostly unemployed, occasionally violent and always financially irresponsible.

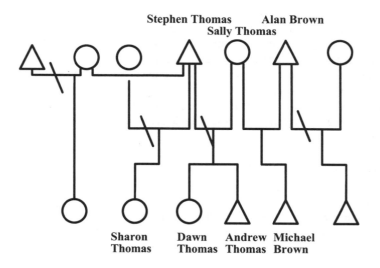

Figure 2.2. The 'family' of Sally Thomas

Sally left the matrimonial home in April 1987, taking with her the two younger children – Andrew and Dawn – into bed and breakfast accommodation and leaving Sharon behind in the matrimonial home with Stephen. There followed a complex and protracted wrangle over the terms and conditions of custody and access. This was exacerbated by the fact that not only were the couple trying to make arrangements for Andrew and Dawn to see their father, Stephen, they were also trying to enable Sharon to see her step-mother, Sally, as well as seeking to preserve some continuity of the sibling group, that is, allowing all three children to spend some time together. Courts and conciliation services were involved in trying to make this exploded and highly conflicted nuclear family hang together in some form, but without success. Despite the best intentions of all concerned, the attempted arrangements repeatedly collapsed in acrimony. This was further fuelled by Stephen being ousted from the matrimonial home in order to allow Sally to move back in. Stephen was eventually re-housed on the same estate within a couple of hundred yards of his former home.

By the time of the second interview in 1991, Sally and Stephen, now divorced, had each taken up residence with partners who had also been previously married. Sally had recently given birth to a son, Michael, by this new relationship. The contact between Andrew and Dawn and their father was continuing to be a source of major conflict and anxiety. Sally's assessment of the situation was that things had deteriorated since her new partner had moved in, at which point Stephen had become jealous, vindictive and obstructive.

. . . we were talking quite well and then he found another partner and that was OK, I even went over there for a Tupperware party, but when I found myself a new partner that was when the trouble started. He started making trouble over the children and that's when the communication stopped.

As a result, and at Stephen's insistence, they only communicated through solicitors, despite living very close to one another. Also, Dawn refused to visit her father ever again. Her allegiances had been substantially transferred to her mother's new partner:

. . . my daughter, as far as she is concerned that [i.e. the new partner] is her dad, she thinks the world of him. She calls him dad and her dad over there Stephen, she calls him by his first name. As far as she is concerned my new partner brings her up, he buys all her clothes and food, he gives her the love and attention she wanted from her other father but never got. So far as she is concerned, that's it, that's her dad.

The intensely negative feelings of Dawn towards her father were further exacerbated by the fact that she disliked both her father's new wife and her daughter and also was upset at the shabby treatment that Sharon, her half-sister, received in their father's house. Stephen had accused Sally of putting pressure on Dawn to effect this break in relations. However, Sally was adamant that anger and resistance was coming entirely from Dawn.

Andrew's position was less clear. Whereas Dawn had opted for the newly emergent nuclear family group, Andrew felt ambivalence. He had a history of emotional and behavioural problems which were attributed by Sally to her first husband's inconsistent and inept handling of his relationship with the boy. The availability of two father figures, a seemingly inept *genitor* on the one hand and a perfect *pater* on the other, was proving a major dilemma. As Sally said 'Andrew is at the stage where he's split between the two dads.' Later she added he sometimes gets 'torn' between the two.

Sally's image of the splitting and tearing of her child suggests an understanding of the situation in terms of something that should be in one place or the other but not in both. The polarities between which Andrew is drawn are those of his mother's husband and his 'real dad' as Sally described her first husband. *Pater* and *genitor* are no longer one and the same and Andrew can seemingly have one but not both. Sally's use of the term 'stage' implies structured process and possibly preferred outcome in the resolution of this conflict. However, Andrew is not of an age where he can assert his opinions with quite the impact that his sister seems to have done. He remains caught in a prolonged liminality.

> [when with his father] he gets spoilt rotten . . . [ ] . . . one minute I'm confident, he's happy here and at other times perhaps I think he would like to be with his dad . . . [ ] . . . but there again if that made him happy I'd have to let him go – not that I think his father's capable of looking after him because I don't think he knows how to, and his partner don't seem to know how to either.

Any possible future decision to allow Andrew to live with Stephen is based upon the cultural elaboration of the irreversible fact of bio-genetic parenthood. Stephen, in Sally's words, is Andrew's 'real dad', a potent relationship especially in view of the fact that the relationship in question is one between a male parent and a male child. This dictates that there will always be the element of legitimacy and legality in the desire of Stephen and Andrew to have a relationship. This consideration is powerful enough for Sally to consider taking steps which are not necessarily in Andrew's own best emotional and material interests as she sees them.

The outcome hoped for is the child's happiness realised through *his* own conscious choice. However, in her deliberations as to which parent Andrew should be living with, there can be discerned a subtle shift from Sally's use of 'dad' to describe Andrew's relationship with Stephen to her use of 'father' to describe Stephen's relationship with Andrew. It is this latter aspect that Sally sees as problematic.

This point is further emphasised by examining the position of Sharon, Sally's step-daughter. Sharon continued to be a frequent visitor to Sally's house where, it was claimed, she was given the kind of care and attention that she did not receive at home with her father, Stephen and his new partner. Sally described how she had often thought of having Sharon to live with her but how this was rejected on the grounds that, whatever her circumstances in Stephen's house, he was her 'real father'. Furthermore, it would not be 'right', that is *natural,* for her to be a part of Sally's newly constituted family as she would not be biologically related to either of the adults with whom she would be living. However, the memory and indeed the continuity of caring provided by Sally for Sharon was clearly an unresolved issue for them both.

In the case outlined above there are numerous points at which the threat of discontinuities seem to outweigh the fact of continuities as relationships slide back into the nuclear family mould. For Sally, the breakdown of one 'family' was followed by the creation of another 'family' in which efforts were made to make it appear a neat and seamless co-resident grouping. Yet, the continuity of external form in the way Sally presents her 'family' conceals internal discontinuities. The roles may appear to stay the same but the personnel have in fact changed. As a consequence the role expectations which are implied by specific kinship terms are highly significant. For example, Sally is keen to point out that Dawn has in effect relegated Stephen from his status as 'dad' by referring to him by his first name and giving the title of 'dad' to Alan, Sally's new partner. The shift from category to person is seen by Sally as an illustration both of the distance that has developed between Dawn and Stephen and her closeness to her new step-father. Thus, the breaking of ties between husband and wife also brings the role of *genitor* as *pater* into question. The roles of husband and father are too closely bound together in terms of sentiment and practice for either Sally or her ex-husband to discontinue one without undermining the continuity of the other. Thus it was difficult for Sally to establish continuity with Alan as a husband without also inviting him to take up the role of 'father' and 'dad' vis-à-vis her children, particularly when their new baby arrived. Although Stephen was persistent about maintaining his role and relationship with his children, most of the economic and emotional gaps left by his departure were effectively filled by another.

There are numerous alternative explanations which could be developed as to why the relationships between children and parents who no longer live together are so problematic. Sally's narrative centres on an ex-husband who, although recalled with compassion, was seen as irresponsible, inconsistent and immature. Although Stephen was not interviewed, he might well have identified an ex-partner keen to play 'happy families', as an interviewee in similar circumstances described his ex-wife's attempts to exclude him from contact once she had formed a new relationship. Attention could be drawn by either party to a system of welfare support which, in housing and social security terms, makes life very difficult for those who end their marriages but seek to develop patterns of parenting across multiple residences rather than according to bureaucratically straightforward intra-household patterns. Running through these potential explanations is the problem already mentioned, that of disentangling blood and patrifiliation from conjugal love and affinity. The ease with which the rupture of marital relationships can bring about discontinuities of conjugality do not sit so easily with the expected continuities of parent-hood. There is a recurrent conflict between matrifocal residence on the one hand and notions of patrifiliation on the other. The matrifocal orientation is clearly apparent in the unity of the sibling group, that is, the belief that children born of the same mother should remain co-resident with her. The ethnographic record reveals that this belief operates at both the parental level and at the judicial level with contested hearings tending to support what is usually the matrifocal status quo. This status quo however is in conflict with notions of patrifiliation. This is most clearly seen in the scattering of surnames across the different residence groups. For example, when Sally re-married it was likely she would adopt the surname of her new partner, Brown. This name would also be given to their son but her own two daughters would retain the name of Thomas, the surname of their father. The whole sibling group would be domestically united by maternal care and residence but publicly divided by the patronyms they received from their respective fathers.

The Extending Family: The Case of Stuart Smith

Stuart was married for ten years before he left his wife, Rachel and took up residence with another woman. The decision to leave was extremely traumatic and protracted because, although clear about his desire to be with the woman with whom he had been having an affair, he was far from happy about moving away from his three young sons. This was made worse by the fact that the matrimonial home was located in a very isolated part of the country and his new partner's home was some sixty miles away. The situation was further exacerbated by the fact that Stuart's new partner was also friendly with his wife (see Figure 2.3).

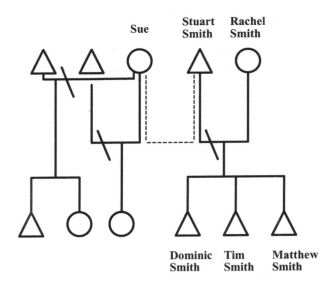

Figure 2.3. The 'family' of Stuart Smith

Stuart reecalls that the early years of the separation were extremely grim for all concerned. For him it involved long weekend trips between his new home and the former matrimonial home. Meetings with his sons took place at the homes of friends where he would stay overnight, or in whose gardens he would camp. The role of friends in providing support was seen as crucial in enabling him to maintain contact at a time when it might easily have ceased. The contact with the boys did indeed continue, and although extremely bitter over the treatment she had received, Stuart's ex-wife was generally supportive of him as 'the boys' father' and recognised the important part that he played in the children's lives.

Where this case differs profoundly from that of Sally Thomas is that the separation took place in the midst of a strong and long established network of mutually supportive friends and relatives. Rachel brought into her marriage the support of a large extended family, although Stuart was apt to see this as interference. Following the divorce, the involvement of these relatives in the lives of both Rachel and her three sons became even greater, raising anxieties for Stuart about his sons being raised in a 'claustrophobic' and 'hermetic' group, although acknowledging that they were 'good' people who had a lot to offer his children. Stuart did not have particularly strong 'family ties' but spoke of a series of important 'family-like' relationships which he had been able to draw upon following the separation. As Stuart commented 'my children are exposed to a wide, varied circle of people'.

As far as the three children were concerned there remained a degree of unity in the circle of kin following the divorce. The two kinship worlds of *mum* and *dad* did not simply bifurcate but continued to function with some degree of coherence. Thus, for example, Rachel took the boys for a Christmas meal with their paternal grandparents. Her father visited the house where Stuart and his new partner lived. More recently, both Stuart and Rachel attended social gatherings hosted by mutual friends, something unthinkable in the early days of their separation. Stuart did odd jobs at Rachel's house and occasionally ate there:

> . . . I've sat down and had meals with them, basically for symbolic purposes, not formally, just snacks, but it all helps.

'But it all helps' refers to Stuart's desire to establish a network of relations that is not fragmented by divorce but merely re-arranged. Consequently, his efforts are primarily aimed at providing evidence of overlap and continuity of parental relationships for his children.

However, the social networks of Stuart and Rachel have not only become more scrambled and intensified, they have also been extended. Stuart's relationship with Sue, his new partner, brings his children into contact with her as a step-parent-figure, with her three children who range from nine to twenty-one and to a certain extent with her family, in this case her siblings, parents and cousins. Whereas in the Thomas case the family of orientation appeared to close down and start up again, here there is a process of accretion whereby functioning relationships are added on to it. These relationships are not perceived as in any way problematic for, or contradictory of, existing relationships. As far as Stuart is concerned, they constitute an expanding network of social opportunity for his children.

In further contrast to the Thomas case, the emphasis throughout the discussion with Stuart focused on persons rather than roles. There was an active attempt by him to eschew kinship roles and thereby flatten kinship hierarchies and power relations which might characterise relationships between him and his children or indeed between him and his new partner's children. Friendship and a history of shared experience provided the basis for relationships and this is typified in the extensive use of first name terms which here mark intimacy and familiarity rather than a dislocation of the relationship between parent and child as in the Thomas case. Consequently, in this case there is a recognition of the value of individual persons in their roles and no question of displacement. Thus, despite a bitter separation, Stuart remains the children's 'father' and has been recognised and supported as such by their mother (although whether this would continue to be the case were she to establish a permanent relationship may be another matter). These feelings are reciprocated by Stuart regarding Rachel's capacities as a 'good' mother. In short, there is considerable mutual trust between them both regarding their ongoing abilities as parents.

Finally, the most distinctive feature of the extending family as illustrated by the Smith case is the desire on the part of all the key actors to ensure the continuity of virtually all those relationships that existed in the past, as well as the new relationships established after divorce. For example, with reference to step-siblings Stuart observed:

It's quite involved because there's six children between us and all six children have a relationship between them . . .

. . . they like the complication of it, working out who's who. The children are familiar with the extended family and they can look at relationships in the same light.

One immediate implication of this view of 'extended family' is the immense amount of energy which is put into the maintenance of relationships on the children's behalf. When with their mother, they are drawn into a large extended family, when with their father they do the rounds of an established network of close friends who Stuart, in the absence of any relatives with whom he would like to be in contact, regards as 'family'. From the children's perspective this can make for an exhausting schedule of movement and socialising.

For Sally Thomas, our first case, there is considerable unease with the messiness of relationships. The unfolding of relationships after divorce took place in circumstances where there was high dependency on the state and few individuals in the 'family' network were in employment. Her ability to shape the configurations of relationships beyond the narrow parameters of the household was greatly limited. Indeed, low-income families may have considerable problems in maintaining kin relations in anything other than the discrete nuclear family variant.[2] Absence of resources for the material expression of relations, whether this be in terms of formal payments of maintenance or informal donations of gifts and money to spend on socialising, may well render relationships precarious and liable to atrophy.[3] Difficult economic circumstances appear to foster a rigidity in the way that family relations are conducted. In ways that are reminiscent of Bernstein's notion of a restricted or closed communication system (Bernstein 1973: 177–80), tender feelings may well be expressed in 'tough terms' precisely because there is no other vocabulary available. Identities and relationships within the changing kinship systems of the poor are positional and context dependent. In network terms, there are numerous points where networks are severed or closed off. Money, goods, favours and sentiments do not flow across the conjugal divide. On the contrary, the way this flow is re-routed at divorce becomes a potent statement of the narrow and tightly bound networks which characterise the nuclear family.

This is in contrast to the Smith case, our second example, in which the re-ordering of kinship relations takes place against a backdrop of relative affluence with most of the adults in employment. For Stuart Smith there was a certain exuberance in his description of post-divorce relationships. For him there was the sense of a controlled expansion of relationship possibilities and permutations consonant with Bernstein's elaborated or open communication systems. Sally Thomas, five years after divorce, appears to be serially recasting her new family in the image of a traditional nuclear family. Stuart Smith on the other hand pays only fleeting reference to conventional family forms. For him the emphasis is on an extending kindred founded on personal identities and relationships; continuities bridge the conjugal divide at numerous points. Throughout Stuart Smith's account there is an apparent denial of material interest when it comes to kinship relations. The narratives he presents portray a network of relationships which are voluntary, individualised and personalised; they are presented as running on and on with very few external constraints.

The Unclear Family

In this chapter it has been my intention to identify and bring into anthropological focus the complex and varied patterns of inter-personal and kinship arrangements which emerge over time as a result of divorce and family reconstitution in Britain. I have referred to these patterns collectively as the unclear family and attempted to locate them within a broader anthropology of marital dissolution. Implicit in this approach has been a critique of the conceptual heritage which emanates from essentialist, ideal-type models of the bourgeois nuclear family. Such models are built on a powerful alignment of co-residence, temporally stable conjugal/parental relationships and the social recognition of fatherhood. Such an alignment leaves little room for agency and the under-pinnings of family life appear to be all but natural.

When viewed against the broader canvas of human social and domestic organisation, however, such arrangements may well be the exception rather than the norm. As Seccombe has recently argued (1993), in the West we may be emerging from a 'golden age' of the family, a period of exceptional stability which reached its zenith in the 1950s and which is now giving way to a period of familial instability. The concentricity of parenting, residence and authority is being progressively de-centred and we are witnessing, if not directly experiencing in our own lives, novel re-arrangements and reconstructions of what were hitherto the certainties of Euro-American kinship. Indeed, Robertson has suggested that in recent times, notions of filiation and responsibility for bringing up children in the West have progressively shifted from the 'compact household to the wider social domain' (1991: 122). The evidence he cites is the fact that increasingly aspects of reproduction are being mediated by civil and market institutions. Here we might draw attention to the considerable machinery which has appeared to assist couples in dealing with marital breakdown, much of which is geared towards sanitising divorce and bringing about an 'embourgeoisement' of its consequences. Divorce law reform, the growth of conciliation services geared to resolving conflict and dispute, the growing expectation of amicable relationships and the emphasis on continued parenting after divorce all point to external pressures to bring particular shape to the form that social and kinship networks take after divorce. In short, divorce generates a host of questions regarding the form and viability of parenthood in circumstances in which family is dispersed and in which there is state participation in key aspects of social reproduction (Donzelot 1979; Goody 1982).

Viewed against such a backdrop, the study of the variations in domestic arrangements after divorce poses some major analytical challenges. The identification of a private domain which is the preserve of the family and a public domain which is characterised by impersonal, market transactions has obscured the two-way traffic between them. Consideration of the arrangements which couples themselves devise or otherwise have imposed upon them requires that we re-think the way that kinship articulates with economy. In other words, the re-shaping of the kinship framework over time is not an arbitrary process. The disaggregation of persons takes place within parameters set by public interests. Fundamental in this regard is the question of resourcing the unclear family. Divorce renders the material underpinning to family life quite explicit; the 'maintenance' of relationships costs money. A network of households in which there are adequate or substantial resources and incomes may be extremely effective in enabling finance and children to flow between households, thus maximising choice and potential in the relational framework which divorce allows. However, in the absence of resources to disperse and disburse, sentiment and the pragmatics of household subsistence often pull in opposite directions. This is nowhere more clear than in the underlying philosophies of the Children Act 1989 and the Child Support Act 1991. Whilst in the Children Act there is an expectation and encouragement of continuing parental involvement after divorce, even though a mother and father do not live together, the Child Support Act sees the non-resident parent as 'absent' and his or her relationship rather more in terms of the pragmatics of financial support. In terms of the case studies presented here one might characterise the Children Act as a piece of legislation ideally suited to a world of Stuart Smiths and the Child Support Act similarly suited to a world of Sally Thomas's. Equally we might begin to understand the fierce and critical reaction that is aroused when these pieces of legislation are applied across all contexts seemingly extending and cutting networks in ways that are favoured in economic, social and moral terms by the state. Thus, as a result of the Child Support Act the likes of Stuart Smith are affronted by being characterised as 'absent' and pursued for maintenance in ways which overlook the quality of their existing relationships with children and former spouse. Conversely, the Children Act means that the likes of Sally Thomas are confronted with a legal framework which puts pressure on them to allow ex-husbands to have contact with their children even though the general climate of economic and cultural expectation moves them to the opposite conclusion, that is, divorce is not just conjugal but parental. In each instance, the law provokes a sense of indignity, because it is attempting to influence and inform areas of family life which are believed to be autonomous, discrete and the object of private ordering.

The unclear family also poses some major methodological challenges. How do we study change in sets of relationships which are themselves characterised by qualitative change and transience? Whereas the nuclear family was usually assumed to speak with one voice, a master narrative, if you will, the unclear family is characterised by a polyphony of voices. The roles, spaces, boundaries and classifications which previously mapped relationships through space and time are subtly transformed to produce competing, contested and often contradictory versions of the kinship network.

In the next three chapters, these challenges, analytical and methodological, are taken up in more detail. Chapters 4 and 5 take up the question of disputes between parents after divorce and in particular the disputes they have over their children. These disputes reveal the fundamental *unclear*ness of family relations after divorce and show the way multiple narratives surrounding parental relationships result in new and complex forms of kinship. Chapter 6 deals with the closely related question of financial support and the role of the non-resident parent.

Notes

1. A notable exception here is Bohannan (1971a) who provides a useful if disjointed collection of articles on divorce in the USA and 'around the world'. Bohannan (1971b) also engages in a series of speculations regarding the longer-term consequences of divorce which pre-figure the idea developed in this paper of the post-divorce kindred as the unclear family. One of the few sociological studies of divorce in Britain is Hart's (1976) participant-observation study of a singles club frequented by divorcees. Hart focused specifically on divorce as a status passage which for most people constitutes a brief but highly anomalous phase between broadly similar married statuses.

2. In the study of non-custodial fathers carried out by myself and colleagues, clear gradients were identified in the levels of contact across social class and income with non-manual workers earning over £300 per week having the highest levels of contact and most likely to have their children on overnight stays. This is in contrast to unemployed men whose relationships with their children from previous marriages appeared to be particularly at risk (Simpson *et al.* 1995: 5).

3. Such an inference is hardly a new one, it has resonances of the culture of poverty debate (Lewis 1966) and more recent discussions regarding the rise of households headed by women (e.g. Ross and Sawhill 1975) in which paternal relations are largely characterised by their transience.

3

Disputing Persons: Constructions of Childhood after Divorce

Given the psychological, emotional and economic investments that are placed in children in contemporary society, the energy expended on contests over them by divorcing parents is hardly surprising. Concerns over children are apt to unleash powerful passions and emotions ranging from immovable stubbornness through to irrational violence. People who are otherwise genial, sensible and reasonable are rendered combative and intractable when faced with the demands and assertions of a former partner regarding the upbringing of their children from a former marriage. But 'Kramer v Kramer' type confrontations and the 'tug of love' headlines which regularly feature in the tabloids are the tip of a rather more massive and mundane iceberg of social relations formed by the breakdown of the conjugal family. Long after the dust has settled on divorce petitions and court orders, disagreements over the minutiae of day-to-day parenting such as dress, discipline and care arrangements for children regularly rise and submerge in the routine chaos of life after divorce.

Fundamental to such conflicts for each parent is the question of what kind of person their child is, ought to be and will become. Divorce introduces vulnerability and uncertainty into these and other areas of personal life where there are high expectations of confidence and predictability. The child as the object of parental duty and responsibility is brought into sharp focus as parenting and residential arrangements take on novel and distributed forms. Psychological, legal and welfare concerns also come into play reinforcing the idea of the child as a 'bundle of needs' (King & Piper 1990: 61). However, how these needs might best be served and just what is in a child's 'best interests' are subject to multiple and conflicting constructions given that objective yardsticks of just how children might be grown into healthy, happy, well-adjusted adults are difficult to come by. Although parents might struggle valiantly to shield their children from the consequences of the breakdown of their relationship, the 'best interests' of the child are invariably someone's version, assembled out of the emotional and practical contingencies which each party is left with when the marriage ends. Rarely do such versions coincide as in most divorces one party is, at the very least, moving out of the marriage more slowly than the other. In the early stages of marital break-down, it is not uncommon to find the reluctant departee claiming that the 'best interests' of the child are served by working to preserve the marriage whereas the initiator claims to be serving the child's 'best interests' by taking the very opposite steps. In the midst of such discrepant perspectives, just how parents engage in the construction of the child as a person is apt to become deeply problematic. At one moment a parent might argue that the child is an autonomous person when it comes to decision making. At the next, the child is treated as a kind of property or possession which it is the owner's responsibility to safeguard and protect with the result that individual agency is denied to the child. Needless to say, assessments and interpretations of the child's autonomy and who 'owns' the child are not simply discrepant but conflicted.

What is 'best' for a child following divorce is readily articulated by mothers, fathers, grandparents, uncles, aunts to say nothing of the legal and welfare professions. However, where parents are concerned, 'best interests' is the subject of a deep passion which is not simply born out of concern for the child but a concern for the self in relation to the child. The child enables parents to externalise and demonstrate, in embodied form, who they are in terms of their values, social status and aspirations. At issue for parents who have divorced is the way that they each, as mother and father, succeed or fail in passing on the essentials of their respective identities onto their children. In this sense, divorce triggers a contest (or in some cases simply exacerbates an already existing one) over the future identity of offspring; it raises questions about the roles of parents, their boundaries of responsibility and the kinds of people their children will eventually grow up to be. For some, this may be a simple accommodation, as for example between couples who simply perpetuate a classic division of parental labour in which the mother is the full-time nurturer and the father is a bread-winning absentee. In such cases, a man might well have a deep belief that his child is and will always remain 'a chip off the old block' despite his or her physical absence. But, in these days of surveillance and doubt over personal and parental competence the child becomes the object of concern *par excellence*: it is thus not simply the quantity but the rather more illusive notion of the quality of parenting that is at issue. Being a 'good' role model and setting the 'right' levels of intervention, direction, discipline, freedom, control and indulgence have become integral to the quest for good parenting. Issues which are in any case problematic within the conjugal family are likely to be considerably amplified in the wake of divorce. Throughout this chapter consideration is given to these issues as they are expressed by parents in interviews. Parents' accounts are considered primarily for what they tell us about the ways that conflict, uncertainty and unpredictability are accommodated into their familial relationships after divorce. Fundamental to this process is the way family members see themselves as linked by essences and resemblances which have to be re-arranged and separated. Before going on to explore this proposition in depth, however, it will be useful to consider the kinds of disputes which were commonly described by parents.

Constructing Childhoods

The concerns that parents express about their children are as varied as their lifestyles and identities and it would be beyond the scope of the present work to attempt a systematic classification of these. What I present in this section is a series of vignettes which reveal the varied concerns expressed by parents over aspects of their children's upbringing in relation to a former partner.

Town Man versus Country Woman

Mrs Ellis described how one of the advantages of the separation from her husband had been that she could now walk in the countryside and at every opportunity took her thirteen-year-old son with her. Her passion for fresh air and walks had always caused problems in the marriage because her ex-husband was a '*town man*' preferring a steady regime of work, television and the local workingmen's club. She saw this as a form of laziness on his part which translated into an unhealthy influence on their son. She was openly critical about Mr Ellis, contrasting her encouragement of their son's outdoor interests with his '*can't be bothered*' attitude. Her other passion was ballroom dancing in which she also involved her son. Mr Ellis was not at all pleased that his son was being encouraged to pursue ballroom dancing as a hobby and identified this as one of the many irritating activities in which his much hated ex-wife involved their son and which threatened his endeavours to bring his son up to have, as he saw it, 'proper' masculine values and attributes.

When Saturday Comes

In Sheffield there is a deep and serious rivalry between the city's two football teams: Sheffield Wednesday and Sheffield United. Mr Evans, a redundant steel-worker, had been a lifelong United supporter and had brought his son and daughter up accordingly. Trips to home matches at Bramhall Lane once a fortnight constituted an important and regular feature of the children's weekend stays with him. At one of our meetings we talked about his concerns over the way the children were brought up when with their mother. He had very few concerns about her competence as a mother but after a long pause began somewhat hesitatingly *'you might think this is a bit daft, but . . .'* He went on to tell me that his wife had acquired a new partner which was not in itself a worry but the man was a 'Wednesday' supporter and what was more had taken his children to see Wednesday play at Hillsborough. Mr Evans, who otherwise seemed a rather easy-going sort, was flushed and angry in recalling this affront. Taking his children to a Wednesday match was taken as an inconsiderate and deeply provocative act which he felt would do little to better relations with his ex-wife or her new partner whom he had not even met. He described how he had suffered a *'double injury'* in that he had recently been forced to give up his mid-week access on a Wednesday evening only to find that his children might be with his wife's new partner watching the opposing team.

Controlling the Body

Belinda Stimson was born with a serious heart complaint and for two years was frequently close to death. The stress of caring for Belinda placed an intolerable strain on her parents and their relationship. Mrs Stimson was unable to cope with the possibility of losing Belinda and withdrew from her emotionally and practically, leaving much of the responsibility for her care and her frequent hospital visits to Mr Stimson. Belinda did survive but her parents' relationship did not and there ensued a bitterly fought battle over custody in which one of Mr Stimson's primary allegations was his former wife's earlier lack of care for and subsequent mistreatment of the children. Mrs Stimson was portrayed as the 'unfit mother' and Mr Stimson raised concerns about the physical abuse of his children with welfare and educational services and in the courts. After a bitterly contested custody dispute, Mrs Stimson was given sole custody and, despite Mr Stimson's persistent attempts to overturn this, his allegations of abuse were deemed to be unfounded. However, his concerns about the physical well-being of his children continued as an abiding theme in our interviews. The problem centred on the fact that he was only able to see the children once per week and in the periods between their visits he suffered extreme anxiety about their well-being. One area about which he felt particularly strong concern was the use of physical violence to control the children. He was constantly worried that his ex-wife was smacking the children and even more concerned when he discovered that her new partner had smacked Belinda as the following extract, recorded some five years after the divorce, reveals:

> There was a little flare up about two months ago when Julie's [Mrs Stimson's] new boyfriend smacked Belinda and that wasn't very pleasant. It had to be said and it was said and that was it. I went down and sorted it out. Belinda phoned me and said that he'd smacked her – he had perfectly good reason to smack her but I didn't think . . . and Julie agrees, it wasn't his job, he wasn't in a position to do that, it should have been left for Julie to punish her. But there again there wasn't any fisticuffs, the kids went to bed and we sat round a table and we chatted about it and he agreed, ok, he shouldn't have done it but he was at the end of his tether, and I can understand that, and we talked about it which was quite good. I mean a couple of years ago I would have just gone in feet first and ask questions after – she's still my little girl and if anyone's going to punish her – I've never smacked my children, never – never had the need to smack 'em. It's like a red rag to a bull. When I went down I was very, very angry.

Mr Stimson was pleased that this difficult situation was resolved without violence and saw it as an important step forward in coming to terms with the re-formed boundary separating his own life from that of his children and his former wife. Nonetheless, the issue of others using violence to control his children remained a concern which bordered on the obsessive. Not to have control in regard to physical discipline would represent a level of marginalisation from his children which he, as the children's *'real'* father, could never countenance.

The McDonaldisation of the Family

Mr McNally is a chef who prides himself on knowing about food: where it comes from, how to prepare it and to how to eat it. His son, whom ʾe sees every weekend, seems unable to appreciate this and demands ʾnvenience foods and sweets whenever he comes to his father's house access. This is anathema to Mr McNally. He expresses his dilemma in ʾollowing terms:

> eating habits are terrible. That's the main battle with him for me, getting ʾo eat proper food . . . [ ] . . . it's all junk food. I can't get him to eat ʾng. It's impossible. I say it's impossible because – I can't handle it cos' ʾ there with him all the time. He's not influenced by me as to what

eating habits he should have. That's really his mum and whoever he's living with – they're the main controllers aren't they. I can't very well, when I just have him for one day, change his whole weekly pattern, and say this is what you should eat . . . [ ] . . . you just have to accept it. Sometimes you might say something to him and you just hope for the best that he might pick it up and he might be alright.

The issue of the boy's refusal to eat anything other than sweets, burgers and chips thus opens up a wider issue of control, or lack of it, brought on by Mr McNally's long periods of absence from his child's life. He went on to say that there was only so much pressure he could bring to his son before he had to *'back off'* for fear of upsetting and alienating him. Apparent in Mr McNally's concerns over his son's eating habits is thus an issue of power in relation to competing life-styles between himself and his former wife. He is evidently not happy that his former wife, as a working mother, appears to resort regularly to convenience foods in order to maintain her busy schedule.

Mr McNally's case is a little unusual in that the concerns he raises over his child's diet and eating habits are ones that usually occur the other way round. It is far more common for women to make critical comment over their former partner's inadequate sense of a child's dietary requirements. Complaints regularly made include providing inappropriate meals, having irregular eating regimes, waiving table manners, resorting to fast-food at every opportunity and refusing to pay attention to special dietary requirements. An area of conflict which frequently develops in this latter regard is seen in arguments over sweets and additives; some fathers are keen to give lots of sweets whilst mothers are keen to restrict this on medical grounds. A father's search for affection through confection might well be seen by the mother as sheer recklessness and lack of concern for the child particularly as sweets are often linked to problems of obesity and hyper-activity in children.

All such allegations imply a basic inadequacy of one parent in the eyes of the other when it comes to dealing with the subtleties of a child's needs. Parental statements that children need 'proper' food is not simply an observation about diet but is rather more crucially a complex cultural statement in which consumption is used to make statements concerning the differential quality of parental relationships after divorce.

Social Hair

A young child's hair can prove to be an important focus for disagreements relating to broader concerns over identity and control. What a child's hair looks like and who makes decisions over the deeply symbolic act of cutting hair makes a significant statement regarding parental status. Mrs Jenkins described her upset when her son returned from a visit to his father to find that his new partner had '*hacked*' at the boy's hair. The same incident came up in an interview with Mr Jenkins who cited the episode as evidence of his ex-wife's tendency to over-react. He described how his son had arrived on an access visit with the instruction: '*You're not allowed to cut my hair, mummy says you're not allowed to cut it.*' Whereas for the mother the act was a serious and provocative affront, for the father, the event was little more than routine maintenance brought about because the boy's hair was getting in his eyes.

Religion

Divorce is apt to pitch individuals into new and conflicting trajectories and this is nowhere more apparent than in relation to religion. Differences which existed within a marriage, or even pre-existed the marriage, often come to their full oppositional florescence in disagreements over the religious and moral orientation of children after the marriage has ended:

1. A question of morality.   Mrs King had always been a regular member of her local Pentecostalist church and it had always been her intention to bring up her three children accordingly. After a bruising separation in which she eventually won sole custody of the children, the church became an even greater support and solace to her. Going to church on Sunday became the centre of her social life. Mr King had always tolerated her involvement in the church when they were married and had not seen it as a particular problem although it was felt on some occasions to be intrusive and prohibitive. After their divorce however, he came to identify the church as being instrumental in causing the breakdown and creating ongoing problems between them. On a practical level, access arrangements were repeatedly stymied because the children's Sundays were taken up with church and Sunday School. He was made furious by her refusal to vary their Sunday regime and her insistence that he must drop them off outside the church after their Saturday staying access. The problem of the children's church attendance rapidly took on an intractable quality and he was left with little option but to accept her diktat. Access persisted against a backdrop of deeply hostile attitudes between the parents. She described him as foul mouthed, bullying and with a worrying attitude towards alcohol. He described her as a neurotic, religious fanatic who was doing a very good job of passing her problems onto their children.

2. Faith in doubt. The Nesbitts had been a model Mormon family until Mr Nesbitt began to doubt the philosophical basis of the Mormon credo. Divorce, when it came, posed its particular problems as there were six children and for him, a serious ethical question of whether they should remain within the Mormon faith. For Mrs Nesbitt there was no question that this should not be the case. The problem was compounded when Mrs Nesbitt became the second wife of another Mormon who already had a large family. The establishment of one large, polgynous family was the realisation of a Mormon ideal for Mrs Nesbitt and a veritable nightmare for Mr Nesbitt. His crusade to extricate his children from what he increasingly saw as the dubious life-style and dictates of Mormonism was seen by her as his attempt to undermine and corrupt the children's faith. The latter situation was one that she was determined to resist at all costs. The result was thus a dynamic in which each propelled the other in ever more drastic actions in order to gain control over the children.

3. Rituals of the body: A case of circumcision. Mr Palmer always suspected that there would be a problem over his sons' relationship with the Jewish faith. He was not a Jew but his wife was. She had never been a devout Jew whilst they were married but she came from a large and enveloping Jewish family which, as he saw it, drew her ever more closely into itself after their marriage ended. This was a situation which caused him some concern. He openly acknowledged the benefits of kin and support for his ex-wife and sons but was also concerned about what he saw as the stifling and unhealthy aspects of Jewish family life. That his ex-wife should drift back into a pattern of life more in tune with that of her relatives was not an issue for Mr Palmer. What was an issue was that she was taking their children with her. The conflict came to a head when Mrs Palmer announced that she had decided to have their sons circumcised. This was a decision which he resisted passionately and a bitter dispute developed. His line was that it was wrong for the children to be subject to a 'bizarre ritual practice' which for him represented his ex-wife's capitulation to pressure from her extended family. For him, the boys' circumcision was an anomalous act which was not in their interests. At some point in the future they might choose their religious orientation but to circumcise them at this stage was to narrow their choice in a way that he saw as irreversible. His ex-wife took the opposite line. Not to circumcise them was an equally anomalous act which would leave them at odds with their extended family and their Jewish identity. Nevertheless, circumcision became a line beyond which Mr Palmer refused to move:

The circumcision was the one thing that we couldn't have a discussion about. I'd say 'no' and she'd say 'but' and she'd assemble all sorts of people to try to convince me of my error. I'd just say I want to talk in rational terms . . .

As is often the case with such difficult issues, the dispute eventually reached the courts in the form of a contest over custody. The prizes in the contest were as follows: sole custody to Mrs Palmer would give her total control over the children's physical well-being and she could have them circumcised with impunity; joint custody would give Mr Palmer, at the very least, the right to be consulted over issues concerning the children's physical well-being. In other words, she was fighting for the right to be a 'good mother' and he was fighting for the right to veto her actions and thereby be a 'good father'. The issue was the subject of a welfare report in which, as Mr Palmer saw it, the Court Welfare Officer took his ex-wife's side. 'Bargaining in the shadow of the law' (Mnookin & Kornhauser 1979), as is common in such cases, the Court Welfare Officer attempted to come up with a compromise solution. His suggestion was that Mrs Palmer should allow joint custody provided that Mr Palmer allowed the children to be circumcised. Mr Palmer expressed outrage at this suggestion as he felt that the issue was not one over which deals could be done. To his dismay, however, sole custody was awarded to his ex-wife and the boys were circumcised. Although this outcome caused great bitterness on his part at the time he saw himself as having little option but to accept that he was powerless to act; ultimately, his children were Jewish whereas he was not and this was something that he had to live with. His desire for them to experience religion as something that they approached from outside as an intellectual exercise and a fascinating attribute of human beings was confounded by the fact that they would only be able to approach from the inside as members of a particular faith into which they had been physically inducted.

Video and the New Technologies of Socialisation

As technology comes to play a more significant part in the home environment, its meaning and consequences in the lives of children become increasingly problematic. Children's ownership and use of powerful technologies of communication and leisure increase the problems faced by parents when it comes to agreeing limits and setting boundaries for their use (Meyrowitz 1984). This is particularly so when parents set about matching their own models of appropriate experience, ageing and maturation to consumer goods which themselves communicate strong messages concerning agency and adulthood. For example, the amounts of time children spend in front of the television, what they watch and how much money should be spent to provide them with personal access to televisions, stereos, computers, compact-disc players and the like are difficult issues for parents to negotiate between each other and their children. For parents after divorce, such problems are even more serious sources of anxiety as different perceptions of what is 'right', 'natural' or 'permissible' for the growing child to see or do are brought into play.

In interviews, videos proved to be a recurrent theme in this regard. A typical treat for many children on weekend access with their fathers is a trip to the video shop and the purchase of sweets and pop. However, the showing of videos, which many fathers saw as an innocent pursuit, was the source of serious concerns for their former partners. For example, concern was expressed that fathers were unimaginative with their access time. It was pointed out many times by mothers that the fathers of their children had fought bitter and determined battles for their right to access but then seemed to have very little to do with their offspring other than sit them in front of a video with a bag of sweets. Being left before a video screen for great lengths of time was felt to be an inappropriate input from a father.

A rather more serious issue surrounding videos arose regarding precisely what children were being allowed to watch when pitched before the screen. The spread of easily available horror and sex videos, the so-called 'video-nasties', throughout the country such that they can now be hired from most corner shops creates serious conflicts between parents. For some mothers the explanation of their ex-partner's behaviour was in terms of ignorance, with videos a visual equivalent of the dietary problems identified above. In the view of some mothers, fathers were simply lacking in awareness as to where their children were in developmental terms and had little sense of what they might reasonably be expected to cope with, particularly as the fall-out from a late night of gruesome horror would more than likely have to be dealt with by the mother on a Monday morning. Children returning from weekend access and describing videos they had seen were apt to send mothers into apopleptic rage with vivid accounts of videos rated way above their age group.

> . . . they were coming home with stories about the videos they were watching and I was very concerned over that because I wasn't quite sure what they were watching but from what they were telling me they weren't the kinds of video that I would want my children to watch . . . [ ] . . . I confronted him with that and, it's very difficult to know what he himself thought because he'd say one thing and go and do another.

Material which might have been uncontested and quite safely digested within the nuclear family proves to be a source of great uncertainty when set within the dispersed network of parental rights, roles and responsibilities after divorce. Controls are weak; the woman quoted above is uncertain about a number of things that she clearly felt she ought to be more certain about.

The deeper issue which underlies the conflict over watching videos is thus one of disputed regulation and the breakdown of shared controls between parents. One can readily imagine fathers on their access weekend negotiating desperately in the middle of a video shop over which film to take out and finding it very difficult to say 'no' for fear of jeopardising a brief period of contact. Whereas mothers would cite the official age categories as the proper guide for what children should be watching, it would seem that many fathers are tempted to ignore the ratings and indulge their children.

> I don't like them watching some of the videos they watch but he says it's up to him what they watch . . . [ ] . . . I try and say but whether he would listen or not I don't know.

For some fathers, this was seen as a necessary and legitimate role – testing boundaries and introducing children, or more accurately sons, to pleasures which tend towards the adult and illicit. But, as one woman complained '*they are being turned into mini-adults*'. Arguably, this is exactly what some fathers want. They wish to see their children uncoupled from the normal constraints of physical and emotional maturation so that they might realise their full potential as autonomous agents. As such, it is assumed there will be more opportunity for father and child to be free of the mediating influences of the mother.

Children in Society

Above I have provided some brief vignettes illustrating the difficult and often painful disagreements which parents enter into over their children. Such disputes are in many respects unprecedented and form part of a progressive shift in the role and position of children within the family. These shifts have arisen out of the dispersal or fragmentation of family relations on the one hand and the emergence of children as vehicles of consumption and adult identity on the other. In pre-industrial times children were valued for their economic contribution to the family and as active contributors to the household with the attitude and responses of parents shaped accordingly. Throughout the industrial revolution children were increasingly directed away from productive activities and into new structures of economic, emotional and educational dependence (Aries 1979[1962]; Seccombe 1993). Indeed, the construction of childhood as a separate category of experience has augmented and extended to such an extent that nowadays children are carefully contemplated as an emotional and economic cost to the household rather than an essential benefit. The decision to have children is thus far more likely to be linked to notions of psychological utility rather than any economic utility they might bring. In a world increasingly beset by uncertainties, children represent a longer-term project which offers adults the chance to demonstrate emotional control and social responsibility. In other words, children anchor parents in the present and, more importantly, in the future in ways that are more real and authentic than all else.

Begetting sons and daughters makes husbands and wives into mothers and fathers. The birth of a child suffuses these relationships with a sense of the 'natural' and grounds adult relationships in something deeper than voluntary and contractual obligations. This elemental act of sharing is also given metaphorical expression in couples wanting to have a child in order to 'cement' their relationship. Reference to children as a kind of conjugal glue is one I have often heard among divorced people who have re-married and for whom the arrival of a child is a powerful statement of authentication, legitimation and connection. In such cases the birth of a child is seen as a vital means of triangulation, the way in which a couple can give future and direction when navigating what might otherwise turn out to be finite, shallow and falsely premised relationships. Whereas in the past marriage might have laid the tramlines along which parenthood eventually ran, now it appears to be parenthood which provides the essential and paradigmatic framework of family life. But, just as the birth of a child might be a statement of commitment between adults, marriage is also apt to become a statement of commitment by parents on behalf of their children. For some couples interviewed, the birth of children or the decision to become parents was the point at which they decided to convert a cohabiting relationship into conjugal relationship. Their action was usually presented in terms of forestalling a child's potential confusion in later life over status and identity, for example, in relation to surnames.

However, the model upon which family life is nowadays based is not the centrifugal family dominant in the nineteenth century in which considerable effort was directed into spheres beyond the household such as community, extended kin and long and arduous occupational struggle. At the heart of family life as currently conceived lies the centripetal family, a private domain in which members' energies fold back onto themselves in ever more intense, complex and emotionally charged relationships. Children occupy a highly valorised role in these arrangements for they are the empty screen onto which their parents will project their hopes, expectations and aspirations. Children provide the opportunity for adults to be the kind of parent their own parents were not; to allow their children the kind of childhood they themselves were denied and to become the kinds of people they themselves never quite became in terms of education, wealth, happiness, fulfilment, health, experience and so on. Similarly, children by virtue of their 'nature' and their spontaneity provide adults with a potential means to escape from the demands for rational and responsible behaviour expected in the world of work. Citing the work of Zinnecker, Beck and Beck-Gernsheim (1995: 106) suggest that 'the more the objective foundation of life crumbles, the more prominent the "imaginary" becomes in the relationship between the generations'. In such terms, parenthood is no longer merely a service to children and society but in itself becomes a way of life, considerably aided and abetted, one might add, by the possibilities for consumption that surround children and childhood. Parenthood is thus a means to construct and authenticate oneself as a person through the project of creating other persons.

In contemporary society, there are continual reminders of the weighty responsibilities which accompany parenthood. In view of the foregoing discussion, it is also necessary to be mindful of the enormous load and responsibility which parents foist onto their children. Parents bring up their children, but in crucial ways children also bring up their parents. Marital separation impacts on this process in ways that are extremely complex. When parents are no longer even nominally yoked together in the shared project of parenting, a child, as the screen for parental aspirations, becomes the focal point of two projectors rather than one. Each parent must work with, round or against the parallel projections of the other and the child must also work to accommodate multiple models of what his or her parents want them to be in the light of what they themselves wish to become.

Individuals, Dividuals and the Question of Identity

In western society, marriage and parenthood are linked by an assumption that each adult is a unique yet equally contributing individual to the edifice of family life. Marriage, whilst joining the couple, does not obliterate the different birth origins of each of the parents (Strathern 1982: 86). The child born out of such ideas and expectations is a hybrid, a unique individual assembled out of the distinctive inputs of each parent (cf. Young and Wilmott 1973). Indeed, it is the responsibility of parents to work to create and foster this uniqueness. As Bernardes suggests: '"Family ideology" supports a child rearing process that creates individuals, and which simultaneously closes off any alternative paths of human development. The rearing of children in a non-individualistic manner is simply unthinkable' (Bernardes 1985: 282).

But, whilst the creation of individuals may be a dominant ideology under-pinning parental aspirations, it is surely over-stating the case to suggest that alternatives are unthinkable. The inability to think in this regard is not shared by divorced parents for example, who of necessity devise all manner of creative solutions which transcend or subvert dominant familial ideologies in order to sustain their own particular aspirations regarding the individuality of their children. The constraint, in as much as there is one, is analytical and arises largely from a tendency, prevalent in earlier sociologies and anthropologies of the family, to construe the family as a mere assemblage of role-bearing individuals. However, the view of families as made up of bounded individuals performing 'roles' is only one side of the story. Family is an important site for the construction of gender, identity and personhood and role-type theories are wholly inadequate to capture the subtlety of this interactive process. To view the family as a collectivity, with role-bearing individuals as its composite elements, tends to introduce a conceptual distinction between individuals and the relations that bring them together. Family members are knitted together by a variety of exchanges and investments which continually blur and compromise autonomous individuality.

Strathern, following Marriot, offers the notion of 'dividuality' as a means of conceptualising the way that the interpenetration of persons operates in non-western contexts: 'To exist, dividual persons absorb heterogeneous material influences. They must also give out from themselves particles of their own coded substances – essences, residues or other active influences – that may then reproduce in others something of the nature of the persons in whom they have originated' (Marriot 1976: 111, quoted in Strathern 1988: 348n). However, Strathern's analysis is suggestive in western contexts also. Thinking of persons in relational terms, Strathern evokes a contrast between western notions of individuality in which persons are discrete, physical entities and Melanesian notions of personhood which arise out of the effects of multiple relationships. In this conceptualisation, individuality is in no way prior as persons are made up of multiple beings refracted through multiple relationships developed over time (ibid: 185). However, it is not clear that the western context is necessarily that different. A child might end up with her mother's nose and her father's temper and within a marital relationship this hybridity can be a cause for celebration and wonderment. After divorce however, the facts of bio-genetic connection and the hybridity this implies often become a painful and persistent irritant and potential source of conflict. Networks have to be cut but it is far from clear where decisive lines should be drawn (Strathern 1996).

For each parent, their child is a powerful vehicle for the memory of shared experience; an embodiment of the things about their former partner that in the past made them extremely happy, deeply unhappy or, as is most often the case, a complex amalgam of emotional extremes. The child is a nodal point in a network in which the identification of old connections and old traces of dividuality is a source of discomfort and disturbance. New traces of dividuality can be equally troubling as evidence of influences of new partners, grandparents and other kin begin to manifest themselves in the behaviour, attitudes or deportment of one's offspring. As one woman commented:

> They're alright except for Emma, even my eldest daughter says he (ex-husband) picks on Emma . . . [ ] . . . Emma resembles me so whether he picks on her because of that.

And later in the interview:

> He (ex-husband) is such a domineering man that I don't think I could approach any subject with him really. It doesn't create any problems but I wouldn't like my son to grow up being like him to be honest.

Within the nuclear family household in which this particular woman had previously lived there was a classic division of domestic labour. She described a situation in which she was at home and a full-time mother; he was in full-time employment, retained control of the family coffers, drank heavily and was not averse to using violence on his wife in order to maintain this arrangement. His presence in the home was described as bullying and controlling whereas his absence after the separation brought calm and relief. What was radically altered by his departure was the opportunity for him to exercise power and dominance in the domestic sphere. However, despite his removal, his presence and influence persisted in her relationship with the children. Unwelcome patterns begin to manifest; the daughter is bullied by her father because of 'resemblances' to her mother and the son begins to show worrying parallels with his father.

Reciprocal concerns are also evident in the observations of non-custodial fathers, as the comments of Mr Stimson who was encountered earlier in the chapter illustrate:

> . . . the actual way the children behave and the way they speak is their mum's, they've got their mum's sayings. I wouldn't say I would rather have my ways put onto them but I would like to have seen a bit more of a sparkle from their dad. I mean Nick has got my temper, he really has, so he's just a chip off the old block. But some of the sayings he's come out with is all his mum. Which, she's got more contact with 'em anyway . . .

A little later on in the interview Mr Stimson is reflecting on the fact that he had lost a battle to have his children permanently resident with him. He begins by acknowledging his wife's effectiveness as a parent:

> . . . they are a credit to her. They'd be a credit to me if they were here with me but . . . I would have liked to have been in a position to take more credit . . . they're highly influenced by their mother and I suppose if I'd have been living there perhaps a little bit of my influence would have rubbed off.
> [BS]: Do you feel that people don't give you credit for what you have done?
> Yes, my dad says 'oh, they are a credit to her' and I think 'well, hang on a minute, there's parts of me in there as well'.

A dominant theme throughout my interviews with Mr Stimson was his feeling of forced inadequacy as a parent. The overwhelming discrepancy between himself and his ex-wife in the levels and quality of their contact with their children meant that he could never be the kind of parent he so desperately wanted to be. Regular weekend access was deemed wholly inadequate to enable him to make the kind of imprint on them that he would have liked — 'parts' of himself were not manifesting themselves as much as he felt they should be nor was his influence 'rubbing off' and all this translated into an absence of 'credit' for himself as a parent.

What is at issue in such cases is how and in what proportions the things which parents believe they pass on to their offspring are regulated or rather interfered with by the other. Whereas within the family prior to divorce there is a strong presumption that mothers and fathers will provide their children with a coherent and complementary package of parenting comprised of love, support, guidance, discipline, affection and the like, the picture changes fundamentally following divorce. There is no question that parents will go on agreeing that the above list constitute the essentials of 'good' parenting but what is meant by these in practice is often subject to radically different interpretations and expressions. Any sense of a united front vis à vis the children is at the very least difficult to sustain and for most is quite simply an impossibility given the problems of communication that exist between them as former husbands and wives. In the following example, the woman is reflecting on the different responses between herself and her ex-husband to their son's lack of competitiveness at games:

> And I was discussing this problem with Stephen [ex-husband] and Stephen said 'you know I had to encourage him to be competitive because the world was competitive, and that ought to be encouraged'. And I was arguing that if it wasn't in Michael's nature to be competitive then it really ought to be left alone, and for him to develop as he wants to develop. Cos the middle child's very competitive, especially when it comes to sport and things, and he's very good at it too. So, there are certain ways of bringing them up, or certain ideologies that are very different. But I don't think that's particularly harmful because they get one side from me and one side from him, and then they can sort it out for themselves.

Under such circumstances it is easy and all too common for fathers and mothers to perceive one another as not simply being different but inappropriately influencing their children or indeed failing to influence them appropriately. It is also common for parents to feel they are doing their bit only to have it undone when the child passes from one sphere of parental influence to another. The project of bringing up children under such circumstances involves building a relationship which is fraught with parenting black holes. As children move between different spheres of parental influence they are subject to regimes which are mutually unpredictable and to some degree out of control. Fathers thus tend to express concerns about the domination of their former partners who, as custodial parents, are likely to play a much greater role in bringing up their children. Mothers in turn express anxieties when children are with their father on access. Parental concerns cover a wide range of minor but persistent irritants which reflect conflicting expectations regarding their children's politeness, eating habits, dress, behaviour, attitude, values and many other manifestations of unwanted or questionable dividuality. These influences are notoriously difficult to change because they are seen not simply as arising from physical contacts but from inborn and inchoate resemblances between parents and their children. As the following quotations from fathers and mothers reveal, the character of post-divorce relations in this regard is one of simply working round and enduring the conflicts which arise over differences in attitude and approach to parenting:

I don't really ever discuss with her how she brings the children up unless I am really annoyed and there is something that I feel has to be said. I can't just go on and say 'they haven't brushed their teeth this week', I wouldn't say that to her. There are issues that I would like to say to her that I don't in order to keep harmony. (father)

If he wants to act in a certain way with the children then I just have to let go of that. (mother)

There are so many things that go on that at the end of the day I just can't be bothered with it all. If you documented it all and put it all down there would be 101 things that would annoy you. But at the end of the day you just get so fed up with that you don't bother. (father)

. . . this is what they do, they wear you down and wear you down and you think is it all worth it, is it worth my health and putting the children through all of this trauma about this. You just cave in . . . I thought I was fairly strong in that department but . . . (mother)

In these instances, levels of tolerance of parenting differences and discrepancies would appear to be high not least because there is a keen awareness of the emotional and financial costs of conflict should it be actively expressed rather than passively endured. However, there are also far more serious discrepancies which it is impossible for parents to put up with as the following account of one mother reveals:

I'm quite strict on most rules and he says (to the children) 'I couldn't give a damn what your mother does, when you're over here you do as I say.' He used to let them watch horror films and 18 rated films. They're forbidden to watch anything over a PG here. My son's under a psychologist now he was getting nightmares over some of these x-rated films. And he was told he was having nightmares and he said 'oh, don't be so stupid' and when Andrew (son) bedwets and he says 'mummy baths me' his response is 'I'm not your mother' . . . [ ] . . . They run riot over there; he has the wrong sort of discipline . . . [ ] . . . he let's them play unsupervised. All my rules he purposefully breaks over there . . . if they swear he laughs, every time they say daddy says they're allowed to do it.

For this woman, the movement of her children back and forth was not simply an uncomfortable but necessary exposure to the quirks and foibles of their father. The contact had disastrous consequences for her children which made her own life as a single mother far more stressful than it already was. Furthermore, she was of the opinion that this was precisely his intent in acting the way he did. Whereas for most couples the problem is one of how to deal with the passive and often unintentional undermining of one another's parental endeavours, this woman had to deal with the rather more serious problem of hers being actively undermined. As she saw it, her attempt to construct a particular family ethos for her children with its distinctive 'values', 'rules', 'discipline' and codes of acceptable behaviour was consistently and maliciously wrecked by her husband.

In a similar case, a woman described how she had run into a series of behavioural problems with her teenage son which resulted in a major confrontation with him. The way that this was dealt with by his father reinforced her sense that she was on her own as a parent:

> We had a big World War Three row, and he (the son) said 'I'm not eating that tea then' I said 'Well please yourself' – so he rang his father, and I heard him say 'Dad can I come and have tea with you?' Well off he went. So I was furious, I actually wrote to Colin and I said 'Could you not have stopped to think why he was ringing you at 7 o'clock, in a state, "Dad, can I have tea with you?" Couldn't you stop and think that there'd been some problem?' I said that you were undermining my authority as a parent. [Sighs] I didn't have a reply, and he didn't talk to Keith. Oh yes he did! He said, Keith said 'dad showed me the letter', he said 'and he laughed'. So I mean, I get, I've had that, so I think now if there's a discipline problem I'd sort it out on my own. I wouldn't dream to say 'oh I shall tell your father' . . . [ ] . . .

Men who are on the other side in cases such as this tend to express a deep antagonism towards the 'extending family' ideology described in chapter 2. It would seem that there is a deep uncomfortableness when it comes to acknowledging or co-operating in a former partner's parental endeavours. Such a stance is indicative of a considerable investment in the maintenance of clear, firm boundaries between former spouses. The conclusion one is tempted to draw from this observation is that for many men, to allow boundaries to become fluid and fuzzy is in some way to capitulate to a matricentric view of the world. Mr Evans, the former steelworker referred to above, described how he had told his children that they were not to refer to their mother's child by a new partner as 'brother', as their mother had told them to do, but must refer to him as their 'half brother'. This patrilineal 'skew', as Strathern once described it (1982: 72), amounts to defining siblingship in terms of paternity rather than in terms of the fact that the three children in question had all emerged from the same womb. Furthermore, he had anticipated the day that his children's 'half brother' would want to come with them to his house and he had warned them well in advance that he would never allow such a visit to take place. The children had comprehended the message well. Indeed, he commented on how good his children were in that they never talked about the living circumstances at their mother's house:

> I think they've adjusted great because they've got this life and they've got that life.

Use of the notion of different 'lives' appeared to be a common rationalisation of a father's position vis à vis his children after divorce. As another man commented: '*ok, she shows 'em one way of life, I'll show 'em the other*'. The construction of parallel and discrete 'lives' for children, in which different values were assumed to prevail, different relationships functioned and between which there was little transfer of information at the adult level, was seen as the most satisfactory way forward for many fathers and furthermore was not seen as in any way problematic for the children who had to negotiate this fundamental duality.

Women faced with the predicament of their children's movement between separate environments run in radically different ways proved particularly problematic. Faced with this situation they were apt to express irritation and distress at their former partner's lack of support or communication about the children. A common response to this absence-cum-presence on the part of a former partner was a sense of expanded responsibilities and roles. Indeed, several women commented they felt that they had had to become '*both mother and father*' to their children following divorce. Of necessity they had attempted to widen their activities and responsibilities to encompass those of the largely absent father. Thus, activities previously undertaken by a husband, or rather activities which it is assumed a 'good' husband should have undertaken, are performed by a mother who is more often than not anxious to compensate for the assumed inadequacies of her single-parent status. The activities commonly identified in this regard range from the demonstration of benign authority over children to practical home maintenance. It is also highly likely that this expansion of roles has something to do with blocking out the disruptive influence of a former partner. Indeed, it may well be that being '*both mother and father*' enables a woman and her children to slip easily into the label of lone or single-parent family with all the connotations of self-sufficiency and isolation which this title carries (Strathern 1992a: 79, cf. also Wilson and Pahl 1988). It is perhaps significant in the quotation above that the father felt it necessary to point out to his children '*I'm not your mother.*' The man's apparent refusal to countenance becoming father and mother to his children is in stark contrast to many women's preparedness to fill the day-to-day absences of their former partner in their children's lives.

I am your Father

Interfering with the expected patterns of dividuality proves to be a particularly powerful and emotive issue for men in general and divorced men in particular and one which touches the mainsprings of masculinity and identity. Houseman (1988), in a refinement of an argument earlier made by Barnes (1973), suggests that the biological imperatives of reproduction place important constraints on the possible conceptualisations of parenthood. Quite simply, mothers will always know they have become pregnant and given birth whereas the role of fathers in this process is always open to doubt. Paternity must always be backed by culturally elaborated and reinforced statements in a way that, leaving new reproductive technologies aside, motherhood rarely is. For fathers, divorce often means that they become even more marginal to the hub of domestic and childcare activities than they were formerly. It is hardly surprising therefore, that divorce and its implications raises important questions of dividuality and the way in which men see themselves as linked to their offspring. Indicators of this connection such as shared physical features, genetic paternity and patronyms begin to take on heightened relevance. Of particular significance are the substances which in western kinship signify closeness of relationship and commonality of inheritance. For many men with whom I talked, issues of consubstantiality (Pitt-Rivers 1973: 92), as evidenced by references to 'flesh' and 'blood', were common and especially so in circumstances where relationships had been reluctantly attenuated. Where other aspects of a relationship, such as cohabitation and communication, had ceased between a father and his child, 'blood' may have been the only thing left for him to evoke. Indeed, invocation of a 'blood' relationship was often presented as the 'natural' basis of a man's desire and indeed his assumed right to have contact with his children (cf. Modell 1986).

Generally speaking, fathers with whom I spoke were angry at being 'pushed' into situations in which their relationships with their children were challenged and called into question as a result of problematic contact. Needless to say, the problems were rarely seen as originating from their own actions or activities but those of their former partners. To threaten the paternal relationship was seen by many men as a wife's ultimate 'weapon' in a bitter divorce. To jeopardise the father-child relationship was seen at worst as a cruel denial of that which can never be denied, that is, a 'flesh and blood' link. At best the paternal relationship was being rendered totally peripheral to the child's emerging identity. This was seen by fathers as a particularly malicious act and the spleen vented by men about their partners in this respect was considerable. Most of the invective, incidentally, involved moving an ex-wife into a variety of non-human categories, animal and supernatural, such as cows, sows, bitches and witches. Bloch (1973: 78) comments that among the Merina of Madagascar those who fail to follow the moral dictates implied by kinship are classed as witches; they are inhuman. In this regard, I was fascinated to note recently a sticker on a plumber's van which bore the slogan 'my ex-wife drives a broom stick' — as with the Merina, to be outside of kinship is to be beyond the acceptable limits of morality and sociability. The problem, is of course, according to whose definitions of kinship? The dilemma faced by mothers in this regard would appear to run in the opposite direction:

> . . . at the back of my mind was the thought that he really is their father (i.e. their biological father), but he didn't realise that fathering children isn't enough, you've got to earn your rights with them.

Whereas mothers might argue for the achievement of paternal status, men are more likely to fall back on straightforward ascription. Furthermore, this would appear to be particularly so where the offspring are male. An important finding of earlier research into fatherhood after divorce was that fathers were three times more likely to lose contact with their children if they were all girls than if they were all boys (Simpson *et al.* 1995: 20). This finding is hardly surprising given the 'conspiracies' that exist in many families linking men to their sons and daughters to their mothers (Newson and Newson 1978: 288 also cf. Steinberg 1987). Nonetheless, this gender loading reveals some important cultural dimensions of post-divorce conflict over children.

Basically, there is a powerful expectation that sons will be brought up as 'proper' males and for many fathers there is concern that mothers, without male assistance and guidance can not do this properly. This is expressed by fathers and indeed by mothers themselves, in terms of the absence of a 'male role model' in the home. Consequently, fathers diagnose their son's problems in terms of a need to be drawn away from their mothers who might otherwise hang on to them too long with dividually catastrophic consequences. The ultimate concerns in this respect are to be seen in the comments of one man who described his relief at hearing that his son had kissed a girl behind the bicycle sheds at school. Prior to this he was concerned that his son was growing up 'soft' and might have homosexual tendencies; a direct consequence as he saw it of his own forced absence from his son's life coupled with his ex-wife's smothering and exclusive attachment to their son. In their less extreme form, such attitudes might well account for the frantic activities to which sons are subjected on their access weekends – football, swimming, camping, climbing and general rough and tumble are primary components of many fathers' access periods. Some fathers quite explicitly identified this as counter-balancing their son's more sedentary mid-week life-style with their mothers. This analysis would appear to be confirmed by some members of the judiciary. One woman interviewed had been adamant that her six-year-old son and thirteen-year-old daughter should not be seen by their father whom she felt had caused them distress and health problems in the past. When the case eventually came to court the judge accepted her arguments on behalf of the daughter but told her that 'little boys need to see their fathers' and ordered a period of supervised access.

'Clear' ideas about the bringing up of sons is in stark contrast to the confusion which daughters tend to spell for their fathers. In general the camaraderie between fathers and sons would appear more difficult to sustain with a daughter, bringing to mind the song from Rodgers and Hammerstein's Carousel – 'you can have fun with a son but you've got to be a father to a girl'. The lyric is somewhat prophetic in that it captures the difficulty which many fathers feel when it comes to developing relationships with their daughters after divorce. The gender discrepancy is typified by the response of one man with male and female teenage children:

Very, very close, . . . [to the son] . . . I think partly it's because I, I treated him, it's a cliché to say he's more of a mate than he is a son, but I tried to treat him appropriate to his age rather than a baby or anything, so now that he's sixteen he is more like a mate than a son. We have a lot of laughs, but there's an unbridgeable gulf between me and Meg [daughter] partly as I say because she's a different sex, and partly because we missed out on that bit because of the state of the marriage which I regret bitterly.

And commenting on the children's access activities:

Unfortunately they tend to involve Chris more than they've involved Meg I'm afraid, but I think it's the bond. That makes her sound like a second class citizen but I don't mean that. It's just that there's a rapport between Chris and I which there isn't between . . . , now and again it happens, and it's very rewarding when it does, but it's almost an exception whereas with Chris it's almost normal . . . [ ] . . . but you try to sort of see what she's about, to the best of my ability, but it's something you do actually think about, knowing that you're never going to get there, but you try.

Comments by fathers who had retained contact with daughters give some indication of the difficulties that are entailed in maintaining this relationship. These difficulties are particularly apparent during adolescence when, under any circumstances, a daughter might be exploring her emergent identity and sexuality through parental conflict in general and paternal conflict in particular.

After divorce, then, the structures which integrate the diverse aspirations of parents into a coherent and workable whole are at best problematic and at worst rendered redundant and defunct. Other arrangements must come into play which have the effect of wresting individuals out of their familial and dividual contexts. This process is inevitably a painful one, touching as it does on fundamentals of identity and emotion. The process of disaggregating persons is evident in the various disputes over children after divorce. As we have seen, these disputes point to deeper conflicts over the kinds of persons children will in future become. For parents, the problems which result from these disputes are complex but they are made significantly more so when the views of the child as a maturing and autonomous individual are also taken into consideration.

Pure Choice and the Problem of Agency

The only time I'll be really settled is when they are 16 or 17 and then they can make up their own minds, but until then I'll always be worried about her, the effect, the influence that her family's having on them and the influence that I don't have on them but would perhaps like to have. But when they're of an age they can basically decide for themselves . . . [ ] . . . they can relax over here if the regime over there is such that they can't handle it.

In this chapter, concerns expressed over children have, broadly speaking, been treated as bi-partite disagreements and disputes between mothers and fathers over their children. However, a theme to run through parental discussions and disagreements over child-rearing is the question of whether a child should actively contribute to decisions over his or her 'best interests'. In other words, the extent to which these exchanges are in fact tri-partite ones which incorporate the agency of the child. What the examples presented at the beginning of this chapter demonstrate very clearly is that a major problem for divorced parents is one of reaching agreement over the age at which the attributes of full personhood such as autonomy and power in decision making should be bestowed on the child (cf. Hockey & James 1993 chapter 2). The disagreements described amount to a painful pushing and pulling of the child back and forth across boundaries which each parent sees as appropriately separating childhood dependency from adult autonomy. Whereas such conflicts are not uncommon between parents who are bringing their children up in conventional nuclear family settings, once again, the particular circumstances of the post-divorce family considerably amplify these alternative perspectives and their consequences for the child. The child no longer occupies a single location within the life-cycle but might well end up managing multiple locations simultaneously as each parent brings into play different constructions of personhood and agency. What appears to be at issue in such disagreements is the nature of choice and its relationship to personal autonomy. Each parent wishes to push the child's autonomous decision-making capacity beyond the dividual constraints laid down by the other so that the child might make pure choices. Such a view is in many ways resonant of the views of Jean-Jacques Rousseau on human nature. For Rousseau the child was born a virtuous innocent who was then subject to the corrupting influences of society; in this instance it is parents themselves who perceive one another as obscuring and distorting the child's true nature.

Arguably such tendencies are part of a wider historical trend in which children have come to be valued less and less for their obedience to structures and institutions and more for their ability to act as autonomous individuals (Gullestadt 1996). Within western market capitalism, for example, children have been increasingly separated out as market consumers in their own right with their own spending power and cultures of consumption. Children are increasingly expected to make choices for themselves and express what they see as being in their own 'best interests'. As the Cleveland Child Abuse Enquiry famously declared and the Children Act (1989) subsequently echoed: 'the child is a person and not an object of concern' (Butler-Sloss 1988). The child is necessarily expected to have his or her own view of how things ought to be and is increasingly expected to act accordingly. Some sense of where the growth of this particular ideology might lead is to be found in the case of Gregory Kingsley reported in *The Observer* (27 September 1992). The twelve-year-old Kingsley was able to exercise the enterprise shown by many husbands and wives in re-ordering their adult relationships by similarly applying to the courts to re-order his own. In an unprecedented decision, a court in Washington DC allowed Kingsley to divorce his mother and become the son of a Mormon middle-class lawyer and his wife.

In the absence of an agreed version of how the child's world ought to be, parents are easily caught up in the construction of alternatives in which children are surrounded by competing stimuli and life-style possibilities. Children are unwittingly cast as consumers of the different parenting and domestic alternatives offered by a mother and a father. This might be in terms of an absolute choice of life-styles in which children are under pressure for most of their young lives to commit themselves totally to one parent or the other or, as is rather more common, the alternatives are integrated with the child subject to periodic shifts back and forth between radically different contexts. Thus, from Monday to Friday a child may be an only child living as part of a single parent household on a run-down council estate and at weekends may join three or four step-siblings to be part of a rather more conventional looking, two parent household which is considerably more affluent. Conversely, a child may spend all the week in such a household and leave it each weekend to visit a father living isolated and alone as a single person in a high rise block.

The management and negotiation of these periodic changes have important implications for the child. As Alanen (1993) has demonstrated, the post-divorce family provides the child with a significantly wider range of opportunities to build up autonomous and individualised social relations than in the nuclear family context. Given the right conditions a child can develop a level of social and practical competence which would be difficult to emulate in the traditional family setting. Children have to develop abilities to manage diverse social arenas and develop skills of diplomacy, confidentiality, discretion and tact in dealing with their parents. After all, whereas an ex-husband and wife must operate with what is at best partial information regarding one another's attitudes, circumstances and motivations after divorce, the child is likely to operate with full knowledge of both contexts. They routinely pass through the social worlds of their mother and their father and often carry a heavy load in preserving their trouble free access to both. Similarly, children may take on important practical tasks from an early age as they assist parents in their survival within their unclear family. This might include activities such as cooking, managing money, looking after self or siblings, making travel arrangements, shopping, arranging school activities and such like. The grown-upness of children, seemingly long before they are expected to be grown up, is readily acknowledged by many parents when they speak proudly of their children's maturity, sensibility and self-reliance. However, these qualities are invariably presented as being in spite of the break-up of the family rather than because of it.

The psychological and child development literature abounds with research reports detailing the negative impacts of this accelerated maturity both whilst it is happening and on into later adult life. Wallerstein, who has probably been the most influential in conveying the bad tidings of divorce for children, speaks of an 'overburdened child syndrome' (Wallerstein 1985 also see Wallerstein and Blakeslee 1989), that is, a cluster of pathologies which results from children carrying the emotional and practical stresses and strains which their parents, disabled by their own anger and grief, are unable to deal with. Wallerstein and Kelly (1980) associate this condition with 'a diminished capacity to parent' with mothers and fathers temporarily or, in some instances, permanently in regression and thereby estranged from the emotional and practical needs of their children. Under these circumstances, adults become child-like and children more like adults with the latter under considerable pressure to achieve their own moral growth and independence (cf. Meyrowitz 1984). Faced with this radical disordering of the life-cycle children's coping and survival strategies might result in angry and conflictual interactions with parents, a partisan affiliation with one parent to the exclusion of the other or a complete withdrawal from family relationships as a way of avoiding being at the centre of damaging parental conflicts. The costs of such strategies to the child are likely to be measured in terms of their physical health, mental health, behaviour problems, impaired educational performance and an increased likelihood of relationship problems and divorce in later life (Emery 1988; McCallister 1995: 24–31).

Some voices have been raised to counter the bleak prognoses made by many researchers into divorce and its impacts on children. Kelly, for example, suggests that much of what has been written about the impacts of divorce is inferred from cases in which there is already a serious pathology such as endemic conflict or emotional disturbance which pre-exists the divorce (Kelly 1988). This, she suggests, has led to a tendency to generalise these findings to the wider divorcing population with the result that divorce is readily associated with a variety of pathological conditions rather than with the powerful adaptive and coping mechanisms it is apt to engender in parents and children. Whilst the impacts of divorce may have indeed been over-played, the cases discussed in this chapter would tend to suggest that divorce does play a fundamental role in transforming the structures within which the socialisation of a child takes place. Particularly in circumstances where active father-child contact is sustained, arrangements of considerable complexity emerge in which the child is both the subject and object of multiple and competing constructions of personhood. Under these circumstances children may indeed be subject to an unbearable torque as they struggle to reconcile their place in diverging parental biographies. However, it is also the case that what we are currently witnessing is a rather more widespread and thoroughgoing shift in the social construction of childhood or more precisely the ways that the categories of adult and child articulate with one another. Not that long ago the dominant image of childhood was, as Holt put it, 'a kind of walled garden in which children, being small and weak are protected from the harshness of the world outside until they become strong and clever enough to cope with it' (1975: 22). What I have described in the context of post-divorce family relations here however points to new patterns of dependence and autonomy in the relationships between adults and their children. Such changes are symptomatic of a significant development in the way children are socialised in the western world. The framework within which socialisation is increasingly taking place is one which, in many respects, is far more in keeping with that experienced by most children in non-western societies. For example, James draws attention to Inuit socialisation practices which seem cruel and harsh by western standards but which are crucial in ensuring survival (Hockey and James 1993: 70). She cites the ethnography of Jean Briggs to drive the point home:

> [Inuit children] can't sit back comfortably, passively absorb the fruits of adult wisdom and experience, and conclude that the wisdom embodies final and permanent answers. Instead of learning to depend passively on the 'authorities' and 'experts', they learn to rely on their own sense of interpreting their own experience, to be watchful, doubtful, alert to hidden meanings and intentions and to keep testing adults as adults have tested them (Briggs 1990: 38 cited in Hockey and James).

The experience of many children after divorce is similar to that portrayed by Briggs for Inuit children. From an early age Inuits are prepared for the perils of a harsh social environment through being teased and generally made suspicious regarding the apparent certainties of the social and physical environment. The cumulative input of parents after divorce amounts to a similar although largely unintentional effect. Shared parenting after divorce is difficult to plan and co-ordinate and an important consequence of this is seen in the way that children are subject to new forms of empowerment and facility in the conduct of their social relationships. If the family forms I have described are indeed in some sense post-modern then one day the children of these families will grow up to be post-modern adults — flexible and fragmented in their social histories and interactions. In this chapter I have sketched some of the processes which underpin these emergent forms of social being. In the next chapter I examine the implications of these developments for the conduct of parental roles and relationships and the way in which these arise out of disputed notions of what is in the child's best interests after divorce.

—4—

The Fractured Triangle:
Disputes after Divorce

There are three lives here and we all have to live as best we possibly can and
that involves a certain amount of co-operative effort in knowing who's doing
what when. If not the one who'll miss out is the one with the least power . . .

Disputes are fundamental breaches in the normative social order and as
such are important sources of anthropological insight. The disputes arising
from divorce and separation throw light on the values, norms, morals,
ideas of personal agency and assumptions that surround family and
parenthood in contemporary society. Consideration of disputes and
grievances after divorce thus provides an important perspective on the
ways in which broader patterns of social and cultural change implode
into private lives shaping the basic currency of inter-personal relationships.
Fundamental in this regard is the fact that disputes are in themselves social
relationships and imply communication, interaction and the mutual
attribution of motive, intent and causality. As such, disputes feature
repeatedly and, in some senses, necessarily after divorce as a mechanism
for restructuring and redefining kinship networks. Disputes are essential
when it comes to expressing, adjusting and managing closeness and
distance between former intimates who in some sense continue as co-
parents of their children.

At one level the conflicts which arise after divorce are simply a
continued expression, albeit in an amplified form, of the conflicts which
tend to arise within nuclear family households (cf. Smart 1984) and which
often figure prominently in the aetiology of its demise. Money, debt,
childcare, stifled aspirations, power, sex and the abuse of trust all figure
as regular sparking points for more consuming conflagrations. In contemporary society, such conflagrations are readily fuelled by the unstable
relationship between gender, the management of resources and the
increasingly fraught project of bringing up children. After divorce the
dominant pattern to emerge for men and women in regard to their children
and the control of resources that were previously shared is invariably a

reflection of what went before: women usually live with their children in the former matrimonial home with greatly reduced access to resources whereas men do not reside with their children but live away from the matrimonial home with their access to resources, such as the former 'family' wage, relatively unimpeded. Extensive experience interviewing men and women in these circumstances reveals that both parties see themselves as having substantial grounds for grievance and injury. What is the point of money for a father who has 'lost' home and family? Where is the joy of home for a mother struggling week after week to bring up children on a low income only to see them disappear at weekends with their father on an access visit? Grievances may translate into spectacular legal battles but they mostly become part of the fabric of ongoing relationships to be worked round and accommodated in an ongoing struggle to manage continuity and discontinuity in relationships after divorce.

Of central importance in this regard are the broad range of disputes which develop between former partners over children and child related issues after divorce. For many couples, 'the children' are invariably presented as 'the only thing that really matters' in the turbulent times which follow the dissolution of marriage and household. As was demonstrated in the last chapter, issues concerning children prove to be the most intense and emotive areas of dispute for, although marriage might have fallen apart, parenthood remains as the basis for ongoing communication and contestation. Just at the point where a husband or wife might begin to feel relief at never having to deal with an ex-spouse ever again, there is a compelling expectation from relatives, counsellors, judges, solicitors and society at large that a former couple will co-operate emotionally and economically over their children and perhaps in ways that they had never done before. As one woman described her feelings about her husband's access to their children following divorce: 'it's a bit like bereavement, only difference is the corpse keeps appearing at the garden gate'. As was pointed out in chapter 2, a couple may not be husband and wife any more but they are expected to be 'mum' and 'dad' for the rest of their lives.

The paramount dispute, from which all others in some sense stem, concerns contact between a parent and his or her children or, more precisely, the critical evaluation of this relationship by the parent who is looking on. Thus, problems may be because one parent feels that there is too much contact or too little, the relationship is too intense or too diffuse, there is too much influence being asserted or too little and a host of other finely tuned but contested judgements concerning the best way for a former partner to bring up one's children. However, the vast majority of parents who remain resident with their children after divorce are in fact mothers.

In longitudinal research carried out by the Newcastle team, for example, the proportion of women reporting that they had custody of all of their children remained over 80 per cent at each of the three time stages considered over a five-year period (McCarthy et al 1991: 4). The predominant role of women in terms of their time, commitment and influence in parenting arrangements means that disputes tend to take on a particular character and the gender roles upon which the nuclear family is built cast long shadows over the form and content of disputes after divorce. As we shall see, a powerful theme running throughout these disputes is the changing role of fathers in contemporary family life: how ought the continuities of kinship be expressed between a divorced father and his children?

In public and private discourses on the family, the notion of fatherhood has been rendered deeply problematic. The 'absence' of fathers from family life has turned the notion of fatherhood into a political and emotional battleground (Burgess 1997: 27–34). For some, the progressive disengagement of men from the family is seen as a self-inflicted wound. Indeed, the alienation of fathers from family life has resulted in a desperate attempt on their part to sustain redundant models of masculinity in the face of profound socio-economic change (Campbell 1993). For others, men are not so much the villains but the victims, subject to a loss of role, power and self-esteem brought on by changes in employment patterns; the bread-winning *pater familias* has been rudely and unjustly toppled (Dennis and Erdos 1992). Either way, there is a clear identification and concern about the growing numbers of men seemingly drifting outside the practical and emotional responsibilities which previously centred on the nuclear family.

To counter what is perceived as a growing disengagement of fathers from their families as a result of divorce there have been a variety of moves intended to re-assert the importance of their role. The reaction is seen both in terms of men's structural position within the family and the affective content of paternal relations. As a result, there has been a convergence of three distinct ideologies. Firstly, the political discourse of the New Right seeks to relocate and reinforce obligations of care and support within the nuclear family with the *pater familias* at its social and economic centre (Anderson *et al.* 1981; Morgan 1986). Secondly, fathers' rights movements, and in particular 'Families Need Fathers', have campaigned to increase the legal rights of fathers following divorce, their objective being to ensure a legally enforceable parity when it comes to each parent's relationship with their children after separation. Finally, there has emerged in the realms of popular culture an ideology of 'new' fatherhood which seeks to project positive images of masculinity and nurturant paternity (Smart 1989).

The convergence of these three trends has been influential in recent far-reaching reforms in family law which ostensibly serve to establish and reinforce the bonds between parents and children following divorce. A recurrent theme in the Children Act 1989, the Child Support Act 1991, and the recent changes in British divorce legislation is that of parental responsibility. The general thrust of these legislative changes is to replace a rhetoric of rights with one of responsibilities and furthermore to ensure that these responsibilities persist irrespective of marital status and living arrangements. Whilst the emphasis is on co-operative parenting post-divorce, the underlying objective would seem to be that of encouraging or enabling non-residential parents, usually fathers, to play a more central role in their children's lives and thus to diminish the role of the State in policing and providing for lone-parent families. As such, these developments form part of a broader shift in the way that relationships are evaluated in contemporary western society. Whereas previous legislation emphasised the role aspects of relationships, there has been a progressive shift in legislative terms in favour of the substance of relationships. Action and behaviour in inter-personal relationships have come to carry increasing weight in formal evaluations of their significance. For those divorcing in the 1980s, expressions of father-right, mother-right and child-right all seemed to be seriously at odds with what men, women and children wanted to do, what they thought they were legally expected to do and what they actually ended up doing. This confusion is particularly apparent regarding the two main areas of parental concern after divorce, namely parenting and financial support. Before going on to consider these in more depth from the perspective of parents it is necessary to locate these issues within a broader policy context.

Parenting Arrangements after Divorce

One of the major policy issues raised during the eighties was the growing tendency for fathers to move out of the web of family ties and obligations following divorce. Bradshaw and Millar (1991) found that 43 per cent of non-custodial parents, most of whom were men, did not maintain contact with their children following separation and divorce, and it was estimated that in 1991 as many as 750,000 children had lost contact with their fathers (Wicks 1991). There is little reason to believe that this trend has not continued. The prevailing view of the consequences of this loss of contact is that the removal of a father's influence has negative effects on the well-being of children and their behaviour. For instance, it has been suggested that the absence of a father figure for the child is likely to result in maladjustment and/or delinquency. Consequently, the absence of the controlling influence of fathers has been cited as a major cause of increased levels of public disorder and juvenile crime (Dennis and Erdos 1992). This is a theme which could not fail to find its way into the rhetoric of government ministers. For example, Virginia Bottomley speaking to the National Society for the Prevention of Cruelty to Children in her capacity as Health Secretary, spoke of children having to overcome the 'mighty hurdle' which the absence of a father presents to a growing child (*Guardian*, 18 March 1993). Speaking as Home Secretary, Michael Howard was moved to point out in *The Times* (10 November 1993) that even though fathers had been absent from family life in the past, their absence from contemporary families was of a rather different order: '. . . they have rarely before been non-existent as a moral presence in entire communities. A swathe of children is now growing up with no father figures of any kind.'

In the divorce context, such views are to some extent legitimated by research findings which indicate that children who had retained contact with both parents coped better with the break-up of their nuclear family unit than those who lost contact with one parent (Hetherington 1979; Wallerstein and Kelly 1980). Although it is never quite clear just what is cause and effect in this often cited formulation, a powerful consensus has emerged concerning the importance of maintaining links between fathers and children after divorce. This is reflected in a pro-contact ideology which permeates the legal and welfare systems and is firmly enshrined in the practices of judges, probation officers, family mediators, family therapists and social workers. These endeavours are further assisted by a growing network of informal and voluntary services available to assist in the negotiation of patterns of post-divorce family life. Relate, formerly the National Marriage Guidance Council, seeks to counsel those with relationship problems but also plays a major role in laying the foundations for amicable, negotiated separations in circumstances where relationships are irreparably damaged. Family conciliation and mediation services are an increasingly common feature of the divorce experience, assisting couples to arrive at negotiated settlements in disputes over children, property and finances. In many areas divorced men and women can attend 'surviving' divorce courses and workshops run by local mediation services. Finally, access and contact centres exist in many areas to provide a neutral venue for those parents who are having difficulties over parental contact following a separation (Simpson 1994a).

Similarly, there has been a shift away from the notion of sole custody to one which emphasises joint rights and responsibilities towards children (Brophy 1989). It has been argued that sole custody orders disenfranchise fathers and create the potential for conflict between parents (Greif 1979; Maidment 1984; Parkinson 1988). Consequently, joint custody orders have been regarded as more appropriate than sole custody ones, although the shift in favour of such orders has been gradual and marked by confusion and regional inconsistency in practice (Priest and Whybrow 1986). Nevertheless, the proportion of orders made in favour of joint custody doubled between 1985 and 1991 (Lord Chancellor's Department 1985–91). However, joint custody did not necessarily imply joint physical custody. In British law, it simply meant the sharing of legal responsibilities for taking strategic decisions about a child's upbringing. Under such arrangements, one parent tended to be awarded 'care and control' whilst the other was awarded 'reasonable access'. Nevertheless, it was felt that such orders would enhance the likelihood of continued involvement of fathers with their children, and in effect separate the discontinuity of conjugal relationships from the intended continuity of parental relationships (Parkinson 1981, 1986, 1988; Maidment 1982, 1984; Richards 1982; Freeman 1983; Eekelaar 1984). Such arguments were seminal in influencing the Law Commission (1988) in its review of child law relating to guardianship and custody which in turn provided the basis for the present law concerning post-divorce parenting which is embodied in the Children Act 1989. The underlying philosophy of the Act emphasises that bringing up children is a serious parental responsibility and not simply a matter of establishing and enforcing legal rights (Hoggett 1989). This responsibility is unaffected by the marital status of the parents. While the concept of the 'best interests' of the child remains paramount, the Act does not promote a rigid view of what these interests are, but recognises the need for flexibility depending on the circumstances and facts pertaining to each child and family situation. For the most part, it is assumed that parents know what is best for their children, and that the State's role is to help parents discharge their responsibilities for ensuring that the child's best interests are met. Consistent with this view is a presumption that the courts will only make orders in circumstances where problems arise and that most parents will be able to achieve the most effective and beneficial arrangements for their children by agreement between themselves.

As part of this shift from notions of rights to notions of responsibilities a new terminology has emerged. The terms 'custody' and 'access', which were in common usage until 1989, were believed to have proved highly emotive to parents because of the notions of ownership and control which they imply. The legislation is now couched in terms of 'residence' and 'contact', words that are believed to describe the arrangements for the day-to-day care of children in a more neutral way.

Child Support

Alongside arguments which focus on the psychological and developmental well-being of children are a series of economic arguments regarding the cost of resourcing households following the departure of a husband and father. In 1989, only 30 per cent of lone mothers received regular child maintenance from their ex-partner and the cost in real terms to the taxpayer of providing income related benefits for lone-parent families was running at £3.2 billion (*Children Come First*, 1990). In an attempt to reduce this cost, the Child Support Act 1991 was introduced. The Act, cynically dubbed the 'Treasury Support Act' by some, allows levels of child support payment to be calculated by means of a formula. To implement these changes the Child Support Agency was established, which had the power to enforce payments, thereby effectively removing claims for child support from the jurisdiction of the courts. The stated objective of bringing about a shift from a judicial to an administrative and formula-based system was to make the collection of child support more effective and its administration simpler and more cost-effective. New powers provided by the Act aimed to make the tracing of recalcitrant fathers more effective and the recovery of maintenance payments from them more straightforward. The objective of the Act was to make a moral as well as a fiscal point; as Mrs Thatcher put it, 'parenthood is for life' (*The Independent*, 19 July 1990). Such views were reinforced by research findings which highlighted the connections between payment of child support and the frequency of contact between fathers and children (Furstenberg *et al.* 1993; Grief 1985). Furthermore, some researchers have identified the payment of child support and having contact with children as complementary activities such that 'legal reforms to the child support system will increase the amount of time that non-custodial parents and children spend together' (Seltzer *et al.* 1989: 1027).

In summary then, the officially expected continuities between parents and children after divorce are ideally realised through ongoing physical contact on the one hand and sustained financial support from the non-resident parent on the other. As non-resident parents are mostly fathers the effect of these developments has been to reinforce particular notions of paternal masculinity and in particular that of the 'good father' (Collier 1995: 176–215). The nuclear family is thus, even in its demise, highlighted against a backdrop of changing patterns of residence and relationship. Mothers are expected to remain the primary carers but strenuous efforts are made to ensure that fathers do not withdraw physically, emotionally or financially from parental responsibilities. The pressure to sustain these continuities results in two key areas of conflict and dispute which correspond with the areas of legislative change outlined above, that is, in relation to child contact and child support. In the next chapter the links between financial issues and child contact are considered in more depth. For the remainder of this chapter however, the question of access and contact is considered. Some of the quantitative findings from the Newcastle research are used alongside parental accounts to describe what former husbands and wives dispute about and how these conflicts are expressed.

Disputes after Divorce

Approximately five years after the initial Conciliation Project Unit research was commenced a follow-up study was carried out in which respondents were re-contacted with a view to finding out what had happened in their lives in the intervening period. A survey was undertaken in 1989 which resulted in 369 questionnaire responses and interviews with a sub-set of fifty-nine individuals made up of twenty-four fathers and thirty-five mothers (McCarthy *et al.* 1991: 3). We were also able to interview twenty-six children from fourteen families and the new partners of five of the men in the sample. The follow-up survey provided a third point (Phase Three) for comparison to the two rounds of questionnaires and interviews carried out for the Conciliation Project Unit Research (Phase One and Phase Two approximately 1985 and 1987 respectively).

As Table 4.1 (see page 91) reveals, the general picture to emerge from the longitudinal research was one of a reduction over time of the numbers of reported disagreements. Time would indeed appear to be the great healer. Results from questionnaire returns were confirmed by our interviews in which it was readily apparent that circumstances had changed and passions evident at earlier stages of the research had subsided. Despite the traumas of the initial separation, for most people, life had developed an air of normality and an effective *modus vivendi* had emerged. Others had equally clearly been unable to do so and were either still fighting or had simply given up and reluctantly accepted the status quo. Disputes over custody and care and control, that is, ones over which parent was the legally recognised guardian and decision-maker for the child, were major issues at the beginning of the study but the numbers involved in these types of disputes had reduced significantly between Phase One and Phase Two. By Phase Three, less than one in twelve respondents were still involved in custody disagreements. This reduction reflects the 'once and for all' view of the original settlement of such disputes for the majority of parents. Some parents may have been far from happy with outcomes of custody disputes at the time of separation but once children were physically in residence with a particular parent there was a growing acceptance and settling down of arrangements.

As suggested in the introduction to this chapter, parents who resorted to the courts to resolve their differences over the fundamental issues of custody were likely to encounter a profusion of orders. In a response to the Law Commission's review of custody law at that time King (King 1987) pointed out that the range of orders available amounted to little more than symbolic representations of parenthood which had little to do with the reality of parenting after divorce. Thus, whereas some courts awarded joint custody as a kind of consolation prize to an embittered and disputatious father, others would refuse joint custody in such cases on the grounds that there was no point if parents were not in relationships where they could at least communicate and agree on what was best for the child. Furthermore, argued King, the greater the number of symbols the more that parents would feel compelled to fight over them as powerful public statements of their continuing commitment to their children after marital breakdown. In cases in the Newcastle research in which fathers fought for and eventually won joint custody there was usually a sense of disillusionment. What was thought by fathers as a way of guaranteeing some power and control over children's day-to-day lives proved to be nothing of the sort. Much to their chagrin such orders amounted to little more than a false horizon which really only brought them into play on a limited range of decisions over health-care and education. As Table 4.1 reveals, only a minority of parents had the inclination or indeed the stamina to continue in their attempts to change established custody arrangements.

Any confusion which there might have been at the legal level over who was in parental control, however, was usually in profound contrast to the clarity of issues faced by parents at the pragmatic level of where and with whom children would actually end up living. What for most parents was anticipated as a major battle once separation appeared likely, usually turned out to be a damp squib. For the majority of parents, the initial decision over residence meant that custody was a foregone conclusion, usually arrived at long before parents ever set foot in the courts. Within the Newcastle sample the typical arrangement following divorce and separation was a simple reflection of the division of labour which existed in the former marriage and one which predisposed couples to more or less standard arrangements. Put at its simplest mothers retained day-to-day responsibility for children and fathers left the matrimonial home to parent at a distance with weekly or fortnightly weekend access. Even though many fathers entertained ideas about contesting custody at divorce this was usually a forlorn hope squashed between the contrary advice of solicitors and the stark realities of housing and finance. A man who has never taken primary responsibility for his children prior to divorce is unlikely to be able to make a case in practical or moral terms for taking on such duties, particularly once he has left his wife and children in the matrimonial home. The tender years doctrine and patriarchal expectations about women's roles held by the judiciary have meant that this pattern has tended to be reinforced throughout the legal system. Even in cases where parents might struggle to arrive at creative alternatives, the combined pressure of solicitors, welfare officers and judges in conjunction with the structuring of economic rewards in contemporary society tends to produce a certain uniformity. In a comparative analysis of post-divorce fatherhood in Scotland and Canada, Kruk (1993) was led to infer that fathers who had been highly involved with their children in the marriage were in fact penalised by the courts which tended to steer them towards the reasonable-access model of weekly or fortnightly weekend access. Conversely, this same model for fathers who had only had limited involvement in childcare, tended to result in an enhancement of the amounts of physical contact they had with their children.

Table 4.1 also reveals a reduction in the numbers reporting disagreements over access by the time of the longitudinal study in 1989 (Phase Three). In the early stages of separation the movement of children between parents tended to be a highly charged affair through which a host of other grievances were likely to be articulated. In most instances, such tensions had been greatly ameliorated by Phase Three with access becoming a practical and logistical exercise. Despite this reduction, access still appeared to be a major problem with almost a quarter of respondents signalling disagreement with their partners about existing arrangements. These disagreements were not so much about whether or not access should take place but were more likely to be about its terms and conditions. For example, custodial parents cited length of access (too long or too short), lack of punctuality and the treatment of children when with the ex-partner as the main sources of conflict. Non-custodial parents on the other hand were more inclined to identify their ex-partners as being restrictive and not giving support for their contact with their children as their main source of disagreement.

Table 4.1. * Percentage of Respondents in Disagreement with Partners over Various Issues at Three Points in Time (N=328)

Phases	1 (1985)	2 (1987)	3 (1989)
Custody	31.7	16.8	7.8
Care and control	28.0	14.9	7.8
Access	56.2	37.0	23.3
Child support	39.8	36.0	28.3
Spouse support	34.8	23.0	11.8
Property	36.3	23.0	6.2
Child contact with new partners	39.4	26.1	15.8
Child contact with grandparents	23.3	13.4	9.6
Child education	12.4	6.8	7.1
Paying for child education	5.3	5.0	5.3
Child health care	11.5	9.0	8.7
Religion of children	14.0	10.9	7.1
Mean number of disagreements	3.3	2.2	1.4

(*adapted from McCarthy *et al.* 1991: 9)

At Phase One, access was the major source of dispute and it continued to be marginally so at Phase Two. By Phase Three, however, it had been replaced by disagreements about child support payments. Four years after first filing for divorce, more than one in four respondents disagreed with their ex-spouses about the amount of child support being paid. Suffice it to say at this stage that for the majority of parents who end up with a custody-to-mother-reasonable-access-to-father type arrangement, there is a powerful tramlining effect in evidence which pre-disposes men and women to particular concerns and areas of disagreement over children.

One important consequence of this tramlining effect is the mutual construction of deficit models. Each parent can identify and understand the sources of their own grievances and dissatisfactions in the wake of divorce by means of reference to the apparent benefits retained by the other. The operation of this deficit plays a powerful role in shaping the networks which develop after divorce and the kinds of sentiments, exchanges and assumptions which underpin it. On the whole, women become considerably poorer as a result of divorce (Weitzman; 1985; Maclean 1991) but they are able to sustain important continuities in terms of their maternal role, residence and networks of kin and community (Riessman 1990). Men on the other hand might retain control of what was formerly the family wage but must confront the loss or impairment of many of the taken-for-granted aspects of day-to-day life which hitherto provided the basis for emotional and psychological well-being (Gerstel *et al.* 1985). What is in fact a more profound structural consequence of the foundering of the gendered division of labour upon which the nuclear family is built is readily translated into personal terms with each party able to point to the actions of the other as the source of additional and avoidable grief when marriage ends. Furthermore, the deficit models outlined above are powerfully reinforced by a variety of pressure groups operating in Britain which seek to represent the various and often conflicting interests of the disintegrating nuclear family (cf. Coltrane and Hickman 1992 for an American perspective on this process). For example, the National Council for One Parent Families has been closely identified with efforts to improve the financial position of a growing body of lone parents made up predominantly of single mothers. Conversely, organisations like Families Need Fathers have worked with considerable zeal to further the legal rights of fathers as parents after divorce. The agenda of each of these organisations neatly dovetails into the other but, like the constituencies they represent, they tend to play down or dismiss the reciprocal concerns of the other.

The deficits experienced by men and women after divorce generate clear and distinctive patterns of social and psychological problems for each (Riessman 1990: chapter 4; McAllister 1995). For women, the sense of guilt, self-blame and sadness caused by the ending of the relationship is compounded by their children's distress, dependency and demands. These problems are likely to be cast in individualistic terms such as depression and are part of a wider pathology which Riessman has referred to as the 'feminisation of psychological distress' (1990: 159). For men, this channel of expression is not nearly so culturally acceptable. The result is that emotional problems are obscured leading to a somatisation of stress which manifests in a range of physical problems. Health problems such as these are typically exacerbated by drinking, smoking and over-working in the aftermath of divorce.

Women's tendency to experience stress over family and financial responsibilities and men's tendency to experience distress over the loss of home and family are clearly revealed in Table 4.2. This table summarises responses given by parents to a variety of questions concerning post-divorce problems. It is interesting to note that women record higher levels of problems than men with regard to the following areas: loneliness, money management, establishing long-term relationships, relationships with in-laws, sense of personal failure, meeting new people, mental health, employment, career planning, physical health, feelings of competence and reliance on medication. Men, however, seem to have had greater problems than women when it comes to keeping old friendships, relationships with children, housing, home-making, relationships with parents and reliance on alcohol/drugs. For men the loss of a partner often represents the loss of the one who is primarily responsible for keeping wider social networks serviced and functioning, for example, through remembrance of birthdays and other special events. Di Leonardo (1987) has referred to this aspect of women's activity in the family as 'kin work'. Men who have not actively participated in this 'work' during the marriage are likely to find themselves severely disadvantaged when it ends. Men often have little awareness of what goes into this 'work' as it is largely held in women's memories and accumulated over time.

Table 4.2.* Percentage of Men and Women Experiencing Specific Post-divorce Problems

	Men	Women	All
Loneliness	31.5	36.9	34.8
Money management	28.5	36.9	33.5
Establishing a new long-term relationship	32.3	34.3	33.5
Keeping old friendships	36.2	28.3	31.4
Relationships with in-laws	28.5	32.3	30.8
Sense of personal failure	28.5	30.8	29.9
Relationships with children	38.5	17.7	25.9
Meeting new people	19.2	24.2	22.3
Housing	26.9	17.7	21.3
Mental health	20.0	21.7	21.0
Employment	19.2	20.7	20.1
Career planning	17.7	19.7	18.9
Physical health	16.9	19.7	18.6
Feeling incompetent	15.4	18.7	17.4
Home making	20.8	8.6	13.4
Relationships with parents	9.2	8.1	8.5
Reliance on alcohol/drugs	11.5	6.1	8.2
Reliance on medication	3.1	4.0	3.7
None of these problems	18.5	17.2	17.7
Number of cases	130	198	328

(* adapted from McCarthy *et al.* 1991: 31)

The patterning of post-divorce relationships then, reveals a strong clustering of concerns according to parental status. Custodial parents, who tend to be mothers, are closer to their children in emotional terms and tend to be concerned about practical issues of child care and finance. Fathers on the other hand are likely to be physically, if not also emotionally, distanced from their children and it is this fact that motivates many of their concerns after divorce. For example, non-custodial parents were more likely to consider that their children had been damaged by divorce and reported greater difficulties in maintaining relationships with them. Over 50 per cent of non-custodial parents were dissatisfied with the amount of time they spent with their children and a similar proportion felt they had grown less close to their children over the previous year. It is not surprising therefore that one in five non-custodial parents wanted changes in custody arrangements and over one-third wanted changes in access arrangements.

Access Disputes

By Phase Three of the research, 44 per cent of non-custodial parents saw their children at least once each week. However, the amount of contact which non-custodial parents had with their children had diminished considerably since the study first began. Almost a quarter (23 per cent) of non-custodial parents in the sample claimed that they had lost contact with their children altogether whilst a further 12 per cent claimed that they saw their children less often than once per month. Among custodial parents, 50 per cent reported that their former partners never saw their children, suggesting a tendency to play up absences whereas non-custodial parents appear to play them down. In a minority of cases, non-custodial parents had simply disappeared and were not even traceable by their partners. One woman who was interviewed described her children's confusion as to why their father had left and her inability to provide them with an answer that satisfied them. Despite her anger at being left with this legacy she still wanted him to get in touch with the children and to remain a part of their lives. Such cases, however, are far from the norm and in most instances the breakdown of access is a long drawn out affair perhaps only reaching its conclusion after several years of unsatisfactory contacts.

The levels of contact between children and non-custodial parents appeared to be associated with social class. Non-manual workers had more frequent contact than manual workers who in turn had more contact than those who described themselves as 'unemployed'. There is a certain irony here in that among those who are in a position of enforced leisure and therefore might be assumed to have increased opportunities for contact with children after divorce there is less contact than among those in work. As suggested in chapter 2, the lack of access among unemployed men is in part a reflection of the importance of money in making access arrangements work. Increased opportunities for contact may be confounded by lack of funds to pay for transportation and subsistence, let alone treats and gifts for the child when on access. Access to suitable housing is also a key variable in determining whether access takes place, for without suitable accommodation access and particularly staying access may not be deemed appropriate by the custodial parent (McCarthy and Simpson 1991).

Over time, regular and frequent contact between children and the non-resident parent appeared to correlate strongly with improved relations all round. Among those non-custodial parents who reported regular contact with children there was a tendency to report improved relationships with children and with ex-partners, greater satisfaction with access arrangements, more frequent communication with the former partner about child-related issues and greater levels of satisfaction with the amounts of communication. Where grievances are in evidence over access, however, it would be a mistake to assume that they only arise from disgruntled fathers who do not, as they perceive it, 'see' enough of their children. As the discussion of detailed case material will show, mothers in their role as custodial parents also experience a considerable amount of anxiety surrounding the question of access albeit for different reasons than their former husbands.

For some custodial parents the difficulty coming to terms with the fact that their children spent time with an ex-partner caused a considerable amount of emotional turmoil. Two-thirds of custodial parents claimed to be concerned about children's welfare during access visits. In approximately half of these cases parents said that they always felt such concerns. In cases where contact took place infrequently or never, custodial parents claimed to be satisfied with this arrangement in almost 60 per cent of cases. However, in one-third of cases there were indications of dissatisfaction which would suggest some feelings among custodial parents that their former partners should be spending more time with their children. Conversely, one in five of those custodial parents whose ex-partners had regular contact were dissatisfied with the amount of contact and presumably would have liked to have seen it reduced. Levels of resentment between parents after divorce seemed to be highest in those cases in which access took place infrequently or never and was at its lowest when non-custodial parents had regular contact with children. Access would thus appear to be problematic when it does happen and problematic when it does not but on balance the benefits in cases where it does happen would seem to outweigh the costs. Benefits for custodial parents would typically include support in parenting and relief from childcare when the children are with the other parent. For the non-custodial parent on the other hand the principle benefit appears to be contact in itself and the opportunity to have a direct relationship with the child.

Beneath the broad statistical brush strokes outlined above are to be found a complex tangle of issues relating to how, where and when the non-resident parent spends time with the children. Not surprisingly, the perceptions of the different parties to such disputes reveal radically different constructions and interpretations of what is in dispute and how the problems might be overcome. Each family member has their own story to tell and is anxious to portray their actions and motivations in the best possible light whilst locating the cause of problems elsewhere and usually with a former partner. In cases in which contact has broken down completely, mothers tend to explain the situation in the following terms: fathers are selfish, hostile, inconsiderate and unfeeling and through their own actions, or, more often than not, inaction forgo the right to fatherhood in anything but a biological sense. However, mothers do not see themselves as having ultimate responsibility for the decision to end contact. This is more often than not presented as being in accordance with the wishes of the child. For fathers, the response is equally unequivocal; contact has broken down because of angry, bitter, vindictive ex-wives who prevent them from having a relationship with their children by undermining their efforts at every turn. They further suggest that this is all too often encouraged by a legal system which has an inherent bias towards mothers. Consequently, despite their best endeavours, their relationships will always run the risk of failure. In cases where father-child contact has broken down, mutual constructions of blame such as this appear regularly. However, echoes of these views feature regularly in the accounts of parents for whom relationships are otherwise affable and access reasonably stable. The politics of parenthood are never far beneath the surface. Sniping is common and contentious histories threaten to burst out in a deluge of deeply personal grievances at every turn. In the case study below, the range of factors which underpin problems over access and their expression are laid out. The account is drawn from interviews with a couple for whom father-child access was an abiding problem throughout the period that they were in contact with the research team. Although it is in some respects atypical in that the issues persisted with considerable vehemence over a four-year period, it is in other ways wholly typical. The disputed relationship between parenthood, power and control which this case illustrates is a regular feature of all post-divorce arrangements over children.

The Walkers

Ian and Beverley Walker divorced in 1985 when they were in their mid-twenties, their eldest daughter was six years old and their youngest was less than a year. The cause of the breakdown was ostensibly his 'friendship' with a colleague from work. Ian maintained that this was all it had ever been but Beverley suspected otherwise and precipitate action on both their parts resulted in her leaving the matrimonial home and taking divorce proceedings. He married the said 'friend' shortly after the divorce went through. This, in Beverley's eyes, proved and compounded his deceit and infidelity although he still maintained that his earlier relationship with the woman who was now his second wife had been entirely innocent.

The couple came into the Newcastle sample as a result of their being sent to a conciliation service by a concerned judge shortly after divorce proceedings were initiated. At this time there was a good deal of anger and bitterness over children, property and the ending of the relationship. Beverley reported having had over forty visits to her solicitor over 1985 and 1986 and he reported twenty over the same period. The visit to the conciliation service came about as a result of their attempts to sort out a problem over access which solicitors and eventually the courts had been unable to resolve. Ian's eldest daughter refused to see him. Beverley's view of the problem was as follows:

> He were going to't solicitors now and again and saying I wouldn't let him have access to't kiddies, like, but the eldest one didn't want to go anyway and the youngest one was only five months old when he went so she didn't really know him to go to him.

And later on in the interview:

> she doesn't want to go with her dad now she's told him point blank that she doesn't want to go and I'm pleased that she's finally made the break and he knows it's her and not us that's stopping it. In time to come he's going to notice that he's missed out on that, he's not going to see 'em grow and it's going to irritate him more than ever. Whereas I've had the privilege of seeing 'em grow up.

Beverley repeatedly claimed that she herself was not opposed to access but felt that any arrangement should correspond to the wishes of the child. At conciliation meetings:

> . . . he still said 'the only reason she doesn't want to see me is because she's had it drilled into her'. So what do you do. He wouldn't accept anything coming from Helen (daughter). But I don't think he realises she's as old as she is. He's still taking Helen as being a child — alright, she's only a child but she's eight and she's a grown up eight.

According to Beverley, one of the reasons underlying Helen's refusal to go with her father on access was her dislike of his new wife. At the conciliation meetings an agreement was reached that access would go ahead at Beverley's house. According to Beverley, this arrangement continued quite amicably for a number of weeks but broke down when Ian's new partner objected to the time he was spending at Beverley's house. The problem was further compounded when his new wife became pregnant which had the effect of further alienating his daughters from his new domestic situation. Beverley described Ian making a number of futile gestures to get the girls to go with him during this period. He got angry, he got violent, he got seductive, he showered them with presents, he refused to give them any at Christmas and birthdays. He even tried on a number of occasions to speak with the children as they came out of school which almost resulted in official complaints by the school and police action. All of this as far as Beverley was concerned had the effect of hardening the girls' attitudes towards their father and driving them, much to her approval, into a close relationship with her alone. When Ian decided to drop his attempts to pursue access altogether, Beverley pointed out that the girls' school performance got better and Helen's long-standing problem with overeating eased. For Beverley, however, there was a deep ambivalence over the children's lack of contact with Ian. On the one hand she thought that it was not a good thing for children not to see their father — 'it's not fair on them'. She also went on to point out that she did not think that it was fair on Ian's mother either as the children had not only lost a father but a grandmother too. On the other hand Beverley herself clearly resented the children going off with their father:

> I do think you feel better if you don't communicate, you don't see anything of 'em. It's not sort of whittling you every Saturday when they're coming taking the kiddies away, . . . [ ] . . . so I think you do feel better . . . [ ] . . . you're not thinking 'oh my god, what's he saying to 'em'.

Likewise, she sometimes expressed concern for her ex-husband's mental and physical health whereas on other occasions she all but wished him dead. Such ambivalence appeared throughout Beverley's accounts over the five years that we were in contact with her.

Ian's account of the situation is inevitably pitched rather differently:

> My ex-wife seemed to think that it would be better if I got on with my life and she carried on with hers and I just forgot that the kids existed. I disagreed.

The idea of a boundary which has in some senses been wrongly drawn crops up repeatedly in Ian's account:

> She just got it into her head that I divorced her and that included divorcing the kids as well.

In Ian's eyes, Beverley had major problems dealing with the ending of the marriage and had put all her energies into directing the children against him and his new wife. Ian made numerous references to the children being primed in their responses to him. In conciliation for example:

> . . . Helen was a bit robotic, like a tape-recorder, it was as if she'd got a script and was sticking to it. I think she's had it drummed into her what she'd got to say.

Ian had all but exhausted the available options to get access onto a stable footing. Each time arrangements would work for a spell and then break down with a flurry of allegations as to who had scuppered the fragile encounters. Ian described how he had even resorted to doing jobs, such as car maintenance, for his ex-wife and her father in return for which he would be allowed brief contact with his children. Ian was clear that blame for the situation did not lie with the children but with Beverley:

> I think she'd tell you that the girls didn't like coming. They didn't like Eileen (new partner) and they were feeling that they'd got to come. They'd got to do these things to keep me happy. But I always said that if ever they didn't want to come they'd just got to let me know . . . [ ] . . . but they never said anything like that.

But, Beverley was not entirely culpable as far as Ian was concerned. Many of the problems in his marriage to Beverley and in the divorce which followed could be traced back to the powerful physical and emotional presence of her father. In Ian's estimation, Beverley's father had consistently interfered in their relationship. Although Beverley's father's aim was no doubt to protect his daughter, the effect as far as Ian was concerned was to undermine her capacity to solve problems for herself. Ian had suspected this all along but came to realise it more following the death of Beverley's father after which there was a considerable thaw in his relationship with her. This change was rather disconcerting because the communication that developed with Beverley appeared to be better than when they had been married and opened up to the extent that he could confide in her about problems in his second marriage. By the time of the last round of interviews in 1990, there was a feeling of sadness and regret on the part of both Ian and Beverley that the marriage had ended and with hindsight their actions had perhaps been rather too hasty. However, this easing of parental conflicts did little to solve the problems of access to Ian's two daughters whom he only saw for unspecified periods and on an irregular basis, often going for several months between meetings. Despite improved relationships with Beverley, the damage done to his relationship with the children in the aftermath of his departure was seemingly fundamental and his estrangement from them was almost total. The absence of contact with his daughters had caused him great distress and he had several times been close to a nervous and physical breakdown as a result.

At one level, the case of Ian and Beverley Walker is simply another sad tale of how two young people having embarked on the project of family life became impaled upon the shards of intimacy when it failed to match their aspirations. At another level, however, the case reveals some important characteristics relating to power and authenticity in relationships after divorce. In this post-divorce family as in many others, there is an ardent desire on everyone's part for people to be true, honest and direct in their dealings with one another. However, this characteristically modern quest for purity in relationships is confounded because of the way that other actors within the network of post-divorce relations are perceived to influence one another's relationships. Ian wishes to have a direct relationship with his children but their apparent autonomy is embedded in their relationship with their mother which is in turn embedded in her relationship with her father. Similarly, Beverley claims that she wants Ian to have a direct relationship with the children who she offers up as being able to make up their minds completely on their own. The problem as far as she is concerned is that he is unable to act as an autonomous agent because he is compromised by his circumstances as a husband and father in his newly formed household. It would seem that the price that each is demanding for the possibility of a relationship is nothing less than extrication of the other from their current relationships of dependence and support. This is a price that neither will pay as both are unwilling or unable to jeopardise their embeddedness in other kinds of relationships; their individuality is always shot through with troubling remnants of dividuality. Stand-offs such as this one form part of a tension over the shape, content and autonomy of relationships after divorce: they are characterised by a series of partial and competing versions of what relationships are and ought to be. Thus, a mother might consider her eight-year-old child 'grown up' enough to have made a decisive statement to the effect that she never wants to see her father again. A father might see this declaration of autonomy as spurious because of the extent to which it is influenced and motivated by the mother. What he wishes is a truly autonomous gesture and the only gesture acceptable as such would be the child's expressed wish for paternal contact. He desires and encourages a situation in which his children 'can make their own minds up'. He looks to a future in which he might have a more direct, pure and unmediated relationship with them.

Father, Mother, Child: The Fractured Triangle

Consideration of the disputes which arise over children after divorce reveals the way broader structural issues are worked out in ordinary lives. Central in this regard is the changing position of men within the family. Having moved out of the hub of family life as a result of divorce, or having been moved as men themselves might see it, there follows a desperate attempt to regain entry. For many there is a sudden realisation of just how far outside they have moved. What were hitherto invisible aspects of domestic production become all too visible along with the emotional and economic costs they are likely to have to bear as a result of their loss. Sudden reversals of strategy and intent as fathers come to realise that passive fatherhood is no longer an option are a likely cause of concern to former partners for whom the new found passion and militancy of fathers who were previously dormant is apt to be a source of puzzlement:

> . . . it was very traumatic for Billy because his dad was fighting over him and he never wanted anything to do with him when he was little, he never played with him, he never took him out . . . of course as soon as his son was taken off him it was 'my son' and he became very angry and aggressive.

However, it is clear that once the tramlines typically followed at divorce are laid down, it is men who, in parenting terms, end up on the outside looking in on compact and largely self-sufficient matrifocal units (Smith 1996: 42). Their experience is one of a radical shift from a context in which the power gradient is steeply inclined in their favour to one in which considerable power passes to their former wives. Divorce comes as a profound shock as one redundant steelworker recalls:

> When I worked at BSC I was this married man with a job, with a house, with kids and I was going out a couple of times a week for the last hour and I'd take her out at the week end . . . it seems like thirty years ago and it's not, it seems like another life altogether, it seems so distant, it's strange.

In marriage men might well oversee resources and control space and movement within the family in ways that are subtle and pervasive. After marriage has ended they are more than likely displaced and in exile with the opportunities for the exercise of control over former wife and children greatly diminished if not entirely absent.

Several researchers have suggested that women benefit considerably from the power structures which they create and control in the domestic sphere (Ribbens 1994; Stacey & Price 1981). These findings are no doubt closely correlated with those of researchers into men's perceptions of the home which report that within marriage men are often detached from family life and even envy the close relationships they see between mothers and children (Lewis 1986; Lamb 1987). Within the conventions of the nuclear family, however, the marginality of fathers vis à vis their children is rarely problematised but is woven, along with work patterns, notions of masculinity and the household division of labour, into orthodox constructions of paternal masculinity. After divorce, not only is this marginality highlighted, it is compounded as the full sense of detachment, disengagement and disempowerment in relation to the mother-child dyad is realised (Simpson *et al.* 1995). These feelings are powerfully underlined by the basic distinction between living with and not living with one's children. In a rather revealing phrase one man described how he was no longer an 'in-house' father. In short, the role of the non-custodial father vis à vis his children is an extremely vulnerable one. From the non-custodial father's perspective the custodial mother appears to hold all the cards with the trump card being the children themselves.

For non-custodial fathers there is a rather difficult but obvious conclusion to draw concerning their role as parents, namely, the considerable extent to which their role as fathers is dependent upon their ex-partners (cf. Backett 1982 & 1987). In most marriages, and therefore in most divorces, the role of the father is mediated by that of the mother. Who a father is and what he does is dependent upon the mother; it is through her relationship with the children that the father receives information and cues about his own role. Strathern captures the role of mother as mediator between a father and his children from the other end on, as it were: 'we should not be confused here with issues of legality. The so called "natural" father has to demonstrate a "social" relationship to the mother as much as the jural father whose paternity is established by marriage' (Strathern 1991: 149).

At divorce these dynamics are made highly explicit as women often discover once they step outside of the bundle of constraints which characterise traditional marriage arrangements:

there was at some point a realisation . . . ummm, that somehow I was in control of the kids and they were mine, and, and, he was dependant on my good will. Now that sounds absolutely horrible to put it into words – but I'm sure there was some sort of understanding or belief of that. Then actually I thought, 'OK, I can organise this now', which changed it for me. And I think before that point I had felt very controlled by what he had done . . . there was like some sort of dependency on what he wanted and sort of, I just thought, 'I can do this for myself.' A sort of independence isn't it . . . Emotional independence or something.

In another instance a woman recalled the sense of empowerment she had felt regarding her children:

. . . if I'd still been married. I think I would have just carried on bringing up the children and working one or 2 nights a week at the hospital. Not really learning that much about myself and what else I could do anyway. So I feel in a way that umm, it's a bit like leaving a parent somehow. That sounds a bit strange – but I think when I was 21 I got married for security, not realising I could provide the security myself. . . . [now] . . . I feel more confident that if I have a partner I can actually say what I want, which is something that I could never do, I was not particularly assertive – but now I am, I think – far more so anyway. Particularly when it comes to the children. I find that, if anything partners have tried to dominate me – this isn't just with marriage, you know, it's other men too. After a while they try to dominate me, dominate the situation, see you as some sort of poor little woman who can't cope with 3 children and they do you a big favour, and they don't seem to realise how valuable it is to have children in their lives, they're quite a bonus for people rather than a hindrance. I think people always seem to look at children and think 'Oh that's terrible, isn't that awful. But when I was doing my degree I actually found that the children grounded me somehow . . . [ ] . . . They keep you sane somehow I think. . . . [ ] . . .

Once the structures which underpin and sustain the father's role within the family are dismantled, the support which he might have expected can no longer be assumed. Indeed, it may be actively withdrawn. In circumstances where contact between father and children breaks down, for example, it is common for fathers to blame this on the mothers' failure to support them. Once the mother is removed from the fatherhood equation, the non-custodial father, to a greater or lesser extent, is a free-standing agent and may not have the resources in terms of knowledge, information and emotional insight to be able to relate to the child on his own terms. As one woman commented:

I don't think he knew where to start, he didn't know how to be a father . . . his own experiences were so poor.

It is not surprising therefore that many fathers see themselves as hanging on to their relationships with their children by a precarious thread after divorce. The paradox of patriarchy (Lewis & O'Brien 1987: 6), whereby a father's position and role within the family is also the primary constraint on him being a central character within it, is thus further accentuated for the non-custodial father. The more a man struggles to retain continuity of role and identity as a father following divorce, the more difficult and stressful it becomes to achieve this objective. The alternative, evident in the experience of some fathers encountered in the Newcastle research, is the emergence of new ways of being a father and with this a re-organisation of some of the central planks of masculinity in contemporary society (Simpson *et al.* 1995: 78–81). However, the majority would still appear to be locked in tensions previously submerged within the private ordering of the nuclear family but made painfully explicit once marriage breaks down. Men do not normally end up living with their children after divorce, yet they are still anxious to demonstrate continuing relationships with them. As we have seen in earlier chapters, these continuities can be deeply problematic in social and emotional terms. In the next chapter I turn more explicitly to the place of economic considerations when it comes to demonstrating these continuities.

On Gifts, Payments and Kinship
after Divorce

I can tell you a little story what happened last year. I mean we didn't even start the ball rolling on this one. . . . [ ] . . . , he said 'I'm going to buy her a school uniform.' I said 'Dear, dear dear. What's up with you?' [He said] 'How much do you want?' Well I said 'I heard what Helen said' but, I said, 'she's way out'. I said 'Those sort of things you should come to me' I said, 'You're talking £100 Denis, and that's being modest'. I said 'It's a lot more – but I have started to buy her things.' And I said 'We'd be very grateful if you could buy the bulk of it.' 'Right! Be in on Friday, such and such a time, and I'll bring the money up.' 'OK. Thank you very much.' And off he went. The child was excited – we waited a week – he didn't turn up – we waited another week – he didn't turn up – and she was like a little animal waiting at the door. If I took her off anywhere, we came in, straight to the door! 'I want my father – haven't brought my money!' And of course I lose my rag then, and I think 'Why did he do that! We didn't even ask for it.' You know if I had gone to him and grovelled for it I'd think 'Oh, it's your fault for asking.' You know – but it isn't a fault for asking for your own child, when he should be giving anyway! And this is what I feel – there's nobody to back me up, and nobody to make him sort of stand up and face his responsibility.

A child's move from primary to secondary school is an important rite of passage in British society; it entails the move from a small-scale and familiar school environment into a much larger and impersonal one. For parents and children, it is likely to be a time of apprehension as the child is projected into an altogether different scale and pace of social interaction. As in the account related above, an important parental contribution to this transition is that of 'kitting out' the child with school uniform, sports outfits and technical equipment. Getting the child ready for secondary school in this way is a significant act in that it makes important public and private statements about parental concern, economic well-being and social status. Parents are all too aware of the ways that a poorly turned out child might be type-cast on his or her first day at secondary school with teachers and pupils able to divine the conditions of a child's background from every detail of dress, speech and deportment. Ritual passages such as these, therefore, require that parents mobilise resources in order to make statements to the child and to the world into which the child is about to move. The ways in which this is done reflect the divisions of economic and emotional labour which exist within any particular family. Regardless of what the actual mechanisms are for acquiring cash and translating it into a neat new uniform and shoes, within the conventional nuclear family there is an assumption that parents, together, will provide. In cases like the one reported above, however, the process of provisioning is considerably more complex; the economic imperatives of 'what is' clash with the moral imperatives of 'what ought to be' as interpreted by persons who are not simply located at different points within the network after divorce but have radically different views regarding how that network should be activated and expressed. In this particular mother's story the father sets about the apparently simple task of buying his daughter her new school uniform. This is unacceptable to the mother because in her view his idea of what it would cost is not realistic and it is, in any case, a problem that she has in hand. She portrays herself as potentially self-sufficient but not averse to responding to his overtures regarding financial support. Strategic use of the pronoun in *'we'd be grateful if you'd buy the bulk'* clearly locates him as the subsidiser of a mother-child household and not as the direct provider to his daughter. In the end, despite his offer of help with the school uniform he lets them all down and a point regarding the moral and economic unreliability of ex-husbands is driven home.

Women's accounts of their former husbands' fallibility and their own tribulation appear regularly in the conversations recorded as part of the Newcastle research. In particular, they arise in relation to the occasions when the children of separated parents go to university, get married, go on holiday, come of age and at Christmas and birthdays. In other words, they feature whenever there is a cultural expectation that parents will make joint symbolic statements concerning their children and their relationship with them. As I have argued throughout this book, such statements are apt to become contested and extremely complex once cast onto the uncertain landscapes of family life after divorce. Questions of money and the transfer of resources between former husbands and wives is an area where the pragmatics of family life often come closest to the surface and parents are likely to put one another under pressure; as the woman quoted at the head of this chapter put it '. . . it isn't a fault for asking for your own child, when he should be giving anyway!' In this chapter, I consider specifically the disputes that arise when husbands and wives ask, and attempt to answer, questions of how and by whom their children ought to be resourced once they live apart. The particular focus in this chapter is thus not so much on the transference of resources following marital breakdown as on the meanings which individuals place on their transactions and the items they transact. Once again, the particular patterning of family relationships after divorce means that attention is upon fathers as they are the ones who tend not to live with their children and are more likely to retain access to an income.

Divorce, Property and a Father's Wage

The image of the traditional father (as opposed to the more illusive modern or androgynous father) is integrally linked with the role of 'breadwinner' and family provider. The 'good father' of the classic nuclear family was thus one who through his employment, which usually necessitated long daily absences from the home, provided the financial resources for the domestic sphere to function. It was the father who apparently kept the family from slipping out of respectability by providing a roof over the heads of his dependants, food on their table and clothes on their backs. This image of the 'good father' and benevolent patriarch is part of a domestic division of labour and economic organisation which has dominated family life throughout much of this century. It is an image which is further underpinned by assumptions about property and the control of resources within the nuclear family household. Up until 1870, when the Married Women's Property Acts were passed, women were regarded as having merged with their husbands to such an extent that they were incapable of holding property or performing separate legal acts. Despite the rights which this Act apparently conferred, a century later it was still the case that, where property is concerned, the relationship between a husband and wife was different from any other two people (Wolfram 1987: 111). For example, until 1971 a wife's income was taxed as if it was a part of her husband's.

However, the image of the male 'breadwinner' has been undermined by the profound economic changes which have taken place in recent decades. The welfare system, for the most part, ensures that a father's failure to provide no longer results in destitution for a family. Changes in patterns of employment have shown women's employment increasing considerably alongside substantial increases in male unemployment and uncertainty about employment. What this adds up to is a changing sense of men's financial responsibilities towards the family. These responsibilities are increasingly being seen as shared or, where a man is unemployed, falling either on the state or on a wife or partner. Where families remain in tact this may be construed as a positive restructuring of the division of labour such that the possibilities for a diversification of roles and relationships is made possible; husband and wife can operate with a high degree of economic autonomy within marriage. However, in circumstances where parents separate, the persistence of such attitudes becomes a cause for social (sic. government) concern. A man's assumption that he is no longer financially responsible for his ex-wife and children once the conjugal tie is severed is problematic for the State which, in any case, finds itself deeply at odds with the general drift towards a multiplicity of family forms in Britain today. Indeed, it would appear that it is not marriage per se which currently defines the moral linkages through which financial support is expected to flow but cohabitation. As described in chapter 4, the difficulty that many men appear to have when it comes to committing resources to wives and children with whom they do not live has prompted the creation of an extensive and very expensive bureaucracy in the form of the Child Support Agency to facilitate and enforce such transfers.

The difficulty of separating obligations arising from co-residence from those arising from marriage is seen in attitudes towards monies coming into the household via the husband. Pahl (1983), for instance, identifies three strategies for the allocation of a man's limited wage within a married couple household. These are the abdication of responsibility in which a man simply hands over his wage to his wife in order that she just 'gets on with it'. Second, there is the idea of the 'wife's wage' which is usually fixed according to local conventions. This strategy enables a man to retain extras from overtime and bonuses such that the wage eventually passed on to a wife bears no resemblance to the actual resources available. Finally, there is the pooling system in which resources are brought together in order that joint decisions can be made with either the husband or the wife taking the lead in controlling and organising expenditure. In the event of a divorce or separation, it is clear that the first and last of these options are not appropriate; a man handing over his wage to his ex-wife is as unlikely as a divorced couple pooling their resources and making joint decisions about the resourcing of their respective households. If any model is to prevail it is likely to be the allowance model in which it is seen as legitimate for a man to retain control over 'his' income and furthermore to conceal aspects of it for his own use. After divorce, such concealment is often encouraged by solicitors who are not averse to advising their clients on how to maximise their outgoings in order to ensure that only minimum maintenance claims can be made.

In short, there is a powerful assumption that a wage is paid to the husband and not the household. This is often a difficult point for solicitors, conciliators and judges to get across to men at divorce and occasionally to women who also accept and respect the distinction between patrimony and matrimony – for many men the old adage 'what's yours is mine and what's mine's my own' would appear to hold. At separation limited resources are subject to exacting and often bitter calculations, no doubt driven by a need to survive the economic and emotional trauma of divorce. Each party's inputs and ownership are re-evaluated in an attempt to establish rightful ownership of what was previously in the melting pot of joint conjugal property. This ranges from ownership of the matrimonial home down to the fittings and furnishings within it. Fitted kitchens and tiled bathrooms, for example, featured regularly in men's accounts as 'sweat equity', that is, physical investment in the matrimonial home which perforce has to be relinquished at the point of separation. Likewise, heirlooms and wedding presents would often remain, although not without conflict, within their respective matrilines and patrilines. Such views also extend to other 'family' resources such as pensions, redundancy packages and cars. One man told of his titanic struggle to reclaim a fridge freezer from his ex-wife. The said fridge freezer was bought with **his** redundancy pay which **he** received when he lost **his** job. Likewise, I have interviewed women who spoke of not wishing to make a claim on the matrimonial home because 'he had worked so hard for it'. There are complex issues of natural justice lurking in all divorces and it is not my intention to invite judgements but merely to point up implicit assumptions and symbolic attachments that underpin the process of disaggregating objects and persons from highly compacted family networks (Smart 1984).

An Anthropological Perspective on Family Finances

The idea of the nuclear family household has provided a central theme in academic as well as popular thinking about society and personal relationships in western, industrialised societies. The nuclear family is often characterised, to borrow Lasch's classic formulation, as a 'haven in a heartless world' (1977) and within its walls are to be found the affective antidote to the impersonal world of short-term, market relationships which lies beyond. The boundary between the two spheres of activity is thus frequently and powerfully conceptualised as lying somewhere between a variety of oppositions. Oppositions between public and private, category and person, commodity and gift, market and household, interest and emotion have all been put forward as characterising the quality of relationships one would expect to encounter on either side of this apparent divide. It is assumed that within the nuclear family household of western tradition, husbands, wives and children are generally keen to avoid placing monetary values on the services and gifts they daily transact even though these do have a monetary value in the marketplace. Similarly, there is a reluctance to place strict time limits on the reciprocation of these trans-actions. To engage in the unseemly activity of putting monetary values and time limits on the obligations and sentiments of kinship would be perceived as distinctly odd. Indeed, it is so odd that it provides a source for contemporary humour, as in the car sticker I recently came across which identified the vehicle as 'mum's taxi'.

The opposition outlined above between the domains of family and market has contributed greatly to a tendency to see the family as a wholly natural kind of collectivity which lifts the painful burden of individuality from its members. However, the prevalence of this view has tended to obscure the interpenetration of kinship and economics in complex societies. The internal complexities of family life are seen as governed solely by the normative constraints and obligations of kinship whereas the operation of the market proceeds unimpeded by the irrationalities which these sentiments are apt to engender (cf. Carrier 1992b). This separation of analytical perspectives, originating from a once comfortable disciplinary division of labour, is seriously misleading. The boundary between household and market is far more permeable than such construc-tions allow (Harris 1990; Robertson 1991). As Medick and Sabean (1988: 13) argue, 'emotional needs imply social structure and they can only be fulfilled within relationships whose structure is shaped by complex material forces'. As they point out, the challenge in this regard is to understand the reciprocal relationship between emotions and interests in the structuring of family life. In other words, 'mum's taxi' makes a comic but poignant observation about the classification of service provision. 'Mums' should not be treated like taxi-drivers because this would suggest an inappropriate social distance and conversely, taxi-drivers should not be treated like 'mums' for the same reason; namely, that it would suggest that they should not be paid for their services. The problem, of course, is not that there is much likelihood of taxi drivers being treated like 'mums' but that the reverse is often the case; in contemporary western society the domestic labour of mothers is often invisible, exploited and the subject of deep and persistent conflicts within the nuclear family household (Oakley 1974; Barret & MacIntosh 1982).

Marital breakdown presents an interesting context in which to study interests, emotions and the family because much that is implicit in the vague calculus of family obligations must necessarily be made explicit in the process of dismantling and reconfiguring family and household. In some senses the context which I describe is the opposite of the one dealt with by Belk and Coon (1993). Their research on gift-giving among dating teenagers explores the ambiguities surrounding exchanges which make young people appear like quasi-kin. Here I am interested to explore what happens when couples exit from marriage and set about dealing with the opposite set of ambiguities; namely, those to be found in transactions which convert 'real' kin into other types of kin. In other words, at the ending of a marriage, husbands, wives and children must engage in the messy business of re-evaluating the status and meaning of relationships. This is usually carried out alongside complex material transfers of money, property and goods. However, material interests and the web of emotions which hold family members in place are mostly viewed as separate and distinct rather than in ways which recognise that each provides important idioms for the expression of the other.

My intention, in this regard, is to introduce an anthropological perspective into what are by now some well-worn debates surrounding the issue of fathers' payment and non-payment of financial support for children after divorce. By an anthropological perspective I mean one which highlights the 'relational idioms' created by the transfer of resources between ex-husband and ex-wife. This is in contrast to economistic models of family life which cast familial arrangements in terms of the rational self-interest and altruism of individual family members. The work of Becker (1981) is one of the leading exemplars of this approach. It is also in contrast to the numerous accounts of the legal and social policy issues surrounding maintenance payments after divorce (see for example Eekelaar & Maclean 1986 and Maclean 1991).

One of the distinctive contributions of anthropology in understanding the way that families are re-ordered following divorce is in illuminating the cultural suppositions which guide this process. Where financial considerations after divorce are concerned, this requires a focus on the relationship between the expressive dimensions of relationships after divorce on the one hand and instrumental statements of self-interest and social distance between former family members on the other. Crucial in this respect is some consideration of the role of gift-giving in the classic Maussian sense in the expression and maintenance of relationships. It is my contention that an important aspect of the divorce process is the conscious re-definition of relationship by means of the style and content of transactions. Positive reciprocity, characteristic of familial relations and symbolising long-term relationships, must give way to balanced and indeed negative reciprocity as social distance between former spouses is expressed. However, the nature of this re-definition in regard to children is rarely consensual but, as we have already seen, is highly conflicted. I would further suggest, however, that it is not simply that transactions undergo a transformation but, more significantly, there is often conflict about the very meaning of what is being transacted (cf. Carrier 1992a & 1995: 145). What transactions mean to husbands and wives after divorce differs from what those transactions meant to them as fathers and mothers.

The consequences of this conflict and the efforts that are put into its resolution are of far more than merely academic interest but locate issues of kinship and the meaning of kin-based relationships high on social policy agenda. A growing confusion over the meanings of these relationships and the transactions which define them is increasingly an element in the work of statutory and voluntary agencies dealing with the family. Indeed, there is currently a proliferation of agencies to ameliorate the social consequences of these disjunctions in inter-personal relationships (cf. Giddens 1991). For example, the recently constituted Child Support Agency (Goody and Mitchell 1995) was established in 1993. One of its main objectives was to shift financial responsibility for lone-parent families away from the State and back onto private individuals. This objective reveals, in theory, if not also in practice, the extent to which there is a gap between the way kin ought to behave towards one another and the way they actually do. A guiding principle of the Child Support Act was thus to ensure that fathers, who might otherwise absolve themselves of their financial responsibilities towards their offspring, are made to share the cost of child-rearing after divorce. To realise this outcome the Child Support Agency was given significant powers to retrieve information and enforce compliance with its recommendations. The thrust of government policy has been to drive home fiscally, as well as morally, the long-term aspect of family relations.

Access and Maintenance

In the Newcastle research, it was apparent that by 1989 when the third and final phase of the follow-up study was conducted, the issue of child maintenance had displaced access as the principle source of disagreement (see Table 4.1). One of the main reasons given for the growth and persistence of these disputes over child maintenance was the failure or refusal of non-custodial parents to adjust their contributions over time. Almost half of the custodial parents in receipt of some kind of spousal support at Phase Three (n=203) had not had any change in the level of support since the original agreement. This was primarily an issue for mothers and they complained bitterly about levels of support that had failed to keep pace with inflation, let alone the growing demands made by children as they got older.

> Although I do get regular maintenance it hasn't been altered in five years, you know, they've all grown up, they all eat more, they cost more. But I can't say that I don't get maintenance for the child, I do, and it's always been regular.

Where there had been changes in the support levels this was only rarely an increase with the level of support being raised in only 4 per cent of cases. For the most part the revision was downward either because an ex-partner had ceased to pay (28 per cent) or he was late and erratic with payments (47 per cent). The reasons cited by women as to why the fathers of their children were so tardy in their payment of maintenance included ex-husbands' selfishness, their non-comprehension of the real costs of feeding, clothing and entertaining children and their need to resource second families. For some women however, an ex-husband's inconsistency was seen as having a rather more ominous function in that it served to maintain a residual control and provided an opportunity to harass the woman's new and usually financially precarious household. It is hardly surprising therefore that many women viewed a husband's financial contributions with some ambivalence:

> I didn't want any maintenance because I didn't want any contact with him. That's why I've never bothered to chase him for any maintenance. I think 'Oh I've managed all this time without your money, I don't want your money.'

Needless to say, the perceptions of non-custodial parents (n=108) regarding their support payments were rather different. They claimed that agreements had changed in 64 per cent of cases and that they were paying more than was originally agreed in over 30 per cent of these cases. They were also apt to point out a number of economic factors in their defence. These included the fact that their equity was tied up in the former matrimonial home, that they had had to establish and resource new households; that they had to bear the cost of financing access visits; they had second families to support and such like. In other words, it was rare to meet a non-custodial father who was anything less than punctilious in his payments or in his generosity to his children and, in the same way, it was rare to meet a custodial mother who had ever received everything that she was entitled to from her ex-husband.

Nevertheless, most mothers and fathers were keen to disentangle issues of child contact from those of financial support; it would not be considered fair to deny one solely on the grounds that the other was not forthcoming. However, placing instrumental and monetary valuations on relationships would seem to be an inevitable corollary of conflicts arising in the wake of divorce (Wallerstein and Kelly 1980). Where there are protracted conflicts over contact, the transfer of money between parents is likely to be a critical component of the dispute. Likewise, disputes which are ostensibly over money are apt to draw in other concerns regarding the frequency and quality of contact between parents and children. Indeed, divorce lawyers and mediators spend a substantial amount of their time trying to maximise agreement over differential interpretations of the meanings that time, relationships, money and goods have for their respective clients. The way these contested meanings might appear in the opposed narratives of men and women after divorce is clearly illustrated in the account provided by Ian and Beverley Walker first encountered in the previous chapter.

Ian described how he had spent long periods out of work since he separated from his wife and children in 1985. Consequently, his payment of maintenance had been intermittent. Throughout this period access had been difficult and infrequent with gaps of between a year to eighteen months in meetings with his two children. In his account of why this was the case he identified his wife's bitterness at his departure and her success-ful efforts to 'poison' the children's minds against him and his new partner. When interviewed in 1990 he was staying at home to look after the child from his current relationship whilst his second wife went out to work. He presented this in positive terms as an attempt to avoid the pitfalls of gender stereotyping which had dogged the first marriage. It also gave him the chance to be closely involved with child-rearing in a way that he deeply regretted having been unable to be with his first two children.

Beverley's account of the problems of her children's contact with their father focused on his calculated avoidance of meeting his financial responsibilities towards her and the children over the years. As she saw it, this avoidance even extended to him sending his new wife out to work. At various points in the interview she displayed a deep bitterness over the financial tribulations she and the children had suffered after divorce, made all the worse when he appeared to have achieved relative security. Under such circumstances she would never consider allowing contact as long as he was not paying maintenance. He was equally adamant that he would never consider paying maintenance until he started having contact with his children.

Dual accounts such as the one presented above make explicit the way in which actions and stances are interpreted differently by each of the parties and result in a classic post-divorce stalemate. In most family circumstances, the instrumental exchanges which lie at the heart of this stalemate are obscured by the moral sentiments of kinship – 'sharing without reckoning' as Fortes once described the thickly clustered exchanges which take place between kin (1969: 238). However, the transformation of family relationships which a divorce precipitates begins to expose the instrumentality of these exchanges; there is not much sharing and an awful lot of reckoning. The morality which underlies these patterns of sharing and giving within the family must be renegotiated to accommodate the changed and changing boundaries of family and household. In the event, the membrane which separates emotion and sentiment from rationality and economic calculation proves to be rather more permeable than is often suggested (Morgan 1988). Thus, if a father is not getting the contact to which he believes he is entitled, problems over financial support are likely to follow close behind. The converse of this may also be true. In one case, a man reportedly received a phone call from his ex-wife inviting him to do a deal: 'children for money: I won't screw you for money as long as you don't see the children'. Whereas within marriage and the family one might expect to find 'prescriptive altruism' (Fortes 1969: 246) enacted and reinforced, divorce creates an expectation of negotiation and with this the assumptions that 'nature' can give way to new kinds of voluntarism (Strathern 1992b: 132–5).

Family Relationships and the Spirit of the Gift

In his account of the gift relationship, Mauss placed the exchange of gifts at the heart of all social interactions (Mauss 1925). Many of the most significant relationships in society are expressed and maintained through patterns of gift-giving, indebtedness and repayment. The gift in Mauss's account constitutes a *prestation totale*, that is, an exchange which encompasses the total identities of those involved. The styles and strategies of gift-giving thus provide a crucial indicator of the relationship between the giver and the receiver, the assumed durability of the relationship and the social distance between them. Lévi-Strauss's general formulation of this point proves particularly apposite in the context of relationships after divorce: 'Goods are not only economic commodities but vehicles and instruments for realities of another order; influence, power, sympathy, status, emotion; and the skilful game of exchange consists of a complex totality of manoeuvres, conscious or unconscious, in order to gain security and to fortify oneself against risks incurred through alliances and rivalry' (Lévi-Strauss 1974: 5).

It is these uncalculated transactions which constitute what Bloch referred to as the 'long-term morality' of kinship relations, the all important temporal lag between transactions which binds people together even when they are out of one another's sight (Bloch 1974). In a more recent formulation, Offer (1996) has spoken of gift-giving as part of an 'economy of regard' as distinct from the market economy. Whereas the latter is based on short-term impersonal transactions starkly calculated in terms of their market value, the former is the context in which the most meaningful, lasting and emotionally-laden relationships are given expression. Offer demonstrates some of the ways in which people in regular social interactions go to extraordinary lengths to preserve and indeed maximise the 'economy of regard' by masking the monetary nature of gift-like transactions. Similarly, businesses increasingly personalise their services and communications in attempts to endebt their customers in an economy of 'pseudo-regard' (ibid:4)

Within a nuclear family household the flow of gift-like transactions is many layered and highly complex. On a day-to-day basis, the giving of services back and forth between a husband and wife is seen in activities, such as cooking, caring, sex, cleaning, household maintenance and repair, childcare, household provisioning, transport and shopping. Out of the ebb and flow of these mundane activities is fashioned the edifice of 'family life'. However, conflicts over these activities are often symptomatic of deeper tensions within the nuclear family. For example, the daily practices which define 'family life' often feature as issues of contention on divorce petitions and are captured in revealing phrases such as 'the respondent treated the petitioner like a servant in her own home'. In dismantling the edifice of 'family life' the history of gift-like transactions must be carefully and often painfully given alternative expression. For example, the following exchange was reported to have taken place in the context of a conciliation appointment over child contact problems four years after divorce. The man described how he had appealed to his wife to remember the 'good times' that they had had together when on holiday during their twenty years of marriage:

> . . . and then she says it was her money what took them, to pay for all the holidays because she was working then, you know. I said 'no you weren't working I took you and Peter (the son) to Greece and Majorca' and she said 'no, I think I had an insurance policy up'.

It is in determining the precise meaning of familial exchanges which take place during and after relationship breakdown that major conflicts often arise. The key point here is that it is not simply that there is conflict over what is transacted but there is usually conflict over the meaning of the transaction. Gift-like transactions take on a heightened significance when it comes to expressing continuities and discontinuities at the ending of a marriage. Claims and obligations which were part of a long-term pattern of reciprocity between husband and wife must be terminated. However, this rather blunt operation must be carried out alongside the more delicate operation of maintaining links with children. Asserting and maintaining key kinship relationships must be carried out alongside the extrication, re-definition and possibly the termination of other networks.

In cognitive terms, kinship locates and classifies people. Divorce, however, creates profound disorder (Harris 1983: 14–15). Temporarily at least, people do not know their place and neither do they know what is the appropriate way of expressing their relationships with one another – the practical business of living is made extremely difficult (Finch 1989: 234). One way of altering and giving new meanings to this system of classification in practice is through the exchanges which define the relationships of which it is comprised. At divorce, certain exchanges which were embedded in family relationships become disembedded whilst others remain. Expressed in the idiom of kinship, men and women must set about disentangling the two fundamental axes upon which western notions of kinship rest, namely, 'love' and 'blood' (Schneider 1968). As suggested in chapter 2, relationships based upon 'love' and ultimately reckoned in law and evaluated in terms of conduct must be terminated whilst relationships reckoned in 'blood' and ultimately seen as part of nature must be preserved. Affinal ties are created in law and are reversible; consanguineous ties are brought into existence with the formation of bio-genetic connections between parents and their children and are irreversible. Similarly, the fundamental irreversibility of ties of 'blood' is carried through into an ideology of kinship which sees these as closer than ties of marriage – blood is indeed thicker than water (Firth *et al.* 1970: 88–94). Divorce is the painful re-arrangement of what were previously contiguous spheres of influence, control, exchange and power. However, as we have already seen, the reversal of affinity often heralds the apparent, and often unwanted, reversal of descent and patrifiliation as is evidenced by the large numbers of men who lose contact with their children after divorce (Simpson *et al.* 1995).

Divorce brings to an end the appropriateness of long-term affinal reciprocity. It marks the ending of 'love', that is, the end of a particular kind of morality expressed in the relationship between a husband and a wife. This is rarely a bilateral withdrawal and usually one party is at the very least emotionally unprepared for the ending of the relationship. Actions which unambiguously signal the withdrawal of affection thus come to play an important role in the breakdown of the marriage. One way in which this is marked is in terms of the end of exchanges of affection, gifts, time, labour and money. Significantly, solicitors often advise their women clients who wish to end their marriages but who are finding it difficult to take a second step (the first being going to the solicitor) to end wifely duties such as doing the husband's cooking and washing. These are no longer placed in the realm of generalised reciprocity but are terminated or perhaps relocated in the realm of balanced or even negative reciprocity – allegations of tampering with food, and of domestic harassment, are not uncommon in divorce affidavits of separating couples who find themselves living together in the matrimonial home (cf. Ellis 1983).

On Payments and Gifts

As I have already suggested many of the above issues become clearer if we look at them in terms of the difficulty of disentangling 'blood' from 'love', or, more precisely, of separating the exchanges which express the different moralities which these ties represent. In attempting this painful exercise, a man may wish to signal the ending of the marital relationship by terminating the giving of gifts to a wife, whilst at the same time preserving a gift-giving relationship with the child as part of a long-term relationship. Mothers, on the other hand, will also be keen to discontinue behaviour which implies continuity of the marital relationship. However, what they do require is straightforward financial support from whatever quarter as there are few mothers who are fortunate to escape the 'feminisation of poverty' which divorce brings in its wake (Weitzman 1985; Maclean 1991). In general, mothers living with their children need money and need to maximise their income. Fathers, on the other hand, whilst similarly wanting to maximise their own income, would appear to want to put their resources into gift-like transactions with their children. Their respective attitudes reflect the classic distinction between gifts and commodities. As Gregory (1982) suggests, whereas social exchange establishes qualitative relations between subjects, economic exchange establishes quantitative relations between objects. Particularly for men on low incomes, there is often reluctance and resistance to make payments which smack of renting their children. The payment of maintenance sees the father-child relationship recast as short-term, instrumental and reversible in a way which is at best felt as an undervaluing of fatherhood and at worst its complete denial. This was a perception which many fathers were keen to articulate. For example, when asked how he would describe his relationship with his former partner, one man replied:

> . . . (it's) a business relationship, only thing is she's holding the majority of the shares (i.e. the children), she's holding 90% and I'm holding 10%.

His answer made it clear that neither the form (business) nor the content (unequal shares) of this relationship was what he thought it ought to be. Not surprisingly, competing versions of the way that resources should be transacted between family members is a recurrent theme in conflict and dispute strategies between husbands and wives after divorce (Maclean 1991: 29).

Where there is a flow of support after separation there is a clear desire by fathers to assert a form of domestic ring-fencing so as to preserve and maximise the gift-like nature of the transaction and the personal, emotional and communicative impact of the gift. The following fairly typical quotations illustrate this ring-fencing in action:

> As far as I am concerned the money that I give them goes towards him (the son) and it's not theirs (i.e. the mother and her new partner).

and

> the one thing that does give me some satisfaction is at least I know if I am paying above the maintenance money it's going directly to the children . . . If I pay that £25 to the school, I know it's for the child's trip whereas if I paid her the £25 it could be spent somewhere else.

Attempts by fathers to push this strategy further are often construed by ex-wives as attempts to control, interfere and manipulate: attempts by mothers to resist breaking the household down into budgetary headings of this kind are seen by ex-husbands as belittling their specific role and relationship vis à vis the children. Indeed, allegations made against men regarding non-payment of maintenance were often met with the counter-allegations that it was not being paid because wives were in some way misappropriating monies given for child support and using these for their own ends.

In this regard, some men clearly confuse their own contributions to their children, which they see as part of a gift relationship, with contributions made to the overall running of the household in which they live. This is no doubt related to the fact that men usually have very little 'hands on' experience of managing a domestic budget and hence their assumptions about the extent to which money can be stretched are often wide of the mark (cf. Pahl 1983). In some instances the logic of fathers in this matter is contradictory to say the least:

> She [ex-wife] is still the one person who gets under my skin, even if what she's saying I sometimes agree with. I mean she pleads poverty all the time which I do find irritating, probably because I accept that she is poor and I feel guilty about it, but she'll say to me I've got to get some clothes for the kids. ... [I and my new partner] ... have a combined income of fifty thousand a year and she's supposed to be on social security and puddling around doing some job earning bits. Teresa [new partner] is very good and she loves buying things for the kids ... [ ] ... but Kath [ex-wife] will say 'It's all very well, but ...', I will get a hint from Kath 'it's all very nice you buying all these casual clothes but what I really need is help with their school uniforms'. Its insidious and I find it difficult to cope with. In the house she's in she's just had new kitchen units and new windows and I don't know how she does it. If she can afford new windows she can afford to put shoes on the kids' feet. It seems to me she can afford to buy what she wants to buy.

Contrast this with the ex-wife's version:

> ... they [the children] seem to accept the fact that he's got more money. I do make digs about it from time to time, I can't help it. But I think it's very important that they do realise it's very different. I don't know if they are aware of the subtleties of how it makes you feel. I mean I'm sure I'm more stressed up, I've got piles of bills out there need paying and when things are getting out of hand and out of control and not having the money to pay for them – that's always a niggling worry and it's not a worry for Malcolm [ex-husband]. It's unfair to them [the children] that Malcolm and Teresa have got this huge sum to play with and that to me is unfair to them. He only pays £15 per week each and he's getting away with it. He left the court with a huge grin all over his face, because he probably realised the implications. I think he's got off very lightly from the maintenance point of view. He does pay me that money. I have to ask for it but he does pay it.

The father's view of money is as an expressive gift spent on items such as 'casual' clothes, tried on when the children are visiting at weekends. This view is basically at odds with the mother's more pragmatic view of money as instrumental to the running of a household of which the children are an integral part. This view is reinforced by comments made by the couple's twelve-year-old daughter in interview. When asked about things over which her mother and father disagreed she gave the following answer:

I want a bike but mum doesn't want me to have one but dad says if that's what I want then I can have it. That's the thing at the moment . . . Sometimes they agree that they don't want me to do something but sometimes they, like, have different opinions.

The child is in effect left to weigh her mother's instrumentality (a bicycle is an expensive luxury which carries significant safety risks for a twelve-year-old girl) against her father's expressivity (the bicycle is an appropriate gift from a father to his daughter, particularly if it satisfies an expressed desire).

Similar conflicts over the meanings placed on transactions arise in relation to the physical payment of maintenance. A practice much frowned upon by welfare professionals is that of fathers giving money directly to children in order to be passed on to the mother. The reason put forward is usually along the lines that to put the child in the position of go-between involves the child in transactions that ought to be conducted discretely at parental level and which may cause considerable stress to the child. Once again, things which are in most family circumstances implicit are made troublingly explicit by the changed context of separate households. One man interviewed was quite clear about his duty and his need to support his two daughters aged four and eight. However, he could not bring himself to give the money to his wife. Instead, he insisted on putting the money quite literally into his elder daughter's hand each week when he dropped them off after his contact with them.

Discussions with fathers who did not have contact with their children revealed particularly significant views on the relationship between economics and expressivity. Such fathers would often point out that even though they did not have contact with their children they did nonetheless make some financial contribution towards them. Significantly, this was not one that resulted in immediate benefits for the children but seemed to take the form of putting money 'to one side', for example, in a children's bank account or in a building society which would be given over at a later date. Many fathers were desperate to have a direct emotional and economic relationship with their children but this was felt to be impossible if the children were not being seen and the money was being handed over directly or indirectly, for example via a bank, to the children's mother. The effect of uncoupling economics from expression of kin relations was felt as a denial of a meaningful relationship. In other words, many fathers felt that they had been given little chance of being a player in the economy of regard vis à vis their children. By paying money into a fund to be transferred to the children in future, men were at least making a gesture towards the notion of paternal economic responsibility. After all, there is some sense of failure and shame attached, both by the individual and by the wider society, to the emotional and economic breakdown of the relationship between a father and his children. This opprobrium is to some extent averted by the claim that money is being set aside. Such claims often figure as part of a fantasy among men who have no contact with their children. In this fantasy, the man perceives himself as a 'good father' who is persecuted and denied what is rightfully his. However, he imagines that at some point in the future he will resume his relationship with his children. This happy reunion will invariably occur when the children are older and free of the negative mediating influence of their mother.

Conflicts are particularly apparent when a father becomes that most distinguished of fathers, Father Christmas, who, in this context, comes far more than once a year. Often, fathers are seen by mothers as behaving totally irresponsibly and in such a way that the child's affection is treated like the prize in a contest of competitive consumption. Such behaviour invariably causes annoyance and disruption to the mother. She is usually an unwilling competitor in this game and would rather see money spent on pragmatic resourcing than on grandiose gift-giving. Birthdays, Easter, Christmas and even regular access weekends become conduits through which gifted goods flow to the child, constituting, no doubt, the tip of an iceberg of unexpressed and perhaps unexpressible paternal emotions. The meaning of such occasions can in itself become the source of conflict as in the case of one man who described himself as a 'traditionalist' with regard to 'Birthdays, Easter and tooth fairies'. He also added that he 'resents' his ex-wife because she does not see these as important. In another rather poignant instance I witnessed whilst on duty as a volunteer at a local access centre, a man arrived with a gift for his child whom he had not seen for sometime. It was the height of summer and he had brought a birthday gift which was an Easter egg wrapped in Christmas wrapping paper. For some fathers gift-giving borders on the obsessive, and the giving of gifts is not just expressive of a relationship but actually becomes the relationship. One father, for instance, spoke of how he became upset when he saw a little girl the same age as his daughter riding a bicycle near his house. To my surprise, it was not that this reminded him of his daughter but rather that it reminded him of the absence of opportunities to give gifts to his daughter — 'I could buy my daughter a bike like that!', was his response to the upset. His comment is a powerful reminder of the way that objects 'do not simply depict human beings but depict the relationships between persons' (Strathern 1988: 171)

The desire of men to retain the transfer of resources within one sphere is often countered with equal determination by women to shift them into another. This is seen starkly in the accounts of many women interviewed who showed extreme annoyance when faced with the largesse of their children's father. In some cases, this resulted in the angry rejection by mothers of gifts given by fathers to their children. Such acts fuel disputes which solicitors might then be asked to resolve. For men, and indeed for women, the rejection of gifts is likely to be construed as a powerful statement regarding the short-term or indeed non-existence of the father's relationship. Again whilst on duty at a local child contact and access centre, I have experienced several times a situation in which gifts brought by fathers for their children are discarded by mothers once the fathers have left. At the end of a session, I have discoverd soft toys and dolls stuffed under chairs, in bins or simply left behind following the departure of mother and child from the Centre. Similarly, a complaint from several fathers I interviewed was that gifts which they had bought for their children had been lost or neglected. One man told me that the bicycles which he had bought for his two sons had been left outside his ex-wife's house and stolen, or, as he put it, 'in order to be stolen'.

Conflicts such as the ones described above are made all the more acute when it is remembered that mothers themselves are also anxious to participate in gift-like transactions with their offspring for precisely the same reason as their former partners. However, women in lone-parent households are likely to have limited means to buy presents, luxuries, treats and to pay for holidays – indeed these are the very areas in which economies are likely to be made in the interests of subsistence. The conflict that exists over who pays what and how much is neatly summarised in the following quotation in which a woman is reflecting on the economic difficulties she faces bringing up two teenage sons:

> But, I'd love them to have what their friends have [refers to one friend who received a £105 pair of trainers] I mean he knows that he can't have that, but I'd love my kids to be the same as all the other kids. 'Course I would, I mean, I'm lucky that they don't demand, they know. But I mean they'll say 'Mum, I need, a new pair of shoes 'cos they're flapping open' you know. So it depends on how much money I've got, if I've got it they can have it, if not I have to say 'Ask your father'. Sometimes he might buy it, sometimes he might ask me for half. There is never a strict rule on that. And in a way I wish that we had a strict rule that we all, we both paid for half. But there again I'd like to say well you could pay for half the bills, you could pay for half the food. 'Cos I mean the money he gives me . . . I have £45 a week. Well, I mean my food bill alone is absolutely astronomical you know, what they eat. I mean it doesn't even touch all the other things, gas, electricity, ummm, I do feel that's all very

unfair, you know when, I mean I don't know whether you find this for all the other people, it, it seems so unfair that, – I didn't want the marriage to end. I mean O.K. I wanted the children, yes I very much fought for the kids. But at the end of the day he still wants them to be his children, he still wants to see them but he don't really want the financial burden. Or the financial commitment.

Or, as put rather more succinctly by another custodial mother:

> You often go through this stage of, you know 'well our dad's wonderful because he buys us this, that and the other' and you're bloody awful because you don't do this and you don't do that.

Dismantling family life is now commonplace in Britain, whether in pursuit of freedom, or to escape from oppression, or to achieve something better, or simply in order to have an opportunity to try once again to achieve the 'cereal-packet' ideal of family life (Leach 1968). The conflicts I have identified in this chapter are thus likely to be familiar to the many thousands of men, women and children who engage in the complex and painful business of re-ordering households, resources and relationships following divorce or separation. This process is not, and is never likely to be, a mechanical re-allocation of personnel and resources but will always reflect the deep psychic, emotional and practical investment that individuals make in one another, in their children and the spaces they together inhabit. It will always necessitate a re-negotiation of the basic human qualities of trust, commitment, regard, intimacy and love between a husband and wife whilst at the same time charting the continuities of these qualities in relationships with offspring. I would suggest that exchange relationships across the conjugal divide are crucial when it comes to understanding this transformation. Consideration of the meaning and strategic use of exchanges between ex-spouses is a powerful indicator of how movement out of an earlier web of family reciprocities and responsibilities is achieved.

However, there is rarely agreement between husbands and wives on whether this transformation ought to be achieved at all and, if so, how it might best be brought about. Strategies of separating spouses are likely to be seriously at odds in this regard as different meanings are placed on transactions involving money, time, property, income, networks and information and how these in turn relate to questions of continuity and discontinuity vis à vis children. I have suggested that when conflicts arise after divorce, fathers tend to want to maximise the gift-likeness of their contributions; rather more cynically, they might justify not paying adequate maintenance by claiming thwarted gift-like intentions. They emphasise the gift ethos, I would contend, because they are keen to demonstrate relationships with their children which have both depth and duration. Mothers, however, faced with the same circumstances, want regular, quantified, market-like contributions because they wish to put social distance between themselves and their spouses, and of rather more consequence is the fact that they are usually poor. Similarly, fathers tend to proceed from the idea of a natural relationship which might be elaborated through certain kinds of exchange. Mothers, on the other hand, tend to evaluate that same relationship primarily in terms of conduct, with the father's relationship as *genitor* a problematic secondary feature of who and what they are.

−6−

Dialogues of the Divorced

Divorce is considered to be the second most stressful life event for adults after the death of a spouse (Holmes and Rahe 1967). But, given the extent to which marital breakdown is implicated in ill-health, accidents, suicides and depression among men, women and indeed among children (Dominian *et al.* 1991) it is surprising that it is not the most stressful life event. Divorce is, to use Denzin's terminology, an 'epiphany' (1989: 70); it entails the altering of fundamental meaning structures which impact significantly on many aspects of a person's social and emotional life. As we have seen in earlier chapters, the breakdown of marriage and the fission of households sets in train profound changes in the way that people express their relationships with one another. These changes are not simply about the termination of relationships but reveal complex continuities between former intimates. For many couples, a powerful momentum of shared history and experience means that relationships and the sense of personhood they imply have to be re-negotiated in radically new ways. The object of this book has been to draw attention to these processes, not simply as ones which impact in a measurable way on discrete individuals, but as developments which are fundamentally social in their character and which are expressed within the particular cultural idioms of Euro-American kinship. The way in which I have gained access to people's experience and understanding of these relationships is via an analysis of detailed, narrative accounts generated in interview situations. Up until this point these narratives have been treated as primarily referential, that is, they have been treated as simple accounts, descriptions and illustrations of the events, experiences and feelings that respondents encountered after divorce. In Jerome Bruner's terms they relate to worlds of action (Bruner 1986). In this chapter, I consider the second 'landscape' in which Bruner suggests narrative operates, namely worlds of consciousness. In other words, the construction and delivery of narrative involves an important expression of the narrator's subjectivity. By considering the way that narratives are assembled and how actions, persons and events are evaluated therein it is possible to locate the informant within a particular social and moral space. This space is filled by others whose significance is changing and locates the teller between a contentious past and an unclear future. As I go on to demonstrate, narrative proves crucial in effecting shifts within this space. Such constructions enable their authors to locate themselves in relation to others and thereby re-shape and re-define networks of significant relationships.

The work of the Russian philosopher and theorist Mikhail Bakhtin is useful in conceptualising the links between divorce narratives and actor network theory. The notion of dialogism, as put forward by Bakhtin, highlights the social nature of accounts which we might otherwise think of as purely individualistic and therefore of psychological rather than anthropological interest. Holquist (1990: 29) refers to dialogism as a form of architectonics: the general science of ordering parts into a whole. Whereas an analogy between social life and architecture implies the act of building, but building something which is static, architectonics suggests the creation of structures which are capable of movement and fluidity. To view the complex sociality of family life as a form of architectonics is thus not simply to look for the creation of fixed family structures which persist through time, but highlights the way relations are made and unmade, stretched and concentrated, intensified and attenuated as families and individuals negotiate the increasing uncertainties of the life-course. Throughout this chapter, the telling of stories by informants in the context of the research interview is considered as part of just such an architectonic process with narrative taken as the means by which informants evaluate and communicate their endeavours and thereby map themselves in relation to others. Thus, the narratives recorded here tell about far more than the actual, physical comings and goings of people but also involve a highly imaginative exercise in locating people and events in stories which aspire to coherence and plausibility. The focus of the chapter is an analysis of two case studies each of which is drawn from a single family. The analysis is developed through a consideration of different versions of events and situations put forward by members of the same family and represents an important shift in the level of analysis. In earlier chapters, I have demonstrated the complex linkages which persist at the level of actual social interactions; here the emphasis shifts to incorporate the realm of thought or imagined relationships (cf. Watkins 1986 & Vitebsky 1993). Such relationships are critical components of personal identity and continue to exist long after the typical, two-parent, two-child, co-resident nuclear family has ceased to be identifiable as such. Indeed, what proved particularly fascinating about listening to conversations with respondents once again after several years was the fact that although they were exchanges on a one-to-one basis, respondents often incorporated a variety of devices which implicated them in a much wider social life. The accounts are clearly about self, but crucially about self in relation to others, echoing Carrithers's observation that 'we cannot know ourselves except by knowing ourselves in relation to others' (1992: 1). Thus, running through the interviews are traces of other people occupying other positions; these are the people who previously constituted the family and currently feature in the networks which persist after divorce.

Let me conclude this introduction with a brief example. Respondents would occasionally use, sometimes with the aid of mimicry, the voices of others in the form of reported speech. The following snippet is taken from a woman's account of a meeting with a Court Welfare Officer about an unresolved custody dispute. The following account, although brief, is not untypical of the way in which informants would animate the characters in their everyday tales of adjustment after divorce:

> I took Edward down (to the Welfare Officer) and I said 'don't say you want to stay with me cos I want you to' I says 'I'll not come in the room' and they (Welfare Officers) says 'no stay' and I says 'you speak your mind it's not what I want or what your dad wants'. And he said what I knew he'd say ' I don't want to live with one or the other, I want to live half and half' and his dad says 'oh no, I'm having him' . . .

The reasonable and compliant stance of the woman who knows the mind of her child is countered by the authoritarian and uncompromising stance of the father. The former is captured in the soft tones that she uses to report her own speech which suggest a retreat from conflict. The tones of her former husband, however, are reported as harsh and deep, suggesting aggression and confrontation. Dialogical constructions such as this indicate the way in which social life and mental life overlap to give narrative both direction and force in the structuring of relationships. Similarly, informants would explain the motives for others' actions. They would construct scenarios which explored the consequences of their own actions and the actions of others. They would address all manner of absent audiences such as a former partner, estranged children, the courts and public opinion in ways which went beyond the direct interaction between interviewer and interviewee. Throughout the interviews informants can be heard weaving together characters and plots into narratives which in their telling are simple and elegant. However, in terms of the patterns of human sociality which they reveal they are extraordinarily complex. How to study this important complementary component of social interaction takes us to the interface of social psychology, anthropology and linguistics. It calls into question a division of labour which has prevailed throughout much of the history of the human sciences. This division has seen anthropologists and sociologists mostly concerned with actual social relationships whereas the way that people think about relationships, what might be called the realm of imagined relationships, has been the preserve of the psychologist and the psychoanalyst concerned to understand the nature of the self. However, as Caughey (1984: 17) argues, it is a mistake to see one world as 'inner' and the other as an external 'social' world as the imagined world itself is populated with characters 'felt to be there' and which continually splice into the real world (Hermans and Kempen 1993: 71).

Consideration of narrative and its expression in the form of interview dialogue thus opens up the possibility of understanding important dimensions of human kinship and sociality. As suggested in chapter 1, the conventional paradigms of family and kinship prove quite inadequate once we move into expressions of kinship which lie beyond the axiom of amity. Thus, in the context of post-divorce relationships, it is important that we are aware not only of the actual face-to-face dimensions of social life but also of absent relationships which, in circumstances of conflict and limited communication, become highly significant; as we shall see, out of sight does not necessarily mean out of mind. Before considering the importance of dialogue in more detail I shall begin with a rather more conventional account of the central role of narrative in the representation and articulation of personhood.

Divorce and Narrative

Divorce generates a lot of stories. Stories might be told by the parties caught up in divorce to doctors, social workers, judges and registrars, counsellors, friends and relatives. There are numerous contexts in which a person might be encouraged, required or compelled to give an account of events and occurrences and to engage in the unconscious process of creating layer upon layer of narrative account detailing the who, where, when, why and how of divorce. Interviews conducted with a university researcher are a further context in which such stories are told. In meetings with a researcher over time, stories are told which evolve as the circumstances surrounding the characters in the plot change – new partners enter and leave the scene, children are born, people acquire new jobs or are made redundant, they become richer or they become poorer, hatred and bitterness subside or become more deeply engrained. At a time of radical personal and family change, coherence of self and family relationships can no longer be assumed and, as in any attempt to come to terms with a traumatic life-event, narrative plays a fundamental role both as a means of ordering past events and providing the *telos* for future events (MacIntyre 1981). As Arendt tells us 'all sorrows can be borne if we can put them into a story' (Arendt 1958: 175). Where there is a problematic past or a breach in normative expectations, narrative provides a means of ordering, structuring and making sense of disordered experience (cf. Bruner 1990). In the telling of stories, the complex and dynamic contingencies which accompany life after divorce are briefly given a fixity which can be grasped by both listener and teller.

For Bruner (1986) however, the narrative function goes much further than simply repairing in words what has gone wrong in experience. Narrative is seen as rather more encompassing of human social experience; it is a rudimentary device which subjects routinely use to integrate plots, action, intentions and feelings with the characters in their story. In this approach, a crucial shift is made from seeing narrative as a mode of performance to seeing it as a mode of thought (cf. Widdershoven 1993). In this regard, Bruner distinguishes narrative thinking, which is manifest in storytelling, from propositional thinking which is manifest in argumentation. The object of a good story is life-likeness or verisimilitude; the object of a good argument is to convince someone of rationality and truth. Whereas the former has an imaginative quality and is concerned with 'intention and action and the vicissitudes and consequences that mark their course' (Bruner 1986: 13), the latter proceeds according to the logico-deductive method of western empiricism and aspires to higher levels of abstraction and objectification.

In accounts of divorce, there is clear evidence of both types of thought in action. Subjects tell stories and this is by far the easiest and most economical way for them to communicate the complexities of human experience to one another. They also attempt to present accounts as arguments; passionate attempts to convince the listener of the rightness and justice of their case. Inevitably, however, attempts at objectivity and rational analysis of this highly emotive and deeply subjective process are largely overtaken by narrative forms. Indeed, one of the most profoundly disillusioning consequences for many people who experience conflict at divorce is the realisation that when it comes to dealing with the fragmenting family, the courts, far from being the instrument of rational and objective judgements based upon evidence, are little more than an arena for the telling of stories. Justice happens, or, more likely fails to happen, not because stories are adjudged to be right or wrong but because they are more or less reconciled. At a point where people might have thought they would encounter clear manifestations of structure, power and principle there is a disturbing vagueness; the State appears reluctant to enter in any decisive way into post-divorce family conflict other than as a conduit for proliferating and largely incompatible personal narratives. Stories and not arguments prove to be the most effective when it comes to conveying thoughts and feelings about contested relationships. Stories convey meaning in ways that arguments never can; they explore questions of motivation, commitment, intention and belief and how these relate to the conduct and expression of kinship relations.

However, it would be mistaken to see all informants as equally effective when it comes to telling a 'good story'. Indeed, some interviewees found considerable difficulty when it came to telling their story. For example, one of the most difficult people I ever had to interview was a service engineer from South Wales in his mid-thirties. His marriage had been by all accounts a disaster from its very early stages. His divorce and its aftermath had been painful and protracted involving an interminable dispute over access to his son. The problem that I encountered was that he proved almost impossible to talk with about his divorce. I felt that he liked me and to all intents and purposes we got on quite well but the style of response was one that he would most likely use with work mates or in a bar. In his responses, the intention was clear; he wished to denigrate his wife at every turn and to present her as malevolence incarnate whilst presenting himself as a man who had been grievously wronged. My questions were met with responses which closed off any further questions: '. . . well, you know yourself . . .' or 'huh! you know what women are like'. Such comments would be followed by the kind of silence which in most of his social environments would probably be filled with grunts and nods of a kind that would close down any further discursive utterances because all present would 'know' what women are like. The trouble was that I tended to fill these silences with further questions which rather suggested that I didn't know what women were like and which probably served to confirm to him the fact that people who were apparently educated tended to be rather stupid. In effect, I was being treated, possibly solely on the basis that I am moustachioed and male, as part of his circle of friends, and treated to utterances so filled with the voices of members of that circle that, as far as he was concerned, little, if anything, needed to be said. The narrative of the rejected husband expelled from home and hearth by the 'bad' woman was one which should have been entirely self-evident. Even five years after our initial meeting his account and style of delivery had changed little; it was more akin to a series of discrete, angry and uncoordinated whorls rather than the coherent accounts of people and their motivations evident in the emerging narratives of many respondents. If the ability to construct a coherent narrative of past events is any index of psychological well-being then this man would not have scored highly. It was also no accident that he had repeatedly fallen foul of the people to whom he would have been expected to present rounded and polished narratives regarding his circumstances and his aspirations. Almost from the outset, the man had had serious disputes with his solicitors, probation officers, conciliators and the judiciary, none of whom, as he saw it, would listen to him or understand the deep injustices he felt himself to be suffering.

A second discernible difference in the narrative abilities of informants is one which broadly follows gender lines with men and women adopting very different styles in their relation of events. Useful in this regard is the distinction made by Polkinghorne (1988) between a chronicle and a narrative construction of events. A chronicle is merely a series of events organised in such a way as to reflect a chronological ordering. Narratives, on the other hand, organise or emplot events in combinations that create coherence, giving point and meaning to the actions of protagonists. Thus, a common response of male informants was to try to deliver a chronology of events, often backed up with material evidence in the form of letters, affidavits and court orders which serve to authenticate their chronology in official ways. Responses from female informants on the other hand were more likely to hook the interviewer into personal and emotional accounts centred on the protagonists by highlighting the relevance and immediacy of current and past events (cf. Humm 1987: 20; Hockey 1990: 132). Whereas men tended to organise their accounts around events and the way these events were objectively inter-related, women tended to base theirs upon far more immediate and emotionally grounded evaluations of their experience. As the extended case studies later in this chapter illustrate, when it comes to the 'repair function' of narrative it would appear that men are often more concerned with the re-negotiation of hegemonic hierarchies of value and notions of 'justice' whereas women are concerned with the re-ordering of networks of emotional relations and feelings (cf. Gilligan 1982; Tannen 1991).

Divorce, Dialogue and the Absence of Other

In the previous section, I have treated accounts of life after divorce as if they were quite straightforwardly part of a wider class of sense making stories, that is, the kinds of things all people do, to a greater or lesser extent, when faced with serious personal disruption of one kind or another. However, the narratives under consideration here also reveal another dimension. The accounts that people provide also reveal a capacity or even a necessity for the teller to enter into the life of an absent partner or indeed for the absent partner to enter into the accounts of the teller. Here we begin to move into Bruner's landscapes of consciousness (Bruner 1986) and an altogether different dimension of human sociality. Take for example, the following extract from an interview with a woman whose husband had eloped. His departure was made significantly worse by the fact that the woman was previously her 'best' friend and she was left with two children to bring up. The extract is her response to my question as to whether she thought of her ex-husband often:

Mmmm. Yeah I do yeah, mmm, um. Yeah, I mean quite often, I have to say, I mean obviously not nice thoughts [laughs]. Um, yes, I, they, both of them occupy my thoughts a lot, I don't know why that is, . . . um. I mean somebody said to me the other day 'Do you still love him?' I said 'No I don't. I stopped loving him when he beat me about. Before I left home.' you know, eh? but if I, if I can actually say I think I feel nothing for him, I can honestly say I feel nothing for him, but I absolutely hate her, I mean there is still that which I haven't let go of, which is probably why I still think of them. I mean I think of them most when my children are there you see, I mean like this morning, like the kids, they go to their father's for a long week-end, every third week. So they've been away all week-end, they went – Thursday, Friday, Saturday, Sunday, Monday. . . . So of course I'm bound, I wake up in the morning and I know the children aren't there, in their bedroom. So I immediately think . . . I know it sounds stupid, perhaps very hard for you to understand, but because I know her house, you know, inside and out, I know what bed they're in, so I picture them . . . you know, there, and I mean that, that hurts me. Er, so yes, I hate to say it, yes he does occupy my thoughts. I mean not, not every minute of the day, but almost every day. Mmmm. . . .

Extracts such as this reveal the many-layered qualities of the stories people tell. They are stories told by people about relationships that were once intimate and which are no more. Nonetheless, individuals continue to have a biographical knowledge of one another which is both privileged and deeply entangled. After divorce this knowledge remains but is now applied in contexts where both people have changed, not least because the direct, physical communication that comes from co-residence and regular, habituated contact is now at an end. As I have already suggested, the accounts that will be considered here take us beyond the axiom of amity;

they invite consideration of the points where social life and mental life crucially overlap.

Formerly married couples, then, despite their ardent desire to excise one another from their lives, clearly remain implicated in each other's biographies long after they cease to be formally identified as a conjugal pair. Past intimacy, shared parenting and a shared history of family life lock them together in ways that constrain and determine their actions long into the future. However, these constraints are not only experienced in direct physical contacts but are also felt despite the absence of other. This powerful momentum, in part, explains why it is that separated men and women feel that their former partners continue to have residual and deeply unwelcome power and control long after they have ceased to be husband and wife. This feeling of being violated or 'haunted', as several informants revealingly referred to it, is evident in expressions used to describe encounters with former partners. So, almost seven years after the initial separation a woman can say of her former husband:

. . . he has this terrible effect on me, more so than anyone else in my life.

And, similarly, her ex-husband can make the following statement about her:

. . . she's still the only person on earth that's got the ability to make me so angry over something trivial . . . [ ] . . . she still triggers that and I really don't understand it, I find it so irrational.

Such sentiments are common in the accounts of the divorced and are further evident in phrases such as 'he still knows how to press my explode button', 'all he has to do is give me that look' and 'she knows exactly how to wind me up'. These comments each suggest a precision in communication which can develop only through intimacy. After divorce these communications point to painfully redundant patterns of interaction which leave an echo for many years after the breakdown of a relationship. Thus, whilst relationships with a former spouse continue in the imagination and are occasionally given vent in the form of narrative accounts, the physical contexts for matching these images to actual experience are altered, disrupted or indeed may be entirely absent. The tendency for those who were once intimates to work through dialogues in the absence of other has important consequences for the way that relationships are conducted after divorce. The intermittent connection between dialogues in the head and actual dialogues in social interaction can be seen to exacerbate conflict in situations that are already highly conflicted. Versions provided by parties occupying positions on either side of the great divide reveal how they engage in the hypothetical construction of boundaries, the attribution of motives and various forms of what Carrithers refers to as 'mind-reading' (1992: 54). However, the boundaries are rarely constructed in ways that are shared, the motives are often wrongly attributed and mind-reading is likely to be inaccurate. As the compact sociality of the co-resident nuclear family gives way to the more dispersed sociality of post-divorce family arrangements, the parties must work especially hard to achieve a sense of personal coherence for even simple acts of communication are apt to be misconstrued.

Access to a body of data in which we are able to analyse the narrative accounts of both parties to a conflict is highly unusual. Amongst other things it allows consideration of the ways in which individuals remain enmeshed not just socially but mentally too, long after separation or divorce. The accounts of divorced men and women are not flat and monological but deeply entangled and, in Bakhtin's sense, multi-planar and dialogical (Bakhtin 1986). The respondent, as author of his or her own sense of coherence, is necessarily drawing on the voices of others to establish moral legitimacy and personal authenticity. As Stromberg, speaking of religious conversion narratives, puts it:

> Even if a person has changed, traces of what he was are likely to manifest themselves in his talk. This is because change is constituted above all in talk, in different habits of formulating, understanding, and speaking. Thus one may expect an interview about a life transition to replay to some extent the drama that it tells about, even if that drama occurred decades earlier. Indeed, it is fair to say that a change in the believer's life is sustained only to the extent that it is continually constituted (Stromberg 1993: 15).

Utterances delivered as part of an interview thus feature as part of a chain of communication which both precedes and succeeds a particular encounter. In this thoroughly dialogical view of communication, meaning is not absolute but relative to context and situation, that is, to the flow of utterances in which the speaker participates. The chain is complex for it is not simply literal alternations that shape and constrain any particular utterance; the alternations may take place over long stretches of time and take place with interlocutors who are remote and imaginary as well as immediate and real. Indeed, dialogues may be hidden as well as vocalised and explicit. Any utterance is thus 'furrowed' (ibid: 93) with the traces and reverberations of earlier dialogues. The interview thus becomes a small insertion into a much vaster torrent of words, thoughts and feelings which circulate between those engaged in the architectonics of family life after divorce.

As illustrations of these points I would now like to turn to the consideration of two detailed extracts from interviews conducted with various members of two families: the Coopers and the Jones. The case of the Coopers illustrates a tendency to direct the momentum of the past into the maintenance of a painful disequilibrium in current post-divorce relations. The example shows how there is wide scope for misinterpretation and misunderstanding over roles, intentions and actions amongst those involved. In the second and rather longer example provided by the Jones family, there is an apparent attempt to open out and negotiate new roles and patterns of responsibility within the network of post-divorce relations. As the case study of the Cooper family demonstrates, this endeavour is fraught with difficulties as the parties struggle to reconcile new and emergent meanings of family and kinship with the survivals from the old.

The Coopers

Fred and Audrey Cooper had been married for twenty years before their divorce in 1982. At the time they were interviewed they were having considerable difficulty establishing boundaries and a comfortable *modus operandi* for their lives after divorce. The considerable momentum of a long and intense partnership seemed to intrude into their attempts to develop a regime for Fred to have regular access to Ian, their one twelve-year-old son. Fred lived alone and was having problems coming to terms with Audrey's decision to divorce him after twenty years of marriage. Even four years after the divorce was finalised Audrey reported being confronted by the Book of Common Prayer open at the marriage service whenever she went into his house and she described how he would regularly lecture her on the indissolubility of marriage in the eyes of God. In short, he did not accept the fact they were divorced. His desire for a reconciliation, despite having been legally divorced for four years, meant that many of the actual interactions they had together were the subject of spectacular misinterpretation. Take, for example, the fact that every fortnight Audrey returned to the former matrimonial home along with Ian in order for him to have contact with his father. The visits were often marred by insults and arguments leading Fred to observe 'there's still a spasm of life (in the relationship), there's something there, even if it's only hate!' Her visits to the home were construed by Fred as signalling a residual desire for their previous home life to continue; a logical prelude, as he saw it, to a future reconciliation:

> I went up to the doctor's when they left and she said she'll come back but it might take four years ... and I thought well I'll leave it, but it's been four years now and this August it would've been our 25th wedding anniversary, so I said perhaps we could get back together for then.

The visits led to further confusion for Fred when Audrey would help him with housework. This was a practice he was keen to encourage and did so by 'leaving jobs for her to do around the house'. However, when she eventually stopped helping him it caused considerable concern. As Fred relates:

> I get the dinner and she helps me wash-up or she did. Now she's started doing nothing, and yet when she started coming over she'd go and clean the bathroom, or something like that, or I'd purposely leave something, I'd leave the little washbasin in the downstairs toilet, leave the tiles so they wanted wiping over, so she'd wipe the tiles over, give her something to do, you know, occupational therapy or whatever. She'd go up and make the bed, now she's stopped doing anything, she'll just come in here, sit down and go to sleep.

His concern stems from the fact that she has 'started to do nothing'. Whereas his normative expectation is of her as somebody who is naturally and unconsciously active in the domestic setting, he is now confronted with the worrying prospect of her being unnaturally and consciously inactive. From Audrey's perspective the reasons for her behaviour are viewed rather differently:

> I sit there for hours on a Saturday and never speak. I usually sit there and pick a paper up. I tend to switch off, it just goes over my head. That's the only way I can get back here without feeling utterly crushed and with a thumping headache.

Fred's attempts to bring in 'occupational therapy' are clearly linked to his diagnosis of his ex-wife as in some disordered mental state out of which she will at any moment snap so that they might resume the devoted relationship they had shared for twenty years: 'I'll have you back when your head gets better' he quipped during one interview as an aside to his absent wife. When interviewed in 1987 he was still 'hoping for a miracle' and saw his ex-wife as 'unable to remember the good times' . He spoke at length of the mutual depths of their devotion to one another as evidenced by their previous statements of commitment to one another. He described how, on the few occasions when they were physically separated, they had written letters to one another everyday. He also took me to a large drawer which was literally full of birthday and Christmas cards which did indeed reveal twenty years of regular and deeply affectionate messages exchanged between an apparently devoted husband and wife.

However, Audrey's motivations for coming back to the home on a regular basis were nothing to do with mental imbalance or any desire for a reconciliation but were out of general concern for her ex-husband, whose health, mental and physical, she perceived to be deteriorating. More specifically, she came back regularly because their son refused to be alone with his father. Access was recognised by her as a necessary inconvenience, not least because Fred played relentlessly on the infrequent and poor quality contact he had with his son. Her visits to the former matrimonial home were, as she saw it, principally motivated out of good-will in that they enabled Fred to have access to his son which he might not otherwise have had. Her interpretation of the son's refusal to have contact with his father without her presence was that the boy didn't like his father and was scared of his angry outbursts particularly when they were addressed at his mother. Fred's interpretation of his son's behaviour was that Audrey was lonely due to the separation and was scared to allow the boy to have direct contact with his father for fear they might start a relationship independent of her mediating role. As Fred pointed out:

> . . . you see, I never have a chance to talk to Ian you see . . . well, he feels intimidated probably, he never asks me anything, he always asks his mam if he can do anything, you see.

Ian's demand that his mother be present whenever he met with his father may have had more to do with an unconscious or even conscious strategy to keep all three together as a family. This was especially the case given that the three of them would regularly go out for days together to museums, theme parks and country houses and give every appearance of being a 'normal' family. However, according to Audrey, Ian had come to the conclusion that his father didn't want him there at all really. Having arrived at her own conclusions about the psychology of children, Audrey drives this point home by introducing the voice of the child into the interview:

> Children are quick about who likes them and who wants them. 'He doesn't want me he only wants us to go over so he can get on at you to go back to him and do his housework.'

The upshot of these failed expectations and misinterpretations is a steady state but one founded on a profoundly uncomfortable and potentially damaging instability. The couple, and especially Fred, are enmeshed in ongoing relationships of caring, loving and parenting which are confounded by what they actually do and say to one another. The only logical interpretation for Fred is that his wife is mentally unstable whereas for Audrey his persistent invocation of this theme validates even more her decision to live apart from a man who she sees as bullying and obsessive. As the following quotations reveal, each is able to enter into the thought processes of the other but seemingly incapable of acting to change the dynamic into which they are locked. As Audrey points out:

> I'm downstairs being nagged about going back and how stupid I am, and how I ought to get help and I need to see a psychiatrist . . . I could write his speech for him because I know exactly what he's going to say.

Fred's version offers little to contradict this:

> . . . *and I said 'you're off your trolley, you've lost your marbles', or she was on the verge of a nervous breakdown, and she said 'well, if I am you can congratulate yourself on doing a good job then, can't you?'*

And so, the painful dynamic continued; a social interaction made up of a complex tangle of caring, dependency and hostility. Both Fred and Audrey's stories about their interaction with one another come across as what Harré refers to as 'sustained, ritualised needlings' (Harré 1993: 166). In German, the word *feindschaft* captures the character of these negative but nonetheless stable and ongoing social relations in a way which no English equivalent can. However, as Harré goes on to point out, we actually know very little about the ways human beings set about 'transforming private feelings of enmity into a stable, hostile and publicly realised relationship' (1993: 167). This would appear to be precisely the situation in which Fred and Audrey find themselves.

The Jones

Explicit in the accounts of Fred and Audrey Cooper is a recurrent tension. The tension arises between their ideas of male and female: husband and wife: father and mother as they were within the marriage and as they are transposed into the post-divorce setting. What Beck and Beck-Gersheim refer to as 'feudal gender fates' (1995: 27), epitomised in the opposition between male wage-working and female domesticity, are clearly no longer sacrosanct in the post-divorce setting but begin to be expressed in different ways. As the narratives of family life after divorce unfold it appears that women are the ones who are actively engaged in the process of change and a radical re-framing of private life. Men, on the other hand, find themselves witness to the dismantling of traditional roles and statuses upon which the nuclear family is founded. At the heart of this transformation lies the changing context and meanings of motherhood in contemporary society. As New & David point out: 'In our personal myths home is the place where we are fully accepted, it is linked with the idea of a woman, mother . . . Appeals to defend the privacy of the family evoke powerful memories and dreams, and are thus able to strike chords in many hearts' (1985: 54).

In contemporary western society, hegemonic representations of motherhood are arguably even more powerful than those of family, with the mother constituting the biological hub of the family and the embodiment of the 'nature' axis of western kinship (cf. Schneider 1968 & 1984). Consistent with this is a strong ideology which suggests that a mother's greatest contentment comes about through being with and doing for her family, that is, at the very least, for her husband and children (Ribbens 1994). Motherhood is thus not only the state of being a female parent, it is also a powerful cluster of expectations which occlude reflection on either the individual experience of the condition or the wider historical circumstances which shape this experience (Kaplan 1992).

In the case study of the Jones family which follows, the theme of motherhood and what it means following divorce is explored in the narrative accounts of three different members of the family group. The account is typical of many that were recorded in that it contains some of the most salient themes raised by women as single parents after divorce. For most single parents, there was a desire to communicate their extraordinary struggle and hardship in dealing with loneliness, financial tribulations, the demands of employment and bringing up children but also a certain exhilaration with a newly discovered potential for personal growth, choice and autonomy. The case study also illustrates the counter-narrative, that is, the one produced by ex-husbands, who make sense of their former partner's behaviour by attributing selfish and uncaring motives. As in the case of the Coopers, the narratives presented in this section reveal how each party must take into account the existence of a variety of others, in order to make sense of their situations. Furthermore, they must do so in circumstances where communications with a former partner are intermittent and often hostile.

Wendy and Neil Jones, a working-class couple living on the edges of a major industrial conurbation, were married for ten years before their divorce in 1985. Wendy petitioned on the grounds of Neil's 'unreasonable behaviour'. Like numerous petitions lodged by women on these grounds, it does not contain accounts of drunkenness and cruelty but alleges a basic and sustained lack of regard, sensitivity and perception in dealing with the day-to-day conduct of family life.

In the section of narrative which follows, Wendy is reflecting on her relationship to her two children, Nichola and Sam aged eleven and thirteen (see Figure 6.1). The extract is taken from an interview with Wendy which took place following a crisis which resulted in her son moving to live with his father. The difficulties that Wendy had experienced with her two children following the departure of her husband caused her to review fundamentally what it meant to be a mother. Her account reveals a repeated pattern in which there is a statement of things as they are, a counter-statement of how things were and an attempt to justify what she feels others might see as a moral discrepancy between the two positions. The transcripts are presented verbatim and reveal a soliloquy-like structure in which Wendy is talking to herself, or more accurately 'talking herself', as much as she is talking to me. Yet, even from such a small piece of Wendy's story we might begin to read off some of the voices which inform her assumptions about family and kin.

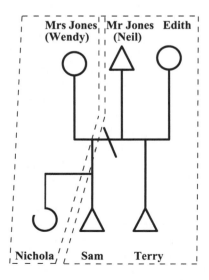

Figure 6.1. The Jones Family (oblique represents divorce in 1985, dotted lines represent households in 1991)

Wendy's Story. The following section deals with a portion of conversation in which Wendy has described the problem that she has in meeting the practical and emotional demands of her adolescent daughter. Wendy sees herself as caught in an invidious trap (cf. Newman 1991) in which she knows that money is the key to running her household satisfactorily but, in order to earn money, she has to be out of the house for long periods only to return drained and exhausted with little energy available to be what she sees as a 'good mother' to her daughter:

> . . . she (Nichola) will come up and she'll say 'look mam I'm really fed up' and we'll sort it out from there . . . but we're all right, I feel guilty now and again, but I find it's as if all my maternal instincts have gone, . . . [laughs] . . . because I think it's just been so hard, they've caused me so much grief, in some ways, I just don't want to know, I just want a quiet life now after all the hassle. It's a case of I love her and I'll do anything for her and I wish I could do more. I wish I had money to spend on her and this sort of thing so she could do the things she wants . . . [pause] . . .

In this extract, Wendy is questioning the very premises upon which her idea of motherhood was previously built. Thus, on one level the relationship with Nichola works well – 'we're all right' she tells us. However, there are feelings of guilt and inadequacy continually rising to the surface which prevent her open, direct and communicative relationship with Nichola being taken at face value. The feeling is that something that used to be there at the level of 'instinct' has gone and the extraordinariness of this conclusion causes her to laugh with incredulity – the idea of running out of instinct is an absurd notion. Being a mother, which used to be something that was automatic and pleasurable, has become something Wendy now finds intensely problematic and even painful. All she wants is 'a quiet life' which conflicts with the selflessness and sacrifice that is expected of working-class mothers living in Wendy's circumstances. The reason she gives for this withdrawal is the 'grief' that she suffered as a single parent who was far from prepared for the reaction that the rejection of her husband would arouse in their children. She is left with the situation in which she does all the right things that a mother should do but despite love, altruism and a profound desire to do more to make her daughter happy and contented there is a discrepancy when measured against the sense of motherhood as previously experienced.

The same themes are re-iterated with further nuances later on in the same interview. We are talking about the prospect of Nichola going to live with her father. Having raised this possibility I have just asked whether she found this a worrying prospect and below is given her reply *in extenso* (I have broken the discourse up as sentences for purposes of presentation and ease of comprehension):

No, because we're at the stage that if ever she wanted to go she could just go and I'd miss her and I'd be upset but I've got to the point where, maybe I'm wrong, but I look after me first and then, I take care of her and I look after her.

I think it's just all the hassle I had when they were here together,

I went through so much. I've done a total about face. I was one of these people who absolutely loved children . . . [pause] . . . but now I haven't got time for them I don't want to know.

I think, in their own way, my two have hurt me so much that I've gone totally selfish . . . [pause] . . . I've never been that way I've always been totally for children but I just seem to look after me first really.

I feel I did my best for them, they've had me while they were young and needed me most, and I'm still here if they need me but I'm looking after my own life. I do feel guilty about it I must admit but I can't seem to be any other way now. I suppose it's an awful thing to say really.

God if I knew then what I know now I would never've had children or got married. I might've had kids later on but I definitely would've had a bloody good career which is what I'm trying to get now.

but they have literally changed my attitude so much, it's hard to believe. I was one of these people who went ga-ga over babies. I don't want any more children, not interested. Towards the end of my marriage I was desperate to have another baby and I'm really glad that I didn't. That's the one thing I can thank him for really . . . [pause] . . .

it's looking after me time, you know, I've done my, sort of, bit. I've had my family, I've looked after them, they're both reasonably independent now.

I mean she does everything for herself, so in a sense I'm not needed, so I tend to look after myself. She looks after me really.

I was in here sobbing my guts up and she heard me crying, she'd gone up to bed, she came down and was looking after me, she made me tea and some toast, I feel as if she's the mother and I'm the daughter . . .

Wendy's account spirals round as before prompted this time by the question of Nichola's independence. Nichola is autonomous and can make up her own mind in opting to be with her father. If she were to make this choice Wendy would feel distress but it would be understandable and, although painful, would ultimately be manageable.

It is the ease with which Wendy envisages the possibility of her daughter's departure that prompts her to engage in a repetitive dialectic. In the emplotment which results she struggles to a position in which her feelings and stance are morally justified and comprehensible. As a mother she is not supposed to take lightly the prospect of her daughter's departure but her feelings contradict this assumption. Her sad but passive acceptance that her daughter may leave her is at odds with what she sees as the dominant expectations surrounding motherhood. This is revealed in phrases like 'maybe I'm wrong', 'I do feel guilty about it I must admit' and 'I suppose it's an awful thing to say really'. This latter phrase is a particularly telling one because it reveals the extent to which Wendy is aware of the discrepancy between her feelings and actions – 'I can't seem to be any other way now', and the way she 'supposes' that these might be interpreted by others in general and me, as interviewer, in particular. She finds herself at odds with the dominant representation of motherhood as she perceives it in others and indeed as she herself once experienced it.

The extent of this transformation is made clear in a series of paired oppositions which contrast how she was then a devoted mother but now views things rather differently. She describes how she was the kind of person who willingly submitted to the unconditional and irrational pull of motherhood; she was one 'who absolutely loved children', was '. . . totally for children' and '. . . went ga-ga over babies'. Reference to 'one of these people' suggests how prominent this representation is in her assessment of her present situation. She 'was' one of these people but is no more. The reason for this is found in the contrast that she then goes on to draw with the present in which she puts her own needs before those of her children. This is seen in a series of phrases such as '. . . but I look after me first', '. . . but now I haven't got time for them, I don't want to know', '. . . but I just seem to look after me first really' and finally '. . . but I'm looking after my own life really'. Wendy drives this point home further by describing how towards the end of the marriage she was 'desperate' to have a third child. Paradoxically however, she finds herself acknowledging that her ex-husband was right to persuade her not to as she now feels that it would have been a mistake to respond simply to the impulse to produce babies.

The making of such statements is clearly painful for Wendy because of the extent to which it runs counter to what mothers should do and feel for their children. Significantly, each of these statements is followed by a justification as to how these honest but potentially deviant responses have come about. Wendy's reaction is primarily triggered by the behaviour of her children after the divorce and the extent to which they 'hurt' her. Incidentally, this also reveals an expectation of Wendy's that children, although supposed to act in certain ways, in this instance did not abide by the expected kin-script either. Her secondary justification for her selfishness makes explicit the implicit instrumentality of parenting and in so doing once again makes statements that border on maternal heresy. She points out 'I've done my, sort of, bit' with 'bit' referring to the package of expectations which anchor a mother within the family unit, that is, as the bearer and nurturer of children. In return for having carried out this task as the dutiful but now disillusioned mother she has arrived in what she describes as 'looking after me time', a period in which she is looking to her own needs rather than the needs of her children.

I would suggest that to see this process of justifying parental selfishness in terms of an exchange is not in itself problematic within the terms of family life conventionally construed and may indeed constitute an important part of the mechanism whereby parents and children establish their respective autonomy. What is problematic in this case is that the exchange is having to be made explicit prematurely; it has come too early for the children and therefore falls outside of the dominant expectations of the life course and its key transitions as they relate to mother-child relations of dependency. The result is that the statement has to be justified and she seeks to do this by means of two illustrations both of which in different ways show Wendy reflecting upon the life-course.

The first illustration begins 'God, if I knew then what I know now . . .' which is followed by a wholesale rejection of the project of family as she came to experience it. Her wish that she had avoided motherhood and marriage is tempered by the admission that she might have considered these later on but she would first have had to have achieved a successful career on her own terms. Indeed, many of the difficulties of recent years have come about as a result of her struggle to earn a living from low paid work, to improve her position in the job market through study and be a 'good mother' all at the same time. It is the bitterness of this experience that leads her to see quite explicitly that there was a life-course or script that she was following and to wish she had put together the sequence of life-course events in a rather different pattern.

Wendy's second reflection on the life-course contains an even more powerful re-presentation of herself as outside the fixities of the life-cycle as it once determined her outlook and expectations. Here Wendy is justifying her tendency to look after herself ahead of her children in terms of their independence and her redundancy – she is quite simply not needed anymore. What is intriguing about this section is that Wendy goes a good deal further than simply spelling out Nichola's independence and illustrates a critical inversion in the life-course. Wendy describes how she was upset and she was comforted by Nichola leading her to feel 'as if she's the mother and I'm the daughter'.

Neil's Story. Narratives such as the one provided by Wendy do not evolve in isolation but are enmeshed in those of significant others such as her ex-partner, her children, her parents and her friends who make up her changed and changing sense of family. In the interviews with Neil, Wendy's husband, there is far less evidence of an emergent narrative of opposition: no re-evaluation of role nor shifting of the life-course. He remained a breadwinner and father throughout the divorce and indeed very soon re-established a new family with a new wife and a new baby in the profound hope that the formulae which failed last time might yet work on this occasion. Throughout his interviews he expressed the simple but ardent desire 'to be a family again'. This rather distinctive and revealing usage highlights the extent to which for Neil, 'family' is part of his social identity and persona.

> In the first few months I missed her a hell of a lot – for company, of being a family with the children. I lived with my parents. I had as much freedom as I wanted but it didn't seem right.

Like many other men who part company with 'family', Neil finds he feels incomplete without its routines and structures. This is in contrast to Wendy, for whom completeness can seemingly only come through a profound re-configuration and re-evaluation of family.

In the early interviews, Neil expressed a degree of surprise that Wendy had felt things to be sufficiently dire to warrant taking divorce proceedings – 'if I'd been a wife-beater, or a gambler or anything like that but I'd done nothing!' Furthermore, the reasons Wendy asked him to leave were, in his estimation, frivolous and seemingly to do with little more than her desire for a 'different lifestyle' which, in his opinion, could have been relatively easily modified had they been prepared to 'work at it'. The lifestyle to which she aspired was one in which his traditional idea of the 'family man', solid, predictable, dependable and committed (but ultimately, in her view, oppressive and stultifying) had no part. In his narrative he casts himself as the good man ejected from his family on the caprice of a cruel and selfish woman. Wendy's life as he occasionally hears about it from her and from the children, and sees it in her behaviour, simply becomes further evidence of her flawed motherhood – she allegedly 'lets the children run wild', 'she comes in at all hours', 'she's a bad manager of money' and, as far as he is concerned, generally does not look to the children's needs as a mother ought. The crowning evidence for him in this regard is the fact that their son chose to live with his father and not his mother. Neil's new partner also echoes these views in her accounts of recent events. Together, Neil and his new partner's accounts appear to re-inforce one another using Wendy, the 'inadequate mother', as a foil to bolster their aspiration to correspond with dominant images of family.

As in the example of the Coopers presented earlier, there is considerable confusion and misunderstanding over who makes decisions particularly where the children are concerned. Whereas he was once central to the conduct of family affairs he suddenly found himself on the periphery and as a result experienced considerable frustration at his feeling of disempowerment. Wendy enters the dialogue through his use of assertive and petulant tones to report her speech. Her lack of negotiation with him over the children is conveyed in his repeated and ironic use of the 'we' pronoun, for example:

> she was the one who was sort of dumping them (the children) on me and then suddenly 'we' decided 'we're not going to do that.'

And, later on in the same interview, he is telling a story which demonstrates how flexible and accommodating he is when it comes to making arrangements for the children in contrast to her capriciousness and intransigence. He concludes with the following:

> . . . it came as a surprise to me when she decided 'we've had enough of this game let's try another one' (and changed the existing access arrangements).

Significantly, a dominant theme throughout the interviews of both Neil and Wendy was the powerlessness each felt in the face of the other. With face-to-face communication intermittent and often problematic both parties were left with nothing but the experience of past interactions to help them manage current crises: Neil found it difficult to see beyond the Machiavellian harpy who had ejected him from home and family and

Wendy found it equally difficult to see beyond the over-grown school boy who had expected her to take over where his mother had left off. Both were engaged in the construction of new biographies which lay outside of the family as previously conceived and lived. Their efforts were no longer directed towards the team-like-ness of family but into the creation of new constructs which would incorporate altered relationships and contexts.

Nichola's Story. In the midst of the competing and contested constructions of how family life will be after divorce are two children, Sam and Nichola. Sam was faring very badly. His behaviour in the home and at school had severely stressed his mother and resulted in her ejecting him from the home and sending him to live with his father. An interview with Sam produced little other than evidence of a very withdrawn and unhappy little boy. His elder sister presented a rather different picture. At thirteen, Nichola seemed to have sized up the situation and worked out ways of getting what she needed from it. In the remainder of this section I turn to a consideration of sections of an interview conducted with Nichola. The extracts reveal the considerable power of narrative and dialogue to construct and maintain absent relationships and how in turn these influence the conduct of actual social relationships.

Over the years that researchers were in contact with various members of Nichola's family a clear pattern of gender relations emerged across the post-divorce kindred. Put at its simplest, all same-sex relations tended to be affable and positive whereas cross-sex relations were fraught with problems. Thus, the father got on famously with his son but had major problems in relating to Nichola; Wendy's relationships with each of the children was the converse. Neil and Wendy had a very poor relationship as did Neil and his new wife. However, Wendy got on well with Neil's new wife who in turn got on well with Nichola but not her brother, Sam. Sam and Nichola could never be left alone together because of their tendency to end up in serious fights. The origins of such a pattern are likely to be rooted in the kinds of gender segregated networks which Bott identified for working-class Londoners (Bott 1971) but which are considerably amplified in the post-divorce context. In this instance, what is of particular interest is the antagonistic relationship between father and daughter or more specifically the way that she describes this relationship in our conversation.

What should be stressed at the outset is the ambiguity Nichola feels towards her father. She is at once fiercely loyal to both her parents yet at the same time deeply bitter towards Neil. The father as an ideal-type construct looms large in her account but the way she feels that she is treated by him falls far short of this ideal, especially when compared with the way he treats her brother. This is in contrast to her relationship with her mother in whom the ideal and the actual would appear to meet. This cordoning off of the former nuclear family as a privileged construction vis à vis other kinds of relations after divorce is evident in comments such as the following:

> . . . I don't like hearing things said about mum or dad, I don't mind about Edith (father's new partner), she doesn't concern me.

[BS]. She's not in the picture?

> . . . it's just like three people at the moment: my brother, my mum and my dad, they are all that matter to me and I'll just defend them, it comes naturally . . . [ ] . . . I'll just build my wall – get over it and you're dead.

However, the ambivalence that lurks behind fortress family is all too apparent:

> . . . my mum, she's helpful, she's kind, she's understanding, it's grand to be living with her. I'd rather live with my mum than my father, even if Edith (father's new partner) wasn't there I'd rather live with my mum. She doesn't ignore me, she loves me and Sam (younger brother) equally. My father will buy things for my brother but he will totally miss me out. My mother says 'you can't buy for one and not the other' my father doesn't see it that way. Living with my mum, it's better that way.

The use of reported speech as illustrated in the quotation above, and as used extensively throughout the rest of the interview, suggests tremendous facility on Nichola's part when it comes to animating and giving voice to the characters in the narrative she presents. Indeed, she conveys a vivid picture of how, from her perspective, things are in her family, dispersed though it is. The picture is far from static and provides important clues about movement and the attribution of intentionality within her evaluation of why things are the way that they are.

In other parts of the interview, the use of reported speech is carried a stage further in that she does not just report the speech of others but begins to enter the realm of reported thought and even to construct imagined dialogues with her father. Her 'self-talk' (Goffman 1981) takes the form of rehearsals of the kind which Vygotsky (1962) and Mead (1936) identified as essential preludes to acts in real situations and particularly where such situations are in some sense irregular or anomalous. In this instance Nichola uses her narration of how things are with her father as part of a strategy to make sense, both to me and to herself, of changing relationships and family boundaries. In the interview she struggles to match powerful ideals with painful actualities. Schwartz (1987) has suggested that when significant others (such as mothers and fathers) become internalised they tend to operate as relatively stable internal standards rather than as 'persons' with a voice. Arguably, Nichola's account reveals the opposite process in action, that is, the tendency of Neil to become a prominent internal voice.

> . . . he was nice for three weeks and then just . . . he went back to normal . . . [ ] . . . I just think 'oh well, taken for granted again' 'she'll come up whenever I want her to come up' 'well you're wrong mate I will not go' I don't want to go, I ain't going to go, nobody can make me do that.
>
> [BS] Would you tell him directly?
>
> Oh yes I'd tell him to his face . . .[ ] . . .

What is clear from this instance is that in our conversations the problematic relationship with her father makes it necessary for Nichola to challenge and confront him. As a consequence, Neil, with whom she has minimal actual contact, regularly appears in our conversation. Nichola reacts strongly to the fact that Neil takes her for granted. She described how on one occasion she protested that if he wasn't going to take any notice she would cease to be his daughter. This produced some change in his behaviour but, as the extract above reveals, he very quickly began, once again, to treat her in ways she found upsetting. Thus, despite Nichola's protests and attempts to assert herself she appears to be largely confined to dialogues that proceed in Neil's absence. Not only does she articulate her own thoughts, she enters into Neil's thoughts and furthermore challenges them – *'well, you're wrong mate!'* – thus presenting a direct rebuff to what she sees as Neil's denial of her as a person.

Nichola, like other children who were interviewed, was particularly adept when it came to animating the characters in her family. Just how adept is seen in the following quotation which captures something of the extraordinary power and elegance of narrative to organise and thereby make sense of large portions of space and time (Polkinghorne 1988):

... he will probably notice me when I'm 103. He will be dead then and he'll be looking down on me and saying 'is that my daughter? I never noticed her' and I'll think 'well thank you'.

Encapsulated in less than forty words is Nichola's capacity to project her story long into the future, to a time when her dead father is looking down, presumably from heaven (which suggests once again that he was not entirely beyond redemption). She goes on to formulate and give voice to the thoughts of her dead father who finally realises the mistake he has made in overlooking his daughter. She responds with a highly ambiguous expression of thanks. To wait until she has reached 103 years to achieve recognition from her father is to demonstrate the magnitude of his inability to express what his daughter craves from him. It is also perhaps to make a rather more subtle statement about the irreversible and long-term nature of consanguineal relationships, even though as an elderly woman whose life is almost over she will still have the powerful *imago* of her father with her.

In summary, this chapter has attempted to throw light on the complex relationships which persist between persons once the physical edifice of the nuclear family is dismantled. At divorce, relationships might appear on the face of it to be brought to an absolute and immediate end but, particularly where children are concerned, this is rarely the case. Relationships which figured in the former family roll forward with a considerable momentum for many years after separation and divorce and consitute an important part of the complex architectonics of post-divorce family relations. The character of these relationships is deeply problematic for they are marked by a troubling mixture of the presence and absence of significant others; they are characterised by conflict and dispute as each party attempts to place their own narrative constructions on past, present and future events. Parties demonstrate the sense they make of these relationships through the stories they tell, that is, narratives which locate others in relation to self. Evidence of how people achieve this complex operation is revealed in the way voices and dialogues are incorporated into their narratives. Engagement with public opinion, an absent partner, the courts, god or some other super-addressee all find their way into the stories told and by entering into this rich mental life we are able to see the way that respondents locate and move themselves within emergent networks of relationship after divorce.

Divorce, Kinship and the History of the Western Family

The study of marriage has had a special place in the history of anthropology. As an institution, marriage has been consistently implicated in questions of classification and status; production and reproduction; inclusion and exclusion; gender and identity, as well as the more particular issues of legitimacy and illegitimacy. As such, marriage has long been identified as one of the paradigmatic institutions of society and upheld as an important basis for cross-cultural comparisons (Mair 1971; Bell 1997). The universalistic definitions of marriage upon which such comparisons have been based, however, have proved to be flawed. One of the best known critiques of such definitions was provided by Leach, who, in a seminal article on the definition of marriage, advocated that marriage be at best viewed as a 'bundle of rights' (1961: 107–108) which defied universal definition. In his formulation the institution is treated as a polythetic rather than an absolute category, that is, one in which different combinations of key characteristics may be present or absent in particular cultural settings (Needham 1971: 6; Barnard & Good 1984: 89–91). Thus, entering into a marriage will, broadly speaking, entail some statement about changed rights in persons and property which is socially, legally and perhaps divinely sanctioned but the size and constituents of the 'bundle' will vary enormously from culture to culture. In western marriage, the change in rights set in place by a marriage ceremony relates to questions of sexual access, residence, domestic labour, shared property, inheritance and the legitimacy and affiliation of children. These changes in roles and responsibilities are fundamental to the formation of the western family. Throughout this book it has been my intention to demonstrate that these issues are no less relevant when it comes to the dissolution of marriage and the altered family forms which arise as a consequence. At the ending of marriage there is some attempt to re-order the bundle of rights that was set in place when the marriage was made and this re-ordering must incorporate important continuities in terms of parenting roles and economic and property relations. In other words, the arrangements which emerge are not simply about the ending of marriage but contain elements which might not be out of place in a polythetic definition of marriage. It is no accident in this regard that some writers have referred to arrangements after divorce as post-marital marriage (Beck & Beck-Gernsheim 1995: 147).

My exploration of this widespread but under-researched aspect of contemporary social relations has been via a group of people who were divorcing at a precise point in British history. They were people who found themselves in 1985 dismantling the products of matrimonial commitment and as a result were engaged in disputes and conflicts surrounding the way that their families should be organised following divorce. These disputes concerned houses, property, finance and how to divide the physical accretions of years of marriage. More importantly, from an anthropological perspective, the disputes were about people or rather the way that people have conflicting ideas over other people's roles, responsibilities and rights and ultimately how they are constituted as persons within networks of relationships, kin or otherwise, once the integument of marriage and co-residence is stripped away. Although this aperture might appear rather small it does enable us to glimpse a much larger picture of changing family and kinship arrangements in the West. By way of conclusion I wish to draw attention to two aspects of this broader picture, namely the relationship between divorce and kinship and the implications of this for our understanding of the history of the western family.

Divorce and Kinship

One of the major problems with which any comprehensive theory of kinship must contend is the question of scope: how are boundaries drawn, how is inclusivity defined and precisely what constitutes a kinship network? Conventional theories of kinship tend to proceed from the assumption that kinship is the social recognition and elaboration of genealogical facts (see Holy 1997: 167). The main problem arising from such an approach is how to assimilate relationships which are undoubtedly of fundamental importance to the actors involved but which are apt to become obscured and excluded by a focus on procreative kinship. Conversely, for theories based on indigenous accounting of relatedness and relationships the problem is where to stop including other kinds of relationship. Kinship ceases to be a privileged and isolable domain of human interaction and becomes dissolved into much more nebulous processes of enculturation and the formation of personhood and identity. The problem is thrown into stark relief if we consider kinship in non-western contexts (Schneider 1984). Thus, if we begin with an assumption that biological relations are not necessarily ontologically prior to social relations, then the notion that individuals are eased into pre-figured networks based on bio-genetic connection becomes highly problematic unless we are talking specifically about Euro-American kinship. In particular, the idea that in the West persons are, by birth, fixed within a pre-determined universe of relatives makes little sense in other contexts (Strathern 1992a). A consequence of this approach is that significant constraints are placed on the way that social kinship might be understood. For example, in the Malay context, Carsten has argued that kinship is not given at birth but is essentially a process of becoming. Central to this process is the practice of living together and eating together. These activities, and particularly the sharing of food, create and reinforce the substance, namely blood, through which people conceive of themselves as being related (Carsten 1995: 224). It is thus not so much western assumptions about the 'thickness' of blood that determine close and enduring kinship in the Malay context but the density of day-to-day exchange. Carsten's analysis begins to throw light on the flexibility of kin relationships and the mutability of kinship identity for her Malay informants. What is of particular relevance to my account of divorce and separation are the arguments that are made in relation to children (Carsten 1991). In Pulau Langkawi, children move freely between houses and act as mediators; they simultaneously divide households from one another because of their exclusive relationship with one set of parents but also unite households through high levels of residential mobility among parents, widespread fostering arrangements and close relationships with grand-parents (ibid: 438). The various illustrations of Malay 'relatedness' which Carsten puts forward (op. cit.) demonstrate very effectively what is of significance to Malays rather than what would be of significance to a western tradition with a focus on genealogical kinship. However, in relation to such approaches, the question arises as to whether what we are being treated to is good ethnography, that is, an account which effectively highlights the particularity of human social and cultural life, rather than good anthropological theory which is capable of simplifying the evident diversity? After all, if attention is switched from kinship to 'relatedness' there is still the problem of its definition and how to make such a definition hold in contexts beyond the specific context under investigation.

Consideration of Euro-American kinship systems ought to make life very much easier when it comes to understanding this problem. Procreative and relativist positions can, in principle, be reconciled, for theoretical talk about English kinship ought to match native accounts of that system. In other words, the folk-models of informants ought to correspond to those of the researcher because, broadly speaking, both have emerged from the same cultural tradition. In western contexts, kinship can be taken as a special domain of interaction which is unequivocally defined and delimited by a genealogical framework fixed at birth and in which the axiom 'blood is thicker than water' holds true. Furthermore, paradigmatic constructs of marriage and family are re-inforced by legal and welfare systems which are also built on these assumptions.

However, the problem with which I have been concerned in this book has been to demonstrate, not so much a convergence, but an interesting divergence between dominant theoretical models of kinship and native practice. One can assume that the people on whose accounts my analysis is based entered into matrimony, shared residence and became parents to children who were legally recognised as their legitimate offspring. In other words, at some point in the past, these people had embraced to some degree or other the dominant ideology of family and kinship. The marriage certificates referred to in the opening pages of this book are one small testament to this fact. Yet, these are also the people who opted to terminate their marriages and set about re-casting and re-thinking the dominant familial ideology to fit their altered circumstances. The arrangements that emerge are shot through with ideas and assumptions about kinship which are clearly rooted in the dominant ideology but which are in other ways novel and analytically challenging. Shadows of the former family can be seen in the way that legal and welfare systems shape and constrain relational possibilities after divorce. They can also be seen in informants' accounts of the nature of genealogical connection and the importance of blood or the role of particular codes of conduct in relation to being a spouse or a parent after divorce. However, the arrangements that emerge are also new and, to a degree, unpredictable; they point to altered configurations of persons, resources and relationships which are radically at odds with the pattern of family life which has been prevalent throughout most of this century. For example, second marriages and the subsequent birth of children often have to be assimilated into the ongoing relationship between a former husband and wife. But, what is one's relationship with a former spouse's latest offspring or more to the point what is the relationship of one's children: step-, half- or full-sibling or denied on the grounds that affinity is at an end? Attempts by each former family member to answer such questions set in train a process of negotiations about and reflections upon the basic currencies of western kinship.

Paying careful attention to these reflections and negotiations opens up two important lines of enquiry. Firstly, considering kinship narratives and discourse under circumstances in which arrangements are to some degree problematised throws light on the dominant ideologies of family and kinship which have, in one sense, been left behind. In other words, in order to make sense of relationships after divorce, people must begin to articulate their former praxis in ways that they might never have had to have done before. Being a parent after divorce, for example, compels a degree of critical reflection on what it is to be a parent under 'normal' circumstances. These voices from the margin are apt to generate perceptions in a way that those who are submerged in more conventional family structures rarely can and they serve to throw new light on areas of family and kinship otherwise taken as 'natural' and self-evident (Harris 1981). Secondly, consideration of these accounts draws attention to the new forms and expressions of kinship relationships which emerge in the wake of marital breakdown. In earlier chapters I have considered some of the relationships left hanging when husbands and wives separate and how these translate into novel patterns of continuity; these have included relationships between former spouses, between siblings old and new, between parents and their children and with former in-laws. They have also included new partners, new children and new sets of in-laws. My analysis has drawn particular attention to the fact that the process of working these relationships into viable arrangements is made considerably more complex by the fact that the meaning and significance of these key relationships is likely to be disputed, challenged or even denied.

What emerges from this analysis is a sense of people engaged in various processes and strategies of conversion. Kin whose relationships were solidly defined, identified and constrained by the norms of consanguinity and affinity must redefine those relationships, or, as the case may be, actively resist acts of redefinition. I have described the way that close family members set about converting one another into other kinds of kin who have different qualities of relatedness. Thus, kin whose relationships were formerly centred on the family might become close and reliable friends, despised adversaries, distant and unwelcome memories or they might fashion wholly new kinds of relationship from an extensive matrix of post-divorce relationships. Throughout this work I have documented how mothers, fathers and children set about becoming different kinds of kin to one another, thereby creating new forms out of the wreckage of the old.

One of the most contentious areas in the processes of redefining the form and expression of relationships is in relation to men and their dislocation as fathers and household heads. As I have demonstrated, in terms of the arrangements which are made after divorce, fathers tend not to live with their children but have contact with them on an occasional basis. Mothers, on the other hand, tend to remain in more or less permanent residence with their children. The relocation of the father outside of the home has significant implications. Indeed, a father's ability to influence and control socialisation and organisation within what he would previously have thought of as 'his family' represents a very significant recent development in the history of the western family. What the disputes considered in this study reveal is an ongoing tension between the ideology of patrifiliation on the one hand and the fact of matrilocality on the other. Active demonstration of these opposed ideas in the kinship of the western family is evident in the contests between mothers, fathers and their children. After divorce, each strives to define and express their relationships according to their own wishes and desires despite the competing and alternative constructions of others. For example, in instances where there is a dispute arising because a custodial mother wishes to deny a non-custodial father access to their child there are often two clearly competing discourses in evidence. For the mother, the father's claim to kinship based in 'nature' is played down in favour of a model of kinship in which conduct is paramount. This is because the man, usually as a result of his behaviour, has, in her view, jeopardised or otherwise diminished his right to be a father. Needless, to say, in such cases the father is apt to reject or dispute conduct as the definitive element in future paternal relations and to maintain the irreversible and irrefutable nature of blood ties as the basis of his moral and legal claim to be able to have contact with his child. There can never be an outright victory in instances such as this but mothers and fathers necessarily engage in radical and ongoing contestations about the meaning and expression of 'relatedness'. The fact that this 'relatedness' is located outside the conventional settings of marriage, family and the home draws attention to new and contested identities within the dominant system of gender and kinship (also cf. Loizos & Papataxiarchis 1991; Cornwall & Lindisfarne 1994). These new identities, often fraught with contradiction and uncertainty, suggest new possibilities for how fathers, mothers and children engage with the longer-term projects of family and kinship. Such arrangements, however, are not spontaneous and unexpected but form part of a much broader development in the way that personal and family relationships are organised in the West.

Divorce and the History of the Western Family

One of the more influential histories of the the family in western society is attributed to the 'rise of sentiment' school (Shorter 1975; Stone 1977; Flandrin 1979). The approach documents a progressive triumph of warmth and affectivity over the brutish and calculatingly functional relationships of families in the past. In the present day, it might thus appear that a number of key transformations have all but taken place and the flowering of sentiment in family relations has come to over-shadow the once powerful collectivities of family and community making the way clear for ever more strident expressions of personal desire. The consequences of these changes impact fundamentally on the meanings of marriage, home and family in contemporary society. For example, throughout this century predictability arising from ascribed kinship roles and prescribed relationships has given way to varying degrees of unpredictability in relation to close kin. As the evidence presented here highlights, increasing amounts of 'working out' are having to be done to integrate and make sense of personal networks of kin. Similarly, long-term commitment has increasingly given way to expediency and contractuality in the conduct of inter-personal relations. Relationships which were formerly embedded in dense networks of kin and community have been distilled into 'pure' relationships held in place by little more than the stuff they are made of. Family-based systems of control have given way to freedom of choice and parental authority is increasingly subject to conflict and negotiation. Under the conditions of 'reflexive modernity' it appears that 'instead of individuals being resources for families, families are becoming resources out of which individuals construct their selves' (Gullestadt 1996: 37); the question which is now asked is 'what can my family do for me?', rather than the question which was asked in earlier times, namely 'what can I do for my family?' Baudrillard gives such developments a post-modern twist in identifying the absorbtion of society by culture: 'the rational sociality of the contract . . . gives way to the sociality of contact' (cited in Wexler 1990: 169). In understanding these grand transformations in western family life, divorce and relationship breakdown occupy a crucial position. The point at which many of the polarities outlined above appear to be maximally opposed is in relation to the breakdown of marriage and the public and private conflicts which are engendered. It is through a careful exposition of these conflicts; how people talk about them, manage them, attempt to resolve them and ultimately incorporate them into the fabric of their social lives that I have been able to bring into more precise ethnographic focus many of the contradictions and tensions which appear to be erupting at the heart of contemporary family life.

It would seem that contemporary family life is teetering towards what Elliot (1986: 133) has referred to as a tragic paradox in which security in personal relationships must always imply commitment and loss of freedom. One of the main forms that this contradiction takes in western society is in relation to increased sexual and conjugal choice on the one hand and the expectation of fulfilment through monogamous partnership and the demands of parenting on the other. Attempts to resolve this paradox in practice is the stuff of marriage counselling sessions the length and breadth of Europe and North America and currently exercises the imagination of a wide range of 'experts' in the field of human relationships. The key to resolving the paradox would appear to be a precarious balancing act which combines personal growth and satisfaction within a close and intimate relationship founded on open communication. As Bellah *et al.* remark:

> The individual must find and assert his or her true self because this self is the only source of genuine relationships to other people. External obligations whether they come from religion, parents, or social conventions can only interfere with the capacity for love and relatedness. Only by knowing and ultimately accepting one's self can one enter into valid relationships. . . . But this search for a perfect relationship cannot succeed because it comes from a self that is not full and sustaining. The desire for relatedness is really a reflection of incompleteness, of one's own dependent needs (Bellah *et al.* 1985: 98).

It is not so surprising therefore that contemporary marriages are often riddled with anxieties brought on by the efforts of husbands and wives to match their individual expectations and life-styles to the constraints of family life (Fletcher 1973). Summed up in the idea of 'for better or for worse', the founding charter of modern monogamy, are the roots of a deep ambivalence. Keenly aware of this, marital therapists point out how contemporary western marriage is as much about the effective management of conflict and disagreement as it is about the maintenance of harmony. From their perspective, marital failure often results from an inability to manage and negotiate the differences which individuals bring to the marital relationship with the shared construct of marriage being insufficiently elastic to accommodate opposing drives; individualism and familism are ultimately beyond reconciliation. Under-pinning such assessments of contemporary marital stability are psychological theories which tend to portray the autonomous self in terms of two basic motivational characteristics. This dual orientation is seen in the use of paired terms such as action and reception; agency and communion; self-enhancement and union (Hermans & Kempen 1993: 147). Such oppositions emphasise the fundamental importance of independence and inter-dependence in human development and in human relationships (Markus and Kitayama 1991). Human existence is portrayed as an uneasy oscillation between these two polarities: the society built on individual self-interest and rational, bureaucratic calculation in the conduct of social affairs is as doomed as the one that tries to submerge them in anonymous collectivities.

These opposed pulls are powerfully encapsulated in ideologies which support and advocate familism and individualism respectively. At the present time, for example, major conflicts are evident in the debates surrounding the status of family in society and that of individuals within families. On the one hand, family living is believed to bring benefits of care and predictability but does so within a structure that demands long-term commitment and fidelity. However, these aspirations are located within a society whose dominant value system is based on acquisition and the pursuit of self-satisfaction (Lauer and Lauer 1994). The longer-term prognosis of some commentators is grim to say the least. Family represents the last bastion of morality, the place where primary social education takes place and the milk of human kindness is first imbibed. Fragmentation of the nuclear family represents the final capitulation of society to the predations of organised capitalism and heralds an inexorable drift towards social anarchy (for example see Mount 1982; Dennis and Erdos 1992; Dennis 1996). A similar conclusion is reached by those who see the social costs of familism being undercut by those of more individualistic social strategies. In societies of the kind traditionally studied by anthropologists and in which family and kinship play a central and pervasive role, the rewards from being alone are few and the costs considerable. In contemporary western society the reverse is increasingly the case. For example, what Goode describes as the 'marginal utility of males' would seem to have declined dramatically such that nowadays relationships between men and women tend to be of shorter duration and typically involve less by way of mutual dependence and investment (Goode 1984: 77). In Britain, these changes in the style and character of commitment are nowhere more apparent than in the substantial increase in single occupancy residences. The biggest increase in such residences is among men under pension age. By the turn of the century it is predicted that one in ten of all households will be occupied by single men (*General Household Survey 1990*). Furthermore, one of the major propellants of this increase is the number of marriages which currently end in divorce (McCarthy and Simpson 1991). At various levels, then, alarm bells are ringing as individualism and instrumentalism in the organisation of personal life appear to displace and destroy an older and more established bedrock of familism. The alarm bells ring all the more loudly given that this bedrock is also the one upon which the key social, legal and economic institutions of modern society have been built.

In terms of the fate of the western family, however, the point of collapse or rather concern about its collapse has been reached many times before in the course of this century (Scanzioni 1983: 27–30). Periods of stability have given way to periods of instability and arguably after the turmoil of the Second World War the nuclear family entered a brief but 'golden' age in terms of conformity and normative values (Gillis 1985: 289; Seccombe 1993). The images of family lodged in this period have remained both powerful and central in the ideological projection of ideal family forms. Tensions, however, soon began to appear and many of these began to be evident throughout the 1960s. Utting (1995) summarises these developments in Britain as follows: a fall in marriage rates as more people deferred or rejected marriage (also cf. Dormor 1992: 8), an increase in divorce, a growth of non-marital cohabitation, more children growing up in families which fall outside of the traditional nuclear family pattern, that is, in ones which are step-, reconstituted or recombinant families, deferred child-bearing, declining fertility, a rise in births outside marriage, an increase in the numbers of lone-parents and, finally, more mothers in paid employment. These important demographic changes were carried along by a powerful cultural undercurrent which channelled the murmurings of discontent among young people into a variety of counter-cultural forms (Segal 1983). The family seemed to be less and less a sturdy vessel for the containment and regulation of persons and their emotions and increasingly took on the character of a delicate and overcharged circuit. As people fed more and more emotional voltage into this circuit in the form of potent desires for love, fulfilment, happiness, security and well-being, the fuses began to blow.

It is not my intention here to speculate on the future of the family as such but it should be clear from the foregoing discussion that ideological projections of the nuclear family are currently, and indeed always have been, predicated upon a far more rich, creative and ultimately varied expression of the possibilities of human kinship. We should not be blind to the many threads of evidence which cut across the more linear narratives describing the development of family forms in the West. For example, Laslett's account of the size of households based on parish registers reveals that large households filled with extended kin were far from the norm in pre-industrial England (Laslett 1972). Similarly, Macfarlane's exploration of the origins of English individualism concludes that, as far back as the thirteenth century, the family was organised along individualistic rather than collective principles (Macfarlane 1978). Such works should signal caution when it comes to understanding the western family without reference to a broader canvas of human kinship and family arrangements.

What I have been at pains to do throughout this book is demonstrate how important changes in contemporary family arrangements connect up with this broader canvas. In order to do this I have described some of the social and cultural forms that kinship is taking as a result of divorce in Britain today. For an increasing number of people, divorce is seen, at least by one of the parties involved, as a way to escape feelings of unhappiness, dissatisfaction and constraint created by marriage and family. However, whilst undoubtedly solving one set of problems, divorce, in the short term at least, ushers in many others. As I have demonstrated, unpacking relationships after divorce might offer the possibility of liberation, freedom and happiness but it is also extremely strenuous, stressful and time-consuming in the years which follow. Husbands and wives rarely exit cleanly and crisply from the obligations and exchanges in which they were formerly situated. Whilst most have a clear idea of which parts of their previous networks they would like to extract and retain for themselves as they enter the realms of the newly liberated, these invariably overlap and clash with those of a former partner. In legal, emotional and practical terms the networks that emerge are partial, transient and, to varying degrees, blurred.

For many politicians and policy-makers, uncertainty and unclearness in the very fabric of family life signal a crisis which has moral, social and economic implications. The rejection of relationships built on a long-term commitment to marriage and the nuclear family opens up a Pandora's Box of personal desires and aspirations which are not easily contained within existing social, legal or economic structures. Another perspective on these arrangements, however, is that they mark the first steps towards new patterns of relationship which are highly fluid and apt to take on multiple and perhaps competing significations for the persons which comprise them. From an anthropological and ethnographic perspective what is of particular interest is what these developments tell us about the social capacities of human beings. In other words, I hope to have revealed something about the family in relation to a broader conception of kinship and human sociality. My analysis of divorce in contemporary Britain has raised questions about the emergence of new expressions of kinship and the way that persons constitute themselves in and through these. The fields of relationship I describe however are not simply spatial, in the traditional network sense, but are fashioned out of intersecting biographies and narratives which fix and locate people in trajectories in time as well as space. These fields also differ in the extent to which they incorporate people who are wholly or partially absent as well as real and imagined relationships with them. These relationships, as well as more conventional social interactions, shape the form and content of arrangements between kin after divorce.

Recent developments in the history of personal life in western society thus make it extremely difficult to talk meaningfully of 'the family' but predispose us to think, at the very least, in terms of 'families', a plethora of arrangements for the organisation of domestic and intimate relationships in which the configurations of gender, space and time are highly variable. Furthermore, what might be thought of as common-sense accounts and explanations of personal motive, expectation and aspiration for living particular versions of 'family life' are nowadays shot through with 'expert' discourses of law, psychology and the social sciences. The seepage of these discourses has been aided considerably by film, television, advertising, chat shows, news reportage and popular magazines which deal repeatedly with the question 'how shall I live?' Giddens evokes the notion of 'reflexive modernity' in attempting to answer this question (1991: 14); he describes a process of self-construction in which responsibility for ontological security rests with the subject and not in the conditions in which he or she finds him or herself. The dramatic rise of counselling, advisory and dispute resolution services is a clear corollary of the load which individuals must now carry as part of their routine existence (Lewis *et al.* 1992; McCarthy 1996). The information available to people about what they might be has become part of who they are and the politics of what they become. Indeed, this book itself might be seen as: '. . . one small contribution to a vast and more or less continuous outpouring of writings, technical and more popular, on the subject of marriage and intimate relationships . . . [ ] . . . they serve routinely to organise and alter, the aspects of social life they report on or analyse' (Giddens 1991: 14).

To turn attention to these aspects of changing family life is to open up significant new areas of research for the social and cultural study of kinship in western society. These areas of research relate to a society which is in many senses after affinity. They invite us to explore macro-economic and policy issues alongside micro-concerns about the social, emotional, psychological and ultimately reflexive constitution of personal life in the late twentieth century and will set significant new agenda well into the next millennium.

Bibliography

Alanen, L. (1993), 'After "the family": Childhood, Gender and Family Change', Paper presented at the XXXth Committee of Family Research, *Gender and Families: Choices, Challenges and Changing policy,* Annapolis, Maryland. USA.

Anderson, D., Lait, J. and Marsland, D. (1981), *Breaking the Spell of the Welfare State,* London: Social Affairs Unit.

Arendt, H. (1958), *The Human Condition,* Chicago: University of Chicago Press.

Aries, P. (1979)[1962], *Centuries of Childhood,* Harmondsworth: Penguin.

Backett, K. (1982), *Mothers and Fathers: A Study of the Development and Negotiation of Parental Behaviour,* London and Basingstoke: Macmillan.

—— (1987), 'The Negotiation of Fatherhood', in C. Lewis and M. O'Brien (eds), *Reassessing Fatherhood,* London: Sage Publications.

Bakhtin, M.M. (1986), *Speech Genres and other Late Essays* (translated by Vern McGee and edited by Caryl Emerson and Michael Holquist), Austin: University of Texas Press.

Barnard, A. and Good, A. (1984), *Research Practices in the Study of Kinship,* London: Academic Press.

Barnes, J.A. (1973), 'Genitor: Genetrix: Nature: Culture', in J. Goody (ed.), *The Character of Kinship,* Cambridge: Cambridge University Press.

—— (1980), 'Kinship Studies: Some Impressions on the Current State of Play', *Man* (n.s.), 15. 2: 293–303.

Barrett, M. and MacIntosh, M. (1982), *The Anti-social Family,* London: Verso.

Becker, G. (1981), *Treatise on the Family,* Cambridge, Mass: Harvard University Press.

Beck, U. and Beck-Gernsheim, E. (1995), *The Normal Chaos of Love,* Cambridge: Polity Press.

Belk, R.W. and Coon G.S. (1993), 'Gift-giving as Agapic Love: An Alternative to the Exchange Paradigm based on Dating Experiences', *Journal of Consumer Research,* 20: 393–417.

Bell, D. (1997), 'Defining Marriage and Legitimacy', *Current Anthropology,* 38, 2: 237–54.

Bellah, R. N., Madsen, R., Sullivan, W.M., Swidler, A. and Tipton, S.M. (1985), *Habits of the Heart: Individualism and Commitment in American Life,* New York: Harper and Row.

Berger, B. and Kellner, H. (1964), 'Marriage and the Construction of Reality: An Exercise in the Microsociology of Knowledge', *Diogenes*, 46: 1–23.

Bernard, J. (1972), *The Future of Marriage*, Harmondsworth: Penguin Books.

Bernardes, J. (1985), '"Family Ideology": Identification and Exploration', *The Sociological Review*, 33: 275–97.

—— (1988), 'Founding the *new* "Family Studies"', *The Sociological Review*, 36: 57–86.

Bernstein, B. (1973), *Class, Codes and Social Control: Volume One. Theoretical Studies Towards a Sociology of Language*, St. Albans: Paladin.

Bloch, M. (1973), 'The Long-term and the Short-term: The Economic and Political Significance of the Morality of Kinship', in J.R. Goody. (ed.), *The Character of Kinship*, Cambridge: Cambridge University Press.

Blustein, J. (1982) *Parents and Children: The Ethics of the Family*, New York: Oxford University Press.

Bohannan, P.J. (ed.), (1971a), *Divorce and After*, New York: Doubleday.

—— (1971b), 'Divorce Chains, Households of Re-marriage and Multiple divorcers', in P.J. Bohannan (ed.), *Divorce and After*, New York: Doubleday.

—— (1993), 'Review of A.F. Roberston: Beyond the Family: The Social Organisation of Human Reproduction', *American Anthropologist*, 95: 175.

Bott, E. (1971), *Family and Social Network*, London: Tavistock.

Bouquet, M. (1993), *Reclaiming English Kinship: Portuguese Refractions of British Kinship Theory*, Manchester: Manchester University Press.

Bourdieu, P. (1977), *Outline of a Theory of Practice*, Cambridge: Cambridge University Press.

Bradshaw, J. and Millar, J. (1991), *Lone-parent Families in the UK*, London: HMSO.

Brophy, J. (1989), 'Custody Law, Child Care and Inequality in Britain', in C. Smart and S. Sevenhuijsen (eds), *Child Custody and the Politics of Gender*, London and New York: Routledge.

Bruner, J. (1986), *Actual Minds: Possible Worlds*, Cambridge MA: Harvard University Press.

—— (1990), *Acts of Meaning*, Cambridge MA: Harvard University Press.

Buisson. M. and Mermet, J-C. (1986), Des circulations des enfants: De la famille à la familialité, *Le groupe familial*, 112: 38–43.

Burgess, A. (1997), *Fatherhood Reclaimed: The Making of the Modern Father*, London: Vermillion Press.

Burgess, E. (1926), 'The Family as a Unity of Interacting Personalities', *The Family,* 7 March: 3–9.

Burgoyne, J. and Clark, D. (1984), *Making-a-go-of-it,* London: Routledge, Kegan and Paul.

Burrett, J. (1993), *To and fro Children: Co-operative Parenting after Divorce,* London: Thorson (Harper Collins).

Butler-Sloss, Lord Justice (1988), *Report of the Inquiry into Child Abuse in Cleveland,* Cmnd 412, London: HMSO.

Campbell, B. (1993), *Goliath: Britain's Dangerous Places,* London: Methuen.

Carrier, J. (1992a), 'The Gift in Theory and in Practice: A Note on the Centrality of Gift Exchange', *Ethnology,* 31: 186–93.

—— (1992b), 'Occidentalism: The World Turned Upside Down', *American Ethnologist,* 19: 195–212.

—— (1995), *Gifts and Commodities: Exchange and Western Capitalism since 1700,* London: Routledge.

Carrigan, T., Connell, B. and Lee. J. (1985), 'Towards a new Sociology of Masculinity', *Theory and Society,* 14: 551–603.

Carrithers, M.B. (1992), *Why Humans have Cultures,* Oxford: Oxford University Press.

Carsten, J. (1991), 'Children in between: Fostering and the Process of Kinship on Pulau Langkawi, Malaysia', *Man (n.s.)* 26: 425–43.

—— (1995), 'The Substance of Kinship and the Heat of the Hearth: Feeding, Personhood and Relatedness among Malays in Pulau Langkawi', *American Ethnologist,* 22(2): 223–41.

Caughey, J.L. (1984), *Imaginary Social Worlds: A Cultural Approach,* Lincoln: University of Nebraska Press.

Child Support Agency (1994), *Press Pack,* London: Child Support Agency.

Children Come First (1990), Government White Paper, 2 vols., Cmn 1236, London: HMSO.

Cochrane, M., Larner, M., Riley, D., Gunnarson, L. and Henderson C.R. Jnr. (1990), *Extending Families,* Cambridge: Cambridge University Press.

Cohen, R. (1971), 'Brittle Marriage as a Stable System: The Kanuri Case', in P.J. Bohannan (ed.), *Divorce and After,* New York: Doubleday.

Collier, R. (1995), *Masculinity, Law and the Family,* London: Routledge.

Collins, J. (1994), 'Disempowerment and Marginalisation of Clients in Divorce Court Cases', in S. Wright (ed.), *Anthropology of Organisations,* London: Routledge.

Coltrane, S. and Hickman, N. (1992), 'The Rhetoric of Rights and Needs: Moral Discourse in the Reform of Child Custody and Child Support

Laws', *Social Problems*, 39: 400–20.

Comaroff, J.L. (ed.) (1980), *The Meaning of Marriage Payments*, New York: Academic Press.

Cornwall, A. and Lindisfarne, N. (1994), 'Dislocating Masculinity: Gender, Power and Anthropology', in A. Cornwell and N. Lindisfarne (eds), *Dislocating Masculinity: Comparative Ethnographies*, London and New York: Routledge.

Corlyon, J., Simpson, R., McCarthy, P. and Walker, J. (1991), *The Links Between Behaviour in Marriage, the Settlement of Ancillary Disputes, Arrangements for Children and Post-Divorce Relationships*, Report to the Nuffield Foundation.

Davies, J. (ed.) (1993), *The Family: Is it Just Another Life Style Choice?*, London: Institute of Economic Affairs.

Davis, G. and Murch, M. (1988), *Grounds for Divorce*, Oxford: Clarendon Press.

Day-Sclater, S. (1997), 'Creating the Self: Stories as Transitional Phenomena', Unpublished MS (presented at the Auto/Biography Study Group Annual Conference).

De'Ath, E. (1992), 'Step-families in the Context of Contemporary Family Life', in E. De'Ath (ed.), *What do we Know? What do we Need to Know?*, Croydon: Significant Publications.

Dennis, N. (1996), 'Men's Sexual Liberation', in R. Humphrey (ed.), *Families Behind the Headlines*, Newcastle: British Association for the Advancement of Science/ Department of Social Policy, University of Newcastle upon Tyne.

—— and Erdos, G. (1992), *Families without Fatherhood*, London: Institute of Economic Affairs, Health and Welfare Unit.

Denzin, N.K. (1989), *Interpretive Biography*, Qualitative Research Methods vol. 17, Newbury Park: Sage.

Di Leonardo, M. (1987), 'The Female World of Cards and Holidays: Women, Family and the Work of Kinship', *Signs*, 12(3): 440–53.

Dizard, J.E. and Gadlin, H. (1990), *The Minimal Family*, Amherst: University of Massachusetts Press.

Dominian, J. (1965), *Marital Breakdown*, Harmondsworth: Penguin.

—— Mansfield, P., Dormor, D. and McAllister, F. (1991), *Marital Breakdown and the Health of the Nation: A Response to the Government's Consultative Document for Health in England*, London: One plus One Marriage and Partnership Research.

Donzelot, J. (1979), *The Policing of Families*, London: Hutchinson.

Dormor, D. (1992), *The Relationship Revolution: Cohabitation, Marriage and Divorce in Contemporary Europe*, London: One plus One.

Edwards, J., Franklin, S., Hirsch, E., Price, F. and Strathern., M. (1993), *Technologies of Procreation: Kinship in the Age of Assisted Conception,* Manchester: Manchester University Press.

Eekelaar, J. (1984), *Family Law and Social Policy,* London: Weidenfeld and Nicolson.

—— and Maclean, M. (1986), *Maintenance after Divorce,* London: Oxford University Press.

Elliot, F. Robertson, (1986), *The Family: Change or Continuity?,* Houndmills: Macmillan.

Ellis, R. (1983), 'The Way to a Man's Heart: Food in the Violent Home', in A. Murcott (ed.), *The Sociology of Food and Eating,* Aldershot: Gower.

Emery, R.E. (1988), *Marriage, Divorce and Children's Adjustment,* Beverley Hills, CA: Sage Publications.

Finch, J. (1989), *Family Obligations and Social Change,* Oxford: Polity Press.

—— and Mason J. (1990), 'Divorce, Re-marriage and Family Obligations', *The Sociological Review,* 38: 219–46.

Firth, R., Hubert, J. and Forge, A. (1969), *Families and their Relatives,* London: Routledge, Kegan and Paul.

Flandrin, J.L. (1979), *Families in Former Times,* Cambridge: Cambridge University Press.

Fletcher, R. (1973), *The Family and Marriage in Britain,* Harmondsworth: Penguin.

Fortes, M. (1969), *Kinship and the Social Order,* Chicago: Aldine.

Franklin, S., Levy, C. and Stacey, J. (eds) (1991), *Off-centre: Feminism and Cultural Studies,* Hammersmith: Harper and Collins.

Freeman, M. D. A. (1983), *The Rights and Wrongs of Children,* London: Frances Pinter.

Furstenberg, F.F., Petersen, J.L., Nord, C.W. and Zilli, N. (1993), 'The Life Course of the Children of Divorce: Marital Disruption and Parental Contact', *American Sociological Review,* 48: 656–8.

Geertz, C. (1983), *Local Knowledge: Further Essays in Interpretative Anthropology,* New York: Basic Books.

Gergen, K. (1991), *The Saturated Self: Dilemmas of Identity in Contemporary Life,* New York: Basic Books.

Gerstel, N., Reissman, C.K. and Rosenfeld, S. (1985), 'Explaining the Symptomology of Separated and Divorced Women: The Role of Material Conditions and Social Networks', *Social Forces,* 64: 84–101.

Gibson, C.S. (1994), *Dissolving Wedlock,* London & New York: Routledge.

Giddens, A. (1991), *Modernity and Self-identity: Self and Society in the late Modern Age,* Cambridge: Polity Press.

—— (1994), 'Living in a Post-traditional Society', in U. Beck (ed.), *Reflexive Modernity: Politics, Tradition and Aesthetics in the Modern Social Order,* Cambridge: Polity Press.

Gilligan, C. (1982), *In a Different Voice,* Massachussetts: Harvard University Press.

Gillis, J.R. (1985*),* *For Better, for Worse: British Marriages 1600 to the Present,* Oxford: Oxford University Press.

Goffman, E. (1969), *The Presentation of Self in Everyday Life,* Harmondsworth: Penguin.

—— (1981), *Forms of Talk,* Philadelphia: University of Pennsylvania Press.

Goode, W.J. (1984), 'Individual Investments in Family Relationships over the coming Decades', *The Tocqueville Review,* VI(1): 51–83.

—— (1993), *World Changes in Divorce Patterns,* New Haven and London: Yale University Press.

Goody, J. and Mitchell, J. (1995), 'The Child Support Agency: Changing Family Structures in Contemporary Britain', Paper given at the Department of Anthropology, Durham. Nov. 1995.

Goody, E.N. (1962), 'Conjugal Separation and Divorce among the Gonja of Northern Ghana', in Meyer Fortes (ed.), *Marriage in Tribal Societies,* Cambridge: Cambridge University Press.

—— (1982), *Parenthood and Social Reproduction,* Cambridge: Cambridge University Press.

Gregory, C.A. (1982), *Gifts and Commodities,* London: Academic Press.

Greif, J. (1979), 'Fathers, Children and Joint Custody', *American Journal of Orthopsychiatry,* 49: 311–19.

Grief, G.L. (1985), *Single Fathers,* New York: Free Press.

Gubrium, J.F. and Holstein J.A. (1990), *What is Family?,* California: Mayfield Publishing Company.

Gullestadt, M. (1996), 'From Obedience to Negotiation: Dilemmas in the Transmission of Values between the Generations in Norway', *The Journal of the Royal Anthropological Institute,* 2(1): 25–42.

Gutman. H.G. (1984), 'Afro-American Kinship before and after Emancipation in North America', in H. Medick and D.W. Sabean (eds), *Interest and Emotion: Essays on the Study of Family and Kinship,* Cambridge: Cambridge University Press.

Harré, R. (1986), *The Social Construction of Emotion,* Oxford: Blackwell.

—— (1993), *Social Being,* Oxford: Blackwell.

Harris, C.C. (1983), *The Family and Industrial Society,* London: Allen and Unwin.

—— (1990), *Kinship,* Buckingham: Open University Press.

Harris, J.R. (1995), 'Where is the Child's Environment? A Group Social-isation Theory of Development', *Psychological Review,* 102(3): 458–89.

Harris, O. (1981), 'Households as Natural Units', in K. Young, C. Walkowitz and R. McCullagh, (eds), *Of Marriage and the Market,* London: CSE Books.

Hart, N. (1976), *When Marriage Ends: A Study in Status Passage,* London: Tavistock.

Harvey, D. (1989), *The Condition of Post-modernity; An Enquiry into the Origins of Cultural Change,* Oxford: Basil Blackwell.

Haskey, J. (1988), 'Trends in Marriage and Divorce and Cohort Analyses of the Proportions of Marriages ending in Divorce', *Population Trends,* 54: 21.

—— (1989), 'Current Prospects for the Proportion of Marriages ending in Divorce', *Population Trends,* 55: 34.

Hermans, H.J.M. and Kempen, H.J.G. (1993), *The Dialogical Self: Meaning as Movement,* New York: Academic Press, Inc.

Hetherington, E.M. (1979), 'Divorce: A Child's Perspective', *American Psychologist,* 34(10): 851–8.

Hockey, J. (1990), *Experiences of Death: An Anthropological Account,* Edinburgh: Edinburgh University Press.

—— and James, A. (1993), *Growing up and Growing old: Ageing and Dependency in the Life-course,* London and New York: Sage Publications.

Hoggett, B. (1989), 'The Children Bill: The Aims', *Family Law,* 19: 217–21.

Holmes. T.H. and Rahe, R.H. (1967), 'Holmes-Rahe social Re-adjustment Rating Scale', *Journal of Psychosomatic Research,* 11: 213–18.

Holquist, M. (1990), *Dialogism: Bakhtin and his World,* London: Routledge.

Holt, J. (1975), *Escape from Childhood,* Harmondsworth: Penguin.

Holy, L. (1996), *Anthropological Perspectives on Kinship,* London: Pluto Press.

Houseman, M. (1988), 'Towards a Complex Model of Parenthood: Two African Tales', *American Ethnologist,* 15: 658–77.

Humm, M. (1987), 'Autobiography and Bellpins', in V. Griffiths (ed.), *Feminist Biography II: Using Life Histories,* Manchester: Studies in Sexual Politics, University of Manchester.

Hutchinson, S. (1990), 'Rising Divorce among the Nuer, 1936–1983', *Man* (n.s.), 25: 393–411.

James, A., Hockey, J. and Dawson, A. (1997), *After Writing Culture:*

Epistemology and Praxis in Contemporary Culture (ASA Monograph 34), London: Routledge.

Kaplan, E.A. (1992), *Motherhood and Representation: The Mother in Popular Culture and Melodrama,* London and New York: Routledge.

Kelly, J. (1988), 'Adjustment in Children of Divorce', *Journal of Family Psychology,* 2(2): 119–40.

King, M. (1987), 'Playing the Symbols – Custody and the Law Commission', *Family Law,* 17: 186–91.

—— and Piper, C. (1990), *How the Law Thinks about Children,* Aldershot: Gower.

Kruk, E. (1993), *Divorce and Disengagement: Patterns of Fatherhood within and beyond Marriage,* Halifax, Nova Scotia: Fernwood Publishing.

La Fontaine, J.S. (1980), 'The Domestication of the Savage Male', *Man,* (n.s.), 16: 338–49.

—— (1985), 'Anthropological Perspectives on the Family and Social Change', *Quarterly Journal of Social Affairs,* 1: 29–56.

—— (1988), 'Child Sexual Abuse and the Incest Taboo: Practical Problems and Theoretical Issues', *Man,* (n.s.), 23: 1–18.

—— (1990), *Child Sexual Abuse,* Cambridge: Polity Press.

Lamb, M.E. (1987), 'Father and Child Development: An Integrative Overview', in M.E. Lamb (ed.), *The Father's Role: Applied Perspectives,* New York: Wiley.

Lasch, C. (1977), *Haven in a Heartless World: The Family Besieged,* New York: Basic Books.

Laslett, P. (1972), 'The History of the Family', in P. Laslett and R. Wall (eds), *Household and Family in Past Time,* Cambridge: Cambridge University Press.

Lauer, R.H. and Lauer, J.C. (1994), *Marriage and Family: The Quest for Intimacy,* Dubique, IA: Brown Communications Inc.

Law Commission (1988), *Family Law Review of Child Law: Guardianship and Custody,* Law Commisssion No 172, London: HMSO.

Law, J. (1994), *Organising Modernity,* Oxford: Blackwell.

Leach, E.R. (1961), *Rethinking Anthropology,* London: Athlone Press.

—— (1967), 'An Anthropologist's Reflections on a Social Survey', in D.C. Jongmans and P.C.Gutkind (eds), *Anthropologists in the Field,* Assen, Netherlands: Van Gorcum and Co.

—— (1968), 'The Cereal-packet Norm', *The Guardian,* 29 January.

Legal Aid Board (1994), *Annual Report 1993–94: Report to the Lord Chancellor on the Operation of the Finance and Legal Aid Act 1988,* London: HMSO.

Levi-Strauss, C. (1974), 'The principle of Reciprocity', in R. Laub-Coser (ed.), *The Family: Its Structure and Functions,* New York: St. Martin's Press.

Lewis, C. (1986), *Becoming a Father,* Milton Keynes: Open University Press.

—— and O'Brien, M. (1987), 'Constraints on Fathers: Research, Theory and Clinical Practice', in C. Lewis and M. O'Brien (eds), *Reassessing Fatherhood,* London, Sage Publications.

Lewis, J., Clark, D. and Morgan, D. (1992), *Whom God hath Joined together: The Work of Marriage Guidance,* London: Routledge.

Lewis, O. (1966), *La Vida: A Puerto Rican Family in the Culture of Poverty – San Juan and New York,* New York: Random House.

Linde, C. (1993), *Life Stories: The Search for Coherence,* Oxford: Oxford University Press.

Linell, P. (1990), 'The Power of Dialogue Dynamics', in I. Markova and K. Foppa (eds), *The Dynamics of Dialogue,* New York: Harvester: Wheatsheaf.

Loizos, P. and Papataxiarchis. E. (eds) (1991), *Contested Identities: Gender and Kinship in Modern Greece,* Princeton: Princeton University Press.

Lord Chancellor's Department (1985–91), *Judicial Statistics,* London: HMSO.

Lowe, N. (1982), 'The Legal Status of Fathers Past and Present', in L. Mckee and M. O'Brien (eds), *The Father Figure,* London: Tavistock.

McAllister, F. (1995), *Marital Breakdown and the Health of the Nation* (2nd edition), London: One Plus One.

McCarthy, P. (1996), 'Marital Breakdown: Professional Shakedown', in R. Humphrey (ed.), *Families behind the Headlines,* Newcastle: British Association for the Advancement of Science/Department of Social Policy, University of Newcastle upon Tyne.

—— and Simpson, B. (1991), *Issues in Post-divorce Housing: Family Policy or Housing Policy?,* Aldershot: Avebury.

—— Simpson, R., Walker, J. and Corlyon, J. (1991), *A Longitudinal Study of the Impact of Different Dispute Resolution Processes on Post-divorce Relationships Between Parents and Children,* Report to the Ford Foundation (Fund for Research in Dispute Resolution).

Macfarlane, A. (1978), *The Origins of English Individualism,* Oxford: Basil Blackwell.

MacIntyre, A. (1981), *After Virtue,* London: Duckworth.

Maclean, M. (1991), *Surviving Divorce: Women's Resources after Divorce,* Basingstoke: Macmillan.

Maidment, S. (1982), 'Law and Justice: The Case for Family Law Reform', *Family Law*, 12: 229–32.

—— (1984), *Child Custody after Divorce: The Law in Social Context*, London: Croom Helm.

Mair, L. (1971), *Marriage*, Harmondsworth: Penguin.

Mansfield, P. and Collard, J. (1988), *The Beginning of the Rest of your Life: A Portrait of Newly-wed Marriage*, Basingstoke: Macmillan.

Markus H.R. and Kitayama, S. (1991), 'Culture and the Self: Implications for Cognition, Emotion and Motivation', *Psychological Review*, 98: 224–53.

Marriage and Divorce Statistics (1977), Office of Population, Censuses and Surveys, London: HMSO.

—— (1986), Office of Population, Censuses and Surveys, London: HMSO.

—— (1990), Office of Population, Censuses and Surveys, London: HMSO.

—— (1994), Office of Population, Censuses and Surveys, London: HMSO.

Mauss, M. (1925[1954]), *The Gift: Forms and Functions of Exchange in Archaic Societies*, Trans. by I. Cunnison, London: Cohen and West.

Mead, G.H. (1936), *Mind, Self and Society*, Chicago: University of Chicago Press.

Medick, H. and Sabean, D.W. (1988), *Interest and Emotion: Essays on the Study of Family and Kinship*, Cambridge: Cambridge University Press.

Meyrowitz, J. (1984), 'The Adult Child and the Child-like Adult', *Daedalus*, 113(3): 19–48.

Mitchell, J.C. (1969), 'The Concept and Use of Social Networks', in J.C Mitchell (ed.), *Social Networks in Urban Situations*, Manchester: Manchester University Press.

Mnookin, R. and Kornhauser, L. (1979), 'Bargaining in the Shadow of the Law: The Case of Divorce', *Yale Law Journal*, 88: 950–70.

Modell, J. (1986), 'In search: The Purported Biological Basis of Parenthood', *American Ethnologist*, 13: 646–61.

Moore, H. (1988), *Anthropology and Feminism*, Cambridge: Polity Press.

Morgan, D.H.J. (1985), *The Family, Politics and Social Theory*, London: Routledge, Kegan and Paul.

—— (1988), 'Two Faces of the Family: The Possible Contribution of Sociology to Family Therapy', *Journal of Family Therapy*, 10: 233–53.

Morgan, P. (1986), 'Feminist Attempts to Sack the Father: A Case of

Unfair Dismissal?', in D. Anderson and G. Dawson (eds), *Family Portraits,* London: Social Affairs Unit.

Mount, F. (1982), *The Subversive Family,* London: Jonathan Cape.

Needham, R. (1971), 'Remarks on the Analysis of Kinship and Marriage', in R. Needham (ed.), *Rethinking Kinship and Marriage,* London: Tavistock Publications.

New, C. and David, M. (1985), *For the Children's Sake: Making Childcare more than Women's Business,* Harmondsworth: Penguin.

Newman, J. (1991), 'Enterprising Women: Images of Success', in S. Franklin, C. Levy and J. Stacey (eds), *Off-centre: Feminism and Cultural Studies,* Hammersmith: Harper and Collins.

Newson, J. and Newson, E. (1978), 'Cultural Aspects of Child-rearing in the English-speaking World', in M. Richards (ed.), *The Integration of a Child into a Social World,* Cambridge: Cambridge University Press.

Oakley, A. (1974), *The Sociology of Housework,* London: Martin Robertson.

Offer, A. (1996), 'Between the Gift and the Market: The Economy of Regard', Unpublished MS, prepared for the Congress of the European Association of Historical Economics, Venice.

Ogus, A., Walker, J., Jones-Lee, M., Cole, W., Corlyon, J., McCarthy, P., Simpson, R. and Wray, S. (1989), *Report to the Lord Chancellor's Department on the Costs and Effectiveness of Conciliation in England and Wales,* London: Lord Chancellor's Department.

Osmond, M.W. (1986), 'Radical-critical Theories', in M.B. Sussman and S.K. Steinmetz (eds), *Handbook of Marriage and the Family,* New York and London: Plenum Press.

Pahl, J. (1983), 'The Allocation of Money and the Structuring of Inequality within Marriage', *The Sociological Review,* 31: 237–62.

Pahl, R. (1984), *Divisions of Labour,* Oxford: Blackwell.

Parkinson L. (1981), 'Joint Custody', *One-Parent Times,* No 7, London: National Council for One Parent Families.

—— (1986), *Conciliation in Separation and Divorce,* London: Croom Helm.

—— (1988), 'Child Custody Orders: A Legal Lottery', *Family Law,* 18: 26–30.

Phillips, R. (1988), *Putting Asunder: A History of Divorce in Western Society,* Cambridge: Cambridge University Press.

Pitt-Rivers, J. (1973), 'The Kith and the Kin', in J.R. Goody (ed.), *The Character of Kinship,* Cambridge: Cambridge University Press.

Polkinghorne, D.E. (1988), 'Narrative Knowing and the Human Sciences', Albany, NY: State University of New York Press.

Priest, J. and Whybrow, J. (1986), *Child Law in Practice in the Divorce and Domestic Courts,* Supplement to Law Commission Working Paper No 96. London: HMSO.

Rapport, N. (1997), *Transcendent Individual,* London: Routledge.

Reiss, D. (1981), *The Family's Construction of Reality,* Cambridge MA: Harvard University Press.

Ribbens, J. (1994), *Mothers and their Children,* London: Sage.

Ricci, I. (1980), *Mom's House – Dad's House: Making Shared Custody Work,* London: Collier-Macmillan.

Richards M. (1982), 'Post-Divorce Arrangements for Children: A Psychological Perspective', *Journal of Social Welfare Law,* 3: 133–51.

—— and Dyson, M. (1982), *Separation, Divorce and the Development of Children: A Review,* London: Department of Health and Social Security.

Riessman, C.K. (1990), *Divorce Talk: Women and Men Make Sense of Personal Relationships,* New Brunswick and London: Rutgers University Press.

—— (1993), *Narrative Analysis,* London: Sage Publications.

Robertson, A.F. (1991), *Beyond the Family: The Social Organisation of Human Reproduction,* Berkeley: University of California Press.

Rose, N. (1992), 'Governing the Enterprising Self', in P. Heelas and P. Morris (eds), *The Values of the Enterprise Culture,* London and New York: Routledge.

Ross, H. and Sawhill, I. (1975), *The Growth of Households Headed by Women,* Washington DC: The Urban Institute.

Scanzioni, J. (1983), *Shaping Tomorrow's Family: Theory and Policy for the 21st Century,* Beverley Hills and London: Sage Publications.

—— Polonko, K., Teachman, J. and Thompson, L. (1989), *The Sexual Bond: Rethinking Families and Close Relationships,* Newbury Park: Sage.

Schneider, D.M. (1968), *American Kinship: A Cultural Account,* Englewood Cliffs: Prentice-Hall.

—— (1984), *A Critique of the Study of Kinship,* Ann Arbor: University of Michigan Press.

Schwartz, R. (1987), 'Our Multiple Selves: Applying Systems Thinking to the Inner Family', *The Family Therapy Networker,* March/April: 25–83.

Seccombe, W. (1993), *Weathering the Storm: Working Class Families from the Industrial Revolution to the Fertility Decline,* London: Verso.

Segal, L. (1983), 'Smash the Family? Recalling the 1960's', in L. Segal (ed.), *What is to be Done about the Family?,* Harmondsworth: Penguin.

Seltzer, J.A., Schaeffer, N.C. and Charng, H. (1989), 'Family Ties after Divorce: The Relationship between Visiting and Paying Child Support', *Journal of Marriage and the Family,* 1: 1,013–1,031.

Shorter, E. (1975), *The Making of the Modern Family,* London: Fontana/ Collins.

Simpson, B. (1994a), 'Access and Child Contact Centres in Britain: An Ethnographic Perspective', *Children and Society,* 8(1): 42–54.

—— (1994b), 'Bringing the *Unclear* Family into Focus: Divorce and Re-marriage in Contemporary Britain', *Man* (n.s.), 29: 831–51.

—— (1997), 'On Gifts Payments and Disputes after Divorce', *Journal of the Royal Anthropological Institute,* 3(4): 731–45.

—— McCarthy, P. and Walker, J. (1995), *Being there: Fathers after Divorce,* Newcastle: Relate Centre for Family Studies.

Smart, C. (1984), *The Ties that Bind: Law, Marriage and the Reproduction of Patriarchal Relations,* London: Routledge, Kegan and Paul.

—— (1989), 'Power and the Politics of Child Custody', in C. Smart and S. Sevenhuijsen (eds), *Child Custody and the Politics of Gender,* London and New York: Routledge.

Smith, R.T. (1996), *The Matrifocal Family: Power, Pluralism and Politics,* New York and London: Routledge.

Social Trends (1991), Office of Population, Censuses and Surveys, London: HMSO.

—— (1994), Office of Population, Censuses and Surveys, London: HMSO.

Stacey, J. (1990), *Brave New Families: Stories of Domestic Upheaval in late Twentieth Century America,* New York: Basic Books.

—— and Price, M. (1981), *Women, Power and Politics,* London: Tavistock.

Stack, C.B. and Burton, L.B. (1994), 'Kinscripts: Reflections on Family, Generation and Culture', in E.N. Glen, G. Chang and L.R. Forcey (eds), *Mothering: Ideology, Experience and Agency,* New York & London: Routledge.

Steinberg, L. (1987), 'Recent Research on the Family at Adolescence: The Extent and Nature of Sex Differences', *Journal of Youth and Adolescence,* 16: 191–7.

Stenning, D.J. (1958), 'Household Viability among the Pastoral Fulani', in J.R. Goody (ed.), *The Developmental Cycle in Domestic Groups,* Cambridge: Cambridge University Press.

Stone, L. (1977), *The Family, Sex and Marriage in England 1500–1800,* London: Weidenfeld and Nicolson.

Strathern, M. (1982), 'The Place of Kinship: Kin, Class and Village Status in Elmdon, Essex', in A.P. Cohen (ed.), *Belonging: Identity and Social*

Organisation in British Rural Cultures, Manchester: Manchester University Press.

—— (1984), 'Domesticity and the Denigration of Women', in D. O'Brien and S. Tiffany (eds), *Rethinking Women's Roles: Perspectives from the Pacific,* Berkeley: California University Press.

—— (1988), *The Gender of the Gift,* London and Berkeley: University of California Press.

—— (1991), *Reproducing the Future,* Manchester: Manchester University Press.

—— (1992a), *After Nature: English Kinship in the late Twentieth Century,* Cambridge: Cambridge University Press.

—— (1992b), 'Enterprising Kinship: Consumer Choice and the new Reproductive Technologies', in P. Heelas and P. Morris (eds), *The Values of the Enterprise Culture,* London and New York: Routledge.

—— (1996), 'Cutting the Network', *Journal of the Royal Anthropological Institute,* 2: 517–32.

Stromberg, P.G. (1993), *Language and Self-transformation: A Study of Christian Conversion Narrative,* Cambridge: Cambridge University Press.

Tannen, D. (1991), *You just Don't Understand,* New York: William Morrow.

Utting, D. (1995), *Family and Parenthood: Supporting Families, Preventing Breakdown,* York: Joseph Rowntree Foundation.

Vitebsky, P. (1993), *Dialogues of the Dead: The Discussion of Mortality among the Sora of Eastern India,* Cambridge: Cambridge University Press.

Vygotsky, L.S. (1962), *Thought and Language,* Cambridge MA: MIT Press.

Wallerstein, J. (1985), 'The Over-burdened Child: Some Long-term Consequences of Divorce', *Social Work* 30: 116–23.

—— and Blakeslee, S. (1989), *Second Chances: Men, Women and Children a Decade Afterwards,* London: Bantam Press.

—— and Kelly, J. (1980), *Surviving the Break-up,* London: Grant McIntyre.

Watkins, M. (1986), *Invisible Guests: The Development of Imaginal Dialogues,* Hillsdale, NJ: The Analytic Press.

Weiss, C. (1986), 'Research and Policy-making: A Limited Partnership', in F.Heler (ed.), *The Use and Abuse of Social Science,* London: Sage.

Weitzman, L. (1985), *The Divorce Revolution,* New York: Free Press.

Wexler, P. (1990), 'Citizenship in the Semiotic Society', in B. Wilson, (ed.), *Theories of Modernity and Post-modernity,* London and New Delhi: Sage.

Weston, K. (1991), *Families we Choose: Lesbians, Gays, Kinship*, New York: Colombia University Press.

Wicks, M. (1991), 'Research Results of Lone Parent Families', Letter to *The Independent*, March.

Widdershoven, G.A.M. (1993), 'The Story of a Life: Hermeneutic Perspectives on the Relationship between Narrative and Life History', in R. Josselson and A. Lieblich (eds), *The Narrative Study of Lives*, Newbury Park: Sage.

Wilson, P. and Pahl, R. (1988), 'The Changing Sociological Construct of the Family',. *The Sociological Review*, 36: 233–72.

Wolfram, S. (1987), *In-laws and Out-laws: Kinship and Marriage in England*, London: Croom Helm.

Yanagisako, S.J. and Collier, J.F. (1987), 'Toward a Unified Analysis of Gender and Kinship', in J.F. Collier and S.J. Yanagisako (eds), *Gender and Kinship: Essays towards a Unified Analysis*, Stanford CA: Stanford University Press.

Young, M. and Wilmott, P. (1967 [1957]), *Family and Kinship in East London*, Harmondsworth: Penguin.

—— (1973), *The Symmetrical Family*, London: Routledge, Kegan and Paul.

Index

2638